EUGENE O'NEILL
The Unfinished Plays

Notes for
The Visit of Malatesta
The Last Conquest
Blind Alley Guy

Edited and Annotated by Virginia Floyd

A Frederick Ungar Book
CONTINUUM · NEW YORK

1988

The Continuum Publishing Company
370 Lexington Avenue
New York, NY 10017

Editor's text: Copyright © 1988 by Virginia Floyd
All hitherto unpublished writing by Eugene O'Neill:
Copyright © 1988 by Yale University

All rights reserved. No part of this book may be
reproduced, stored in a retrieval system, or transmitted,
in any form or by any means, electronic, mechanical,
photocopying, recording, or otherwise, without the
written permission of The Continuum Publishing Company.

Printed in the United States of America

Library of Congress Cataloging-in-Publication Data

O'Neill, Eugene, 1888–1953.
   The unfinished plays: notes for The visit of Malatesta, The last
conquest, Blind Alley Guy / Eugene O'Neill: edited and annotated by
Virginia Floyd.
     p. cm.
   Bibliography: p.
   ISBN 0-8044-2674-0
   I. Floyd, Virginia. II. Title.
   PS3529.N5A6   1988   87-27766
                                                                                              CIP

THE UNFINISHED PLAYS

First page of notes, dated "Aug. 30, 1940," for *The Last Conquest*, providing an example of O'Neill's minuscule handwriting. (Courtesy Yale Collection of American Literature, Beinecke Rare Book and Manuscript Library)

For all those who suffer under a repressive regime, particularly in South Africa—and for the victims and survivors of the Holocaust—lest, as O'Neill warns, "men forget."

V.F.

CONTENTS

Illustrations	ix
Acknowledgments	xi
Introduction	xiii
A Note on Editorial Method	xxvii

1. *The Visit of Malatesta*
Introduction	1
The Play	12

2. *The Last Conquest*
Introduction	39
The Play	46

3. *Blind Alley Guy*
Introduction	121
The Play	131

Notes for *The Visit of Malatesta*	189
Notes for *The Last Conquest*	195
Notes for *Blind Alley Guy*	199
Work Diary Entries for *The Visit of Malatesta*	205
Work Diary Entries for *The Last Conquest*	205
Work Diary Entries for *Blind Alley Guy*	209
Bibliography	213

Illustrations

O'Neill's first notes, dated August 30, 1940, for the idea he conceived that day to write *The Last Conquest*   Frontispiece

Sketches, dated July 4, 1941 in the Work Diary, that O'Neill drew for the Prologue and three of the scenes for *The Last Conquest:*
Prologue: Hall of Black Mirrors
Scene Four: The Hall of Last Suppers
Scene Five: The Garden of Sadism
Scene Seven: The Hill of Execution
    Illustrations follow   79

Set O'Neill drew for the California house in *Blind Alley Guy*. O'Neill dates the sketch September 1941 in his notes and August 28, 1941 in the Work Diary   166

ACKNOWLEDGMENTS

For permission to publish my transcriptions of O'Neill's last three unfinished plays, I thank Ralph Franklin, the Yale Literary Property Committee, and the Beinecke Rare Book and Manuscript Library, Yale University, as legatee of the Eugene O'Neill Collection. For the original permission to transcribe the plays when I was given access to the restricted material in Yale's O'Neill Collection in 1978, I am grateful to Donald Gallup, then Curator of the Collection of American Literature, and to Anne Whelpley, his assistant, who was so helpful in the long months devoted to transcribing O'Neill's minuscule handwriting.

To Ruth Selden, my editor at Ungar, not only for this O'Neill book but also for two earlier ones, I owe a special debt of gratitude both for her sound editorial judgment and for her efforts to make this book possible. I wish, in particular, to thank James Floyd, whose artwork has made visible O'Neill's drawings of the sets for *The Last Conquest*'s Prologue and scenes. O'Neill's faint sketches, drawn in pencil on what is now fragile aged paper, were carefully retraced for this book. I am grateful also to my colleagues at Bryant College, Vera Froelich and Mary Lyons, and to my O'Neill friend, Tom Olsson for their moral support.

My gratitude is extended in a special way to my family: my mother, James and Delia, William and Pat, Carol and Ben, for their support in my period of illness while I was preparing this manuscript, for their love, patience, and understanding.

V. F.

INTRODUCTION

The year 1988 marks the centennial of the birth of America's foremost dramatist, Eugene O'Neill. It is a fitting time for the publication of this book, which presents previously unavailable outlines and notes for the three unfinished plays O'Neill worked on during his last years as a creative artist. These dramas are part of Yale's O'Neill Collection, which the author's widow ordered be restricted to the public for twenty-five years after the death of her husband in 1953. In 1978 I was given permission to prepare for publication *Eugene O'Neill at Work*, which contains much of this long-withheld material, in particular the collection of notebooks in which O'Neill recorded his ideas for plays. These notebooks provide revealing insights into the author's amazingly productive imagination in a twenty-year span; the first is dated 1918–1920; the second, 1921–1931; and the third, 1931–1938. In their totality they form a portrait of a developing artist, one moving from amateur to craftsman to premier dramatist.

Now, with publication of the three plays that O'Neill sought to complete in his last creative years, 1940–1943, a final mature portrait emerges. These manuscripts provide valuable revelations not only of the creative artist at work but also of the social and political issues that were vitally important to O'Neill the man; they are his mature reflections after a lifetime of deep philosophical contemplation, a summary, so to speak, of the ideas that were most important to him, of concepts that he wished to express in his work.

O'Neill had been criticized in earlier years for avoiding contemporary problems and focusing instead on autobiographical material. This emphasis was perhaps to be expected from a man so deeply haunted and indelibly marred by the memories of past familial tragedies. The dramatist's father, Irish-born James O'Neill, managed to become, after much struggle and discrimination, an illustrious matinée idol, but the poverty and difficulties of his early years instilled a miserliness that deeply affected his family's tragic lives. The elder O'Neill's marriage to the genteel, overly protected Ella Quinlan proved to be a disaster. Acquiescing at times to her husband's wish to go on his long one-night tours through small towns unencumbered by children, Ella left her two sons in the care of their maternal grandmother. When her second son died while the O'Neills were on tour, the grieving mother never forgave herself. During a difficult last childbirth, with the delivery of the ten-pound Eugene, Ella's miserly husband hired an inexpensive and apparently inefficient doctor who prescribed morphine to relieve her pain. Ill prepared for her duties as wife and mother, and intensely dissatisfied with her life, Ella escaped from her problems by becoming a drug addict for the next twenty-five years.

Even James's choice of the location of a home for his family proved to be disastrous. The wealthy and snobbish Yankees of New London, Connecticut, ostracized the O'Neills because they were Irish, lacked background and social connections, and, because they were theater people. Haunted as he was by his family's sorrows and tragic, broken lives, Eugene O'Neill, not unexpectedly, began to use family members as prototypes for characters in his plays. His relationships with his mother, father, brother, wives, children, and friends are dramatized in endless variations in the canon. The four O'Neills appear in various guises in both his early one-acters and the later full-length plays, a few of which include *Beyond the Horizon* (1918), *Desire Under the Elms* (1924), *Dynamo* (1928), *Ah, Wilderness!* (1933), and, most specifically, in *Long Day's Journey into Night* (1940).

Through O'Neill's own herculean efforts, he managed to transform the American theater, directing it away from the frivolous romanticism and crude melodrama of the late nineteenth and early twentieth centuries and into the then current international mainstream of serious tragedy. He experimented with numerous theatrical devices: masks, choruses, interior-exterior sets, and thought asides. He expanded his own dramatic horizons, going from the one-acters, 1913–1919, to the multi-act plays in the 1920s, to the trilogies of the late 1920s, to the Cycle plays in *A Tale of Possessors Self-Dispossessed* in the mid '30s. Tennessee Williams stated, with justification, that "O'Neill gave birth to the American theatre and died for it."

How, in turn, did the American theatre react to O'Neill? In the 1920s and early 1930s the dramatist won national recognition and three Pulitzer Prizes. He received international acclaim in 1936 when the Nobel Prize for Literature was bestowed upon him. In his own country, O'Neill was theatrically alive until 1934; his plays (some great successes, others failures) were being produced. Then followed what has been called the years of the great O'Neill silence. Except for the 1946 production on Broadway of *The Iceman Cometh* and the 1947 road tour of *A Moon for the Misbegotten*, his plays were literally ignored. In 1949 O'Neill's wife Carlotta wrote to a friend: "Most people here have forgotten Eugene O'Neill ever wrote for the American theatre! Europe still remembers and Japan."

Now it appears that America's premier playwright, in the centennial year of his birth, will receive the recognition from his fellow countrymen he so richly deserves. Perhaps these manifestations of praise in 1988 and the various productions of his dramas in repertory and university theatres throughout the country will bring a lasting new awareness of O'Neill's significant contributions.

With the publication of the three previously restricted, unfinished plays, a companion volume to *Eugene O'Neill at Work: Newly Released Ideas for Plays* (1981), O'Neill scholars, theatre practitioners, and theatregoers now have, for the first time, the complete body of the author's creative output, with the exception of the Cycle plays—the myriad host of ideas, outlines, scenarios, and unfinished works in progress his prolific mind conceived. The three incomplete plays should provide new insights into O'Neill's versatile imagination. These plays would have made strong social statements. With the exception of the early draft of *Blind Alley Guy*, the works are totally devoid of any autobiographical reference, indicating that O'Neill could write worthwhile material without an emotional/psychological crutch.

The three dramas are linked by a number of similar themes, the primary one being their strong antitotalitarian message. The author was deeply disturbed during this period by the threat fascism posed to the free world; he was angered by "Hitler's war speech against Poland" (Work Diary, 8/31/39) and his subsequent invasion of that defenseless country. A few months later on January 4, 1940, he records his first idea for a political propaganda play, *The Visit of Malatesta*. Later that year, unable to escape his "war obsession," he jots down ideas for two other antifascist plays: *The Last Conquest* on August 30 and *Blind Alley Guy* on December 16. Evidence exists, both in the Work Diary and in the numerous notes for these works, that he made heroic efforts to complete these political plays, but he was, in these years, continuously plagued by ill health: "sinking spells," prostate pain, "bad melancolia," "sleepless nights," and an illness, diagnosed wrongly as Parkinson's disease, that produced a nervous tremor in his right hand. O'Neill's method of composition was unique. He could only create—in his final days as throughout his career—by writing his ideas himself in pencil in that peculiarly small scrawl of his. At the end in the summer of 1943 when the hand stopped writing, he stopped, too.

In his last four productive years as playwright, O'Neill was, seemingly, pulled in two different creative directions, particularly in the summer of 1939. He put aside any desire to focus on political works, and on June 6 he outlined two highly autobiographical plays: *The Iceman Cometh* and *Long Day's Journey into Night*, the latter destined to unlock many private secrets and painful family memories. Instinctively O'Neill knew that his physical powers and creative faculties were waning, that he had to husband his strength and be more selective about which dramas to develop. In the matter of priorities, the "memory" plays ranked first and were written first.

The release at this time of these three antitotalitarian plays—each of which in some way attacks the denial of individual freedom and political, social, and economic rights—could not be more appropriate. There is a brave new clamor in the world today, a cry for freedom and democracy in a number of countries long ruled by a new breed of oppressive dictators.

The fact that O'Neill conceives three distinctly different concepts to expose the dangers of fascism in the same year indicates the seriousness of the problem to him. Had he concentrated on developing one of these ideas and devoted his time and energy to it alone, he could have, presumably, completed at least one of the three plays. Yet, as his imagination soared in the conception of these works, he seemed to forget his debilitating health problems and remember only the past golden creative decades when he had been able to develop his recorded ideas so easily.

The Visit of Malatesta is something new and different for O'Neill in his late mature period: a comedy. His only other full-length comedy, *Ah, Wilderness!*, was written in 1933. The one thing the two comedies have in common is that both could be called "family" plays. In contrast to the earlier work, however, in *The Visit of Malatesta* O'Neill explores many serious issues and concepts. Cesare Malatesta is the fictitious name the author gives to the real-life Enrico Malatesta, the famous Italian anarchist. The play is set in 1923, the year after Mussolini brutally seized the reigns of power in Italy. In a number of speeches Malatesta reveals the suffering he endured at the hands of the fascists. He had been imprisoned but managed to get out and make his way to the United States to visit the comrades of his anarchist days: Rosa Daniello and her husband Tony, who now operates a lucrative speakeasy; Gus Bascone, a shoemaker; and Pete Gebaldi, a gardener. All four have forgotten the anarchist ideals and have become greedy Americanized capitalists. Comedy ensues when Malatesta undertakes a puritan reform movement to "save" his old friends, who seem to be making their way joyously to perdition. O'Neill uses Malatesta's deeply moving recollections of his ordeal in Italy to denounce fascism and to parallel its violence and lawlessness with those same elements and mentality of mind he finds in this country.

The Visit of Malatesta is the first play in over a decade in which O'Neill depicts a real-life historical figure as a central character. His first historical work, *The Fountain* (1921), can justifiably be labeled a failure. In it the fifteenth-century Spanish explorer, Ponce de Leon, journeys west on a quest to the New World, seeking the legendary Fountain of Youth but finding instead, by the play's end, a mystical fountain of eternity and spiritual harmony with the universe. A few creative years later in 1925 in another dismal but more colorful historical drama, *Marco Millions,* the thirteenth-century merchant, Marco Polo, travels in the opposite direction to the east to besot himself greedily with the luxuries of the Orient, plundering the city the Great Kaan gives him to govern, and returning to Italy an emotionally sterile, self-made millionaire. In 1926 O'Neill wrote a religious pageant, *Lazarus Laughed,* based on the short Biblical story of the man miraculously brought back to life, in which important roles were played by historical figures, the Roman emperors Tiberius and Caligula. Now, fifteen years later, O'Neill portrays another Italian leader of men, totally unlike the Caesars, the late nineteenth- early twentieth-century anarchist revolutionist, Enrico Malatesta. As he did for his earlier historical figures, O'Neill researched Malatesta's life, the period in which he lived, and the anarchist movement. What distinguishes *The Visit of Malatesta* from earlier dramas based on historical figures is that it was to be a comedy. With its assortment of vivid characters and its intricate plot, the play would likely have achieved greater success than the earlier historical plays if it had been completed.

Blind Alley Guy could in its early drafts be considered just another family play, one decidedly autobiographical in nature. Set in 1918, it seems to be a continuation of the saga of the O'Neill family beyond the 1912 period depicted in *Long Day's Journey into Night,* although it is subtly disguised as such by many fictitious details. The author attributes qualities possessed by Edmund, Mary, and James Tyrone/O'Neill to the White family: Walter and his parents Tess and Ed. After several name changes, the central figure emerges a dualistic character, Walter White/Black or, as he is known to his underworld friends, "Blackie." The author apparently intended to focus primarily on the Good-Evil dichotomy of Walter White, but there is nothing commendable or redeemable that could represent the supposedly "good" side of this character. He is portrayed as Evil personified. The play is a seemingly verbal flashback, a look at the entire life of this character, as he waits to be electrocuted for murder, through the eyes of his parents, his sister Cassie, and his wife Dora. There is a kind of shallowness about the early notes for this play. Its concept and its execution are exceedingly inferior to the dramas O'Neill was producing in his mature period.

In July 1941, however, O'Neill switches the course of the play, giving it a new political dimension with a simple one-line statement: "Tie up through interpretation of his [Walter's] character with that of Hitler." He changes the setting to July 1934, the period immediately following Hitler's consolidation of power as supreme ruler of Germany. Walter now becomes a tyrannical, mentally unstable Hitler-like gangster, strikingly similar to the one depicted in Bertolt Brecht's 1941 *The Resistible Rise of Arturo Ui*. O'Neill obviously must have researched Hitler's life thoroughly as the parallels between the historical and fictitious figures are too exact to be coincidental.

In the new scenario Walter "does not appear in the play—but he is the dominant character in it as his whole life is recorded through his effect on each of the four members of his family, his father, mother, sister and wife." O'Neill portrays him as a familial monster, an "ugly and maimed man," translating in personal terms and on a small scale the universal horror and destruction his real-life counterpart is inflicting on mankind. In developing the "character of Walter," O'Neill attributes to him traits found in Hitler: "hatred for society in which he feels alien—hatred for Christ, unconscious ambition to supplant." In his mind he will "become victor anti-Christ—reason he hates Jews." Walter is "an anti-Semite—became Communist, then Fascist—admiration not for social theory but for leaders, Lenin, Stalin, Hitler."

No major conflict emerges in *Blind Alley Guy*. The only point of suspense in the first act is the family's uncertainty as to whether or not Walter will actually visit after so many years of broken promises to do so in the past. The useless waiting of the parents resembles that of the two tramps in *Waiting for Godot*. All keep up the pretense of hoping Walter/Godot will come, but secretly they dread the actuality of the visit and confrontation. Later the only tension experienced occurs after the arrival of Walter's wife Dora at the White home the day before Walter's execution, about which the family knows nothing. Time becomes for Dora a dreaded undefeatable enemy.

The play has but a slender thread of a plot. As the notes

indicate, it lacks a central onstage character strong enough to make up for its inadequacies. O'Neill had used offstage characters successfully in earlier plays: Simon Harford, for example, is ill in an upstairs bedroom throughout *A Touch of the Poet*. However, the blustery Irishman, Con Melody, the central character, makes Simon's absence negligible. *Blind Alley Guy* is the weakest of the three unfinished plays; it seems unlikely it could ever be transformed into a successful drama, even if O'Neill had been able to complete it. The notes do reveal, nevertheless, valuable insights into O'Neill's mind at a particular stage of his creativity. Perhaps nowhere else in his plays and notes does he inject so many political comments on Nazism and Communism. For these revelations alone, *Blind Alley Guy* is a valuable manuscript.

A point should be made here on another similarity between *The Visit of Malatesta* and *Blind Alley Guy*. In addition to the fact that the two have a strong antitotalitarian message, both could be loosely labeled "family" plays. So many of O'Neill's full-length plays, from the mid-twenties *(Desire Under the Elms)* to the late 1930s *(Long Day's Journey into Night)* focus on the family unit, the relationships among members, their conflicts, the particular problems they encounter. Many of the characters in these dramas are badly flawed; some, like Lavinia and Orin Mannon in *Mourning Becomes Electra*, are driven by such strong emotions as hatred and vengeance that they will murder a member of the family. Yet some kind of moral order does prevail in these dramas. O'Neill can state with justification: "In all my plays sin is punished and redemption takes place. Vice and virtue can't live side by side." This statement was made long before the writing of *The Visit of Malatesta* and *Blind Alley Guy* and cannot be said to hold true for them. There are some disturbing realities contained in these two late unfinished plays. Most of the characters are not only badly flawed but also totally corrupt. In fact, the major theme or tie linking these works is the corruption of character by materialistic greed. A corollary of this condition is the general lawlessness that prevails.

On the surface, *The Visit of Malatesta* seems to be a cheerful little comedy until one examines closely the characters and the subtle messages in the play. The immediate setting, for example, is an illegal speakeasy; the year, 1923. The remote setting is the era of the so-called Roaring Twenties dominated by corruption, violence, and graft that followed in the wake of Prohibition. The battles between rival gangsters in major cities of the United States, all seeking the millions to be made by supplying thirsty citizens with illegal liquor, produced bloodshed and death, and the destruction of the legal fabric of society with their bribes and payoffs to officials at every level, from lawmakers to law enforcers and judicial upholders of the legal system. What was occurring at the lowest level, in the cities, was also happening on state and national levels. The most striking examples of the latter could be found in the corrupt era of President Warren Harding, two of whose cabinet members were found guilty of involvement in the Teapot Dome scandal.

Against this background, O'Neill in *The Visit of Malatesta* superimposes the Daniello family and their friends, who are obviously affected and influenced by their environment and are seriously flawed. Tony, in addition to running his speakeasy, has a slender young mistress on his mind and is secretly involved in a scheme to start and operate an illegal brewery. His son, Angelo, is the most violent character in the play. In his attempt to become the Artichoke King of the state, he will use "hired assassins and terrorism by bombs" to succeed. Rosa, Tony's wife, once a promiscuous anarchist promoting free love, resorts to extortion and deceit to acquire the diamonds she desires. The Irish cop Delehanty and his boss, the ward heeler Connor, are "on the take" and involved in the brewery scheme. Into this hotbed of lawlessness, O'Neill injects Malatesta, drawn to the United States by Rosa's letters promising an "atmosphere of untroubled, contented family home," of "happy family life." Of course, he is totally disillusioned when he learns what is really happening in the household and sets out to reform one and all. He urges them to earn "just enough to support the family" and informs them that "laws are necessary—not State laws but the implacable laws within the family."

In the first outline for *Blind Alley Guy*, while the son is depicted as a "born monster," Ed, Tess, and Cassie are portrayed as ethical, religious, upright individuals. In the August 1941 notes, while Tess is still described as an "ardent Methodist," she is actually a religious bigot. When Ed pretends to admire Hitler for his "suppression of religion," Tess claims "the trouble with the world" is that people have "lost God." Her husband tells her "the Portuguese and Italians haven't," and Tess responds: "Oh, them streamlined niggers. Better have religion suppressed than Catholic." She later calls Jews "Christ-killers" and claims "Papists and kikes ruined the country."

In his last notes for the play, after the strong Hitler-Walter White connection is made, O'Neill, in order to sharpen the new focus of the play and give it even greater political dimension, changes his original concept of the other White family members. The Whites are now portrayed as amoral, selfish, agnostic: "Loss of all ethical and moral values by Ed, Tess and Cassie—complete scepticism in which they take pride—no faith in old religion—government all grafting politicians—sex morality of no meaning, ancient bigotry—don't vote except special local issues which affect selfish interests." Cassie sings in the church choir "for money reason only." To O'Neill, the family represents the microcosm that reflects the macrocosm. The new characterization of the Whites emphasizes their loss of moral and ethical values, their bigotry, their indifference to individual freedom and basic human rights. By portraying the Whites now as godless materialists and having them support the ruthless German dictator, O'Neill delineates the prototypes of the apathetic Americans who will later inhabit the totalitarian World State of *The Last Conquest* and willingly submit to its tyrannical "Hitler-like leader."

In his revised Prologue of April 1942 for *The Last Conquest*, O'Neill explains how the present dictator was able to form and control a World State. The author points out that there is "no physical resemblance between him" and other dictators, "like Hitler of Germany, who has preceeded him and whose realistic wars, although they met temporary material defeat in the end, triumphed in principle and so ravaged and maimed and tortured the already sick and faithless souls of men, that they paved the way for final, world-wide, spiritual exhaustion and the acceptance of the new Salvation and the Divine Tyrant Redeemer principle in a Holy and Indivisible World State." O'Neill makes a connection between this play and the third unfinished work in one of Satan's observations about the "Blind Alley into which materialism [leads men] (put into their nature by Lucifer)."

In *The Last Conquest* Christ on several occasions issues one of O'Neill's favorite dictums, a warning the author gave in his last interview just before the 1946 première of *The Iceman Cometh,* which forms a binding link between his early and middle works and the final unfinished trio of the early 1940s: "For what shall it profit a man, if he shall gain the whole world and lose his own soul?" Even the Cycle plays O'Neill wrote in the mid-1930s seem precursors to the late unfinished works in the description he gave of them in that last interview: "a psychological drama of a family against the background of the drive toward material progress and the spiritual degeneration of the American people."

Unlike *Blind Alley Guy,* where O'Neill tried and failed to develop a clear-cut Good-Evil dichotomy within its central character, Walter White, he succeeds in *The Last Conquest.* The author states that all eight scenes of the play "are laid in a secret place deep within the duality of Man's spirit." On this "ancient battlefield of the Spirit," the Good-Evil opposites in man's psyche, Christ and Satan, prepare for another of their many struggles waged throughout the various eras for the hearts and minds of humanity. The swing of the pendulum signals the numerous victories and defeats of the two combatants. At particular times when the world is so besotted with Evil that Good has been totally eclipsed, some twist of events takes place to restore the balance of power. Just such a time occurs when *The Last Conquest* begins. Because of humanity's greed, moral weaknesses, and apathy, the entire world is enslaved by Evil, symbolized by the despotic World Dictator, who is actually a puppet under the control of Satan, the Minister of Spiritual Affairs.

The plot of this "World-Dictator fantasy of a possible future," as O'Neill describes it, is "the attempted last campaign of Evil to stamp out even the unconscious memory of God in Man's spirit." To accomplish this, Satan plans to re-create the scenes preceding and including the crucifixion, to make the Christ figure such an object of ridicule that the lethal weapon of laughter would eliminate the slightest remembrance of God in the human mind.

One of the strangest wonders of the play, and it is due perhaps to O'Neill's supreme skill as an artist, is his magnificent character portrayals, not only of Christ but also of his supposedly fiendish adversary, Satan. What O'Neill in his great wisdom and keen perception of the all-forgiving nature of Christ concludes is that even Satan as being, not Satan as sinner, cannot be excluded from the love of God for His creatures. O'Neill demonstrates this fact by showing the loving bond established between Christ and Satan throughout the centuries as the two forces struggle for the possession of the souls of humanity.

Christ treats Satan with great dignity, compassion, pity, and a spirit of loving brotherhood. Satan, in turn, adores Christ in the purest form of the word; he is deeply moved by the excruciating pain inflicted upon him each time the crucifixion is reenacted and begs Christ to let him take his place on the cross. Like Pirandello's *Six Characters in Search of an Author,* whenever the scene of crucifixion takes place in Time there is no way to stop it until the scene is played out. Once these facts are established, the reader understands why O'Neill retained the title "The 13th Apostle" or Disciple in his notes for such a long period. Satan is such an ardent admirer of Christ that he frequently asks him why he, Satan, must constantly play the villain and defeat Christ, whom he loves.

O'Neill made a heroic effort to complete *The Last Conquest.* Of the three unfinished plays it was the most meaningful and significant to him. As late as 1948, five years after he had ceased writing, he was still absorbed in this "projected work of immense scope," according to his friend Dudley Nichols, who stated: "To me it is tragic that he was never able to complete this magnificent project." Yet the notes and outlines have survived.

There could not be a more appropriate time for the release of *The Last Conquest* and the other two unfinished plays as each, in its own particular way, provides a mirror reflecting certain characteristics, aspects, and flaws of the people of this country; its conclusions are as valid and true today as they were in the early 1940s when O'Neill wrote these works. Numerous examples can be cited of their common theme, the corruption of character by materialistic greed. Many of our major institutions are tainted by corruption: modern robber barons of Wall Street abound; investigations reveal a host of government officials who profit from their positions; religious con artists, who make a mockery of Christianity, line their own coffers, taking from the poor and needy rather than aiding them. A brief comment in *The Last Conquest* provides a method by which people can escape the possibility of a future totalitarian World State: "They don't see that a little simple charity, kindness, and thoughtfulness in the world can conquer all this."

One last comment on the timeliness of the release of these plays, two of which depict characters with strong anti-Semitic attitudes. During the 1980s arrogant, unrepentant individuals who carried out Hitler's genocidal policies have been rooted out of their hiding places, and some have been tried for their crimes against humanity. There are some who resent the reopening of old wounds in the fabric of society. Actually, one of the most important messages of *The Last Conquest* encourages such reminders. At the end of this play, in a new ninth scene added by O'Neill, Satan tries to warn a young couple just released from their world of enslavement through the suffering and death of Christ, that history could repeat itself. The confident young people argue that "Christ is our refuge" and "evil cannot prevail." Satan assures them that they will forget: "The spirit is intangible, unseen, while greed and power are realistic facts to anchor dreams upon." Idealistically, the couple plans to build new temples to "worship the spirit of God in man." Satan urges them to "erect temples to Satan, too" because they could once again be caught "unprepared by the evil" in them. They should always keep in mind the fact that "men forget."

O'Neill makes the same point at the end of his first religious pageant, *Lazarus Laughed*. After Caligula, the comparable force for Evil in this play, has slain the Christ figure, Lazarus, he pleads in the last line of the play: "Forgive me, Lazarus! Men forget!" This admonition is one of the major messages of the last unfinished plays. O'Neill realized in the early 1940s the ease with which a nation and its people could slip their moral moorings and embrace willingly, and even joyously, the doctrines and domination of an evil, monstrous dictator. The unfinished plays should serve as a constant reminder of the dangers and evils of fascist tyranny. There are, unfortunately, many forms of social, economic, and religious intolerance and injustice rampant today. There is, however, and O'Neill knew it, only the slightest "hopeless hope" that the main message of the plays will reach enough people to affect the changes that are needed, that a more peaceful world order can be wrought if enough people remember the past in order to change the future.

There will perhaps be purists who will read the notes and outlines for these three plays to analyze O'Neill's style and writing practices. The works should be evaluated primarily not for form but for content, for the envisioned finality of what O'Neill was attempting to achieve. He spent the least amount of time on *The Visit of Malatesta* and set his ideas down in a kind of shorthand, making great use of dashes rather than normal punctuation to separate his ideas. More time was spent on *Blind Alley Guy,* and after many aborted attempts to complete Act One, O'Neill finally manages to write what appears to be a fairly well-shaped draft of it, complete with standardized dialogue. The author's greatest effort and time were reserved for *The Last Conquest.* He again makes profuse use of dashes in the early notes and outlines but once he begins the revised Prologue, the material is clearly and effectively written.

Obviously, the release of the plays is a major contribution to O'Neill scholarship. Now for the first time scholars, theatregoers, and practitioners have available O'Neill's total body of work, with the exception of some of the Cycle plays, spanning the years 1913 to 1943. It is my hope that reading these manuscripts for the first time will bring readers the same wonderment of discovery, the same excitement and satisfaction at having the plays at last that I experienced.

V. F.

A NOTE ON EDITORIAL METHOD

Eugene O'Neill's method of composition was unique. He always wrote in pencil, and his handwriting, minuscule at all times, was nearly illegible in his last period, 1940–1943, when he made the notes for the three plays that are the focus of this book. It was not an easy task to transcribe these hundreds of pages, but it was an exceedingly rewarding one.

In the presentation of the notes and outlines for *The Visit of Malatesta, The Last Conquest,* and *Blind Alley Guy,* I have not altered O'Neill's text substantively; the content is reproduced intact. Some types of grammatical errors have been rectified; misspellings have been silently corrected. Apostrophes, initial or closing quotation marks, commas, hyphens, and terminal punctuation, where omitted, have been supplied. Colons have been inserted before quoted material when O'Neill fails to provide them. At times he puts a period before the two dashes used to separate the material, and I have retained it; otherwise, merely the two dashes are used. I did not insert semicolons when needed but retained the commas O'Neill uses.

When only the initial of the first name of a character is given, the complete name is stated (as "C" for "Cassie"). When the name of a character speaking a piece of dialogue is omitted but is clearly implied, the name is inserted. The first word in a quotation is silently capitalized when O'Neill fails to capitalize it.

Passages that O'Neill attempts to delete by drawing lines through them are placed in square brackets in the text where they appear and an explanation supplied in a footnote at the bottom of the page. Brackets are also used to add [editor's] words for clarification. Footnotes for lengthy explanatory material have been placed at the back of the book. The letters "W.D." after a passage in quotation marks indicate an entry from O'Neill's Work Diary.

I had considered replacing the many dashes in the manuscripts with appropriate punctuation but realized their removal would have impeded the flow and rhythm of the material. Retaining O'Neill's original shorthand provides readers with valuable insights into the method O'Neill uses in the creative process.

V.F.

THE UNFINISHED PLAYS

·1·
THE VISIT OF MALATESTA

Introduction

Of the three last unfinished plays, developed in the 1940–1943 period, O'Neill spent considerably less time on *The Visit of Malatesta* than on the other two works: *The Last Conquest* and *Blind Alley Guy*. He was, however, enthusiastic about the concept for *The Visit of Malatesta* and the fact that the play was to be a comedy, a word he stresses in the four Work Diary entries made in early 1940 and two of the twelve notations in 1941. The decision to write a comedy marked a change of pace for the author; yet, oddly enough, the idea was conceived in his most creative period, while he was concentrating on two tragic dramas, on January 4, 1940, the day after he finished the last draft of *The Iceman Cometh* and the day before he announced his plan for *Long Day's Journey into Night* "to do this soon."

The dramatist alternated working days on this latter play and *The Visit of Malatesta*, which provided two different views, the tragic and comic, of family life, in late February and early March 1940. This was a particularly pain-racked period for O'Neill, plagued as he was by illness and his "damned sinking spells" (W.D.).[1] *The Visit of Malatesta* appeared to be the easier play to work on at the time, containing, as it did, many carry-over elements from *The Iceman Cometh*. It was, however, a nonautobiographical work, demanding all his mental faculties, his imagination, innovation, and concentration, to construct a plausible plot and set of characters. On the other hand, *Long Day's Journey* was purely a memory play; O'Neill had only to recall his past to envision it. It is understandable, then, that on March 3, 1940, he put aside *The Visit of Malatesta* and took up *Long Day's Journey into Night*,

2 · THE UNFINISHED PLAYS

remarking: "will do this play next, I think, but too low physically now for long stretch of work" (W.D.).

On January 4, 1940, on a single separate page of paper, O'Neill compiled a list of characters—the Daniello family and their friends—and brief descriptions of all but two of them: the real-life legendary Italian anarchist hero Enrico Malatesta, who would be called Cesare Malatesta in the play, and the wife of Tony Daniello, later named Rosa. The Daniellos and their two friends, Gus Bascone and Pete Gebardi, were former revolutionaries in Italy and followers of Malatesta before they escaped imprisonment there and settled in the United States.

In the next notes for the play, kept now in a notebook and dated over a month later on February 23, 1940, in the Work Diary, O'Neill provides more information about his characters, naming and describing them in detail, particularly Malatesta, whose story the dramatist narrates. The basic plot has much comic potential. Tony runs an illegal speakeasy in the era of Prohibition. Because his wife, Rosa, once the slender and free-spirited "flame of the revolution," has grown enormously fat, Tony has acquired an exotic, but mercenary, mistress. Over the years the Daniellos and their Italian friends, having abandoned their early noble anarchist ideals, have become Americanized greedy materialists. Into this world of bootlegging, political graft, and licentiousness comes the sober, ascetic Malatesta who, as the play progresses and his understanding of his environment grows, is compelled to reform one and all. The author had used this concept of the savior figure coming to bring salvation, through the doctrine of alcoholic abstinence and renunciation, to old friends in the just-completed *The Iceman Cometh*.

There are so many similarities between this play and *The Visit of Malatesta* that the latter work seems to be a natural outgrowth of the first: a barroom setting with living quarters upstairs; the concept of graft and corruption, with the two policemen, Pat McGloin and Delehanty, "on the take"; the theme of waiting for a messianic outsider (Hickey and Malatesta) who tries to reform his friends; anarchist mothers (called Rosa in both plays), who may have been the mistresses of former anarchist leaders (Slade and Malatesta) and borne them illegitimate children. Tony's son, Angelo, like his young bartender counterpart in *The Iceman*

Cometh, Rocky Pioggi, will resort to any means, however illegal and violent, to get rich. Connor, the crooked ward heeler, is a younger version of Harry Hope, a former "jitney politician." O'Neill uses a device from *The Iceman Cometh* of having two characters (here the shoemaker, Gus Bascone, and the gardener, Pete Gebaldi) who constantly bicker but who are actually good friends.

Both plays also focus on anarchism. Hippolyte Havel, the prototype for *The Iceman Cometh*'s Hugo Kalmar, has an anarchist background similar to Malatesta's. The two joined the movement early in life, and after years of imprisonment, suffering, and persecution in Europe found refuge and safety in London. Both were friends of the dedicated anarchist Emma Goldman, who, like Rosa Daniello, was called "the flame of the barricades." Two anarchists in *The Iceman Cometh,* Larry Slade and Don Parritt, have given up the movement. Hugo, like the Americanized Daniellos and their Italian-American friends, seems to be paying only lip service to anarchism and may actually be a bourgeois capitalist. This latter group reminisces eloquently about their youthful "acts of propaganda by the deed" in the Old World and discuss vague revolutionary plans to be perpetrated in the New World in some distant future, sitting comfortably, meanwhile, in a barroom in the glow of an alcoholic fervor. All respond negatively to the savior figures, Hickey and Malatesta, who urge them to put an end to illusions and status quo blindness and to become more realistic and involved in the activities of life.

In contrast, however, to the varied ethnic assortment of autobiographical characters in *The Iceman Cometh* who had walked across the stage of O'Neill's own life, playing, in some instances, important roles, *The Visit of Malatesta* focuses primarily on only one ethnic group, Italian-Americans, who seem to have played only a peripheral role in his life. As he notes in his Work Diary, "never have written about Italian Americans although in past have known many of them as close friends" (2/10/41). O'Neill, being Irish, was most familiar with the plight of Irish immigrants, depicted in several of his plays. Yet now he decides not to use the Irish, who are subject to moods of deep despair and gloomy introspection for all their verbal wit and comic antics. He chooses instead the Italian Daniellos, who are not only humorous, happy,

4 · THE UNFINISHED PLAYS

and vibrant but also open in their revelations of self, effusive in their emotions.

O'Neill had at first contemplated setting the play in 1912 or 1913, the same time frame used in *The Iceman Cometh* and *Long Day's Journey into Night*. He later changed the date to 1923 in order to use actual historical events to develop his plot and theme. The year 1922 had been an important one in Italian history; Mussolini in that year seized the reins of power and brought two decades of brutal dictatorship to his country. In July 1922 Italy "was drowned in blood by fascist hordes and official police."[2] The year was also important in the real life of O'Neill's Malatesta. Since his return to Italy from exile in 1919, he had been editing an anarchist newspaper, *Umanità Nova*. In August 1922 the paper was destroyed, and he was arrested. After his release he tried to run other papers, but his voice was silenced forever in Italy when an attempt was made on Mussolini's life in 1923, and all antifascist newspapers were suppressed. Malatesta did not escape to the United States in 1923 as O'Neill depicts in the play but was placed under house arrest. His mail was opened; friends who visited him were arrested. He was guarded night and day by police until his death in 1932.

O'Neill portrays Malatesta, when he arrives in the United States in 1923, as being disillusioned by his recent experiences in Italy where he witnessed man's cruelty, injustice, and greed—all sanctioned by a totalitarian fascist government. He comes here seeking a safe refuge in what seemed to be a land of innocence and promise. As a democracy, the United States advocates justice, equality, and the brotherhood of man but fails to practice these principles and fails to protect the rights of all its people. Malatesta thought he had escaped forever from the persecution of government officials. Now, however, in this "free" society he is harassed and has to disguise himself with a beard and glasses to avoid detection by the American police who, fearing a Bolshevik takeover of this country, were at that time busily engaged in mass arrests and the deportation of large numbers of anarchists, who were either Italian or Russian by birth. He discovers that the political system of America, the arsenal of democracy, is corrupt. In 1923 the tainted administration of an incompetent president, Warren B. Harding, was beginning to unravel. Harding died in

August of that year and was mercifully spared the ignominy of the Teapot Dome scandal, in which his Secretary of the Interior Albert B. Fall and Attorney General Harry Daugherty were involved.

Against this background of public corruption and the licentiousness of the Roaring Twenties, O'Neill purposefully delineates characters who are hopelessly flawed by personal vices. The setting used, the illegal speakeasy, is an ever-present reminder of their indifference to a moral code. Skillfully, O'Neill uses all the elements of the play to illustrate his theme: the corruption of character by materialistic greed. Malatesta had believed there could be a bloodless transition to the ideal society because of man's essential goodness. In the past America had represented for him his Utopian dream of an untarnished society. At the conclusion of O'Neill's 1940 notes, however, Malatesta realizes there are different kinds of enslavement. The tyranny of greed in America can be as destructive to the soul of the individual as the tyranny of power in Italy.

O'Neill put aside the story of the fictitious family, the Daniellos, on March 3, 1940, and began to write *Long Day's Journey into Night*, his own family's tragedy, finishing the second draft later that year on October 16, his fifty-second birthday. He then turned to his massive Cycle, *A Tale of Possessors Self-Dispossessed*, and to other ideas for plays. On February 11, 1941 he again took up *The Visit of Malatesta*, changing its name the following day to "Malatesta Seeks Surcease." Although O'Neill uses this cumbersome title in his Work Diary entries for 1941, it seems unlikely he would have kept it in a final draft of the play. The dramatist explains the new title in a passage labeled "plot (in nutshell)." He states: "Malatesta seeks surcease in the family—all he asks is to be accepted as one of them, forget the past." He is immediately recognized as such a virtuous man that the characters joyously welcome him at the end of Act One when he arrives late in the evening at the speakeasy. Rosa is the only character to realize Malatesta has truly recanted his earlier revolutionary life and now, lonely and sorrowful, he wishes to experience the joys of family life. He regrets not having married the loving, amiable Rosa when they were lovers.

Rosa is a unique mother figure in O'Neill's gallery of women. Her only possible rival as a totally warm, loving woman is Essie

Miller in the sentimental comedy, *Ah, Wilderness!*, the other unexpected anomaly from the pen of Eugene O'Neill. Yet Essie is straitlaced and prudish in her attitude to sex. She is no match for the rotund Rosa who, in her youth, had practiced the anarchist ideal of free love, engaging in premarital sex not only with her eventual husband, Tony, but also with at least three of his friends. She is a truly human, likeable person and is exceedingly wise about life and her family, paying as she says "fat for wisdom." Most of O'Neill's other women are either demanding, nagging wives, neurotic possessive mothers, or, like Ella O'Neill, unhappily a combination of both.

Rosa's cousin and her complete opposite, the puritanical Francina, nicknamed the Black Death by Angelo because of the gloom she casts, is closer to the typical O'Neill mother. Like Ella O'Neill, she is temperamental, given to self-dramatization, and imagines she ruined her life by marrying an unworthy man, socially her inferior. When Malatesta begins his campaign to reform the Daniellos and their friends, Francina aids him in this "Puritan movement," actually blackmailing any individual who, unfortunately, cannot resist some former vice.

It is unfortunate that O'Neill's health prevented him from completing *The Visit of Malatesta;* he had an exciting, colorful array of characters, a potentially hilarious plot, and a well-worn but usually successful theme, the destructive power of greed. Yet he seems unable to coordinate these elements and reveals for the first time in his last period obvious signs of creative weakness. He confuses the names of his characters. Connor, for example, is mistakenly called Farrell; more often Rosa is wrongly named Francina. O'Neill is halfway through his notes before Francina is finally designated as Rosa's cousin and not the eldest daughter of the Daniellos. Even more confusing is the lack of a logical, systematic sequence in the division of the notes into recognizable acts. The material is often unconnected with unrelated ideas and thoughts on the characters tossed here and there. O'Neill's final comment on the play in his Work Diary, "have lost grip on it—trouble is too many good ideas—can't settle on one," accurately pinpoints his frame of mind while writing all the notes.

After O'Neill describes his characters in detail and sets down the story in 1940, he begins on February 10, 1941, to write dialogue, loosely constructed characters, and scenes. Following another "everlasting argument" about the existence of God between the shoemaker and gardener, a conversation that could have occurred in the first act, O'Neill then writes, disjointedly, scenes of confrontations between characters, such as those between Connor and Malatesta and Connor and Tony, that are obviously designed for Act Two. Inserted then are the words "Curtain on 1st (?) Act" and Malatesta's reflections at the end of it, his "reasons for coming." What follows are general notes that provide information about Malatesta's early life, his revolutionary days, and his decision to "compromise with self," to forfeit his utopian dream for love and family life. The notes offer as well a synopsis of the plot, passages and dialogue suitable for either act one or two, a definition of "the main family plot" to get Malatesta "married to Francina," and two brief sections containing thoughts for the end of the play.

O'Neill is halfway through his notes for the play before he begins putting the dialogue and action into a logical sequence of acts. The date appears to be February 17, 1941, as he makes a specific reference in his Work Diary to beginning work on Act One, set in the "speakeasy in back of grocery store." There Tony and his friends, Gus and Pete, speak longingly of Malatesta's coming and reminisce about their youthful revolutionary days in Italy. The two Irishmen enter: the ward boss Connor and later the policeman, Delehanty. After Tony goes to the train station to meet Malatesta, the three women appear—Rosa, May, and Francina. By the time Tony returns, disappointed not to have met Malatesta, the entire cast is assembled for the dramatic entry of Malatesta, who, surrounded by his friends, dramatically faints from weakness as the curtain falls.

Act Two takes place the following morning in the "dining room of house upstairs." Malatesta has been served breakfast in bed by the three women, and gradually the other members of the cast joyously reappear, having declared a holiday to celebrate Malatesta's arrival. In passages that would comprise the second act, he tells those gathered of his desire to seek the simple life, condemns alcohol as "capitalist poison," lectures them on materialism and the need to develop a soul. All present, except Francina, are surprised and disappointed to have a "Probie" in their midst.

O'Neill again digresses with some "general notes" before

8 · THE UNFINISHED PLAYS

beginning Act Three, which takes place a month later. In it, Malatesta, aided by Francina, is "going strong on the reform of the Family." His whole personality has changed; he is no longer timid and gentle but "dictatorial," urging a distribution of "greedy savings" to spread the word that Prohibition is the salvation of the family. A secret meeting attended by all but Malatesta and Francina takes place. The many complaints and despair of the men prompt Rosa to reveal her plan to dispose of Malatesta, but not until she blackmails each of them, extracting the promise of a diamond ring. Her scheme depends on the familiar Shakespearean "bed trick." May will be used as a decoy to write a note to Malatesta luring him to her bedroom. Francina will be substituted for May and, after Malatesta enters the room, Tony and Angelo would enter brandishing a knife and sawed off shotgun demanding, for the sake of family honor, that Malatesta marry Francina.

An earlier insertion about the end of the play, possibly a fourth act, states Malatesta will later try to run away but is confronted by both Francina and May saying: "I am with child." They and the others "have made him into a fiery Anarchist again." The play ends happily with Francina apparently now Malatesta's wife, being interviewed by a reporter. When she boasts of being "the Passion Rose of the Revolution," the others "burst out laughing as the curtain descends."

After reading the notes for this unfinished play, one asks why in a period of chronic illness O'Neill made such an effort on this work. One possibility is that he was trying to show through laughter, as he had previously in a more serious tone, what was wrong with society and his fellow man. The preliminary notes contain many of the major themes he had wrestled with throughout his creative career. He shows once again his fascination with people like Malatesta, alienated by society and condemned to prison and exile. In his previous play, *The Iceman Cometh,* he had depicted the self-alienated from society like the losers in Harry Hope's The Bottom of the Sea Rathskeller. The real-life Malatesta had spent half his life in exile and, as he said once, "ten years in bits and pieces" in prison. The notes state that in jail: "his broodings in solitary have turned back in nostalgic memory to his own family—with remorse, regret—for he had disregarded them." He visits the Daniellos to enjoy the warm, loving family life described glowingly in Rosa's letters. The visit is O'Neill's opportunity to depict again, as he had in numerous plays, various types of conflicts experienced by family members: external struggles with society and with each other and internal ones within specific individuals.

In this play the members of the Daniello family in conflict with Malatesta illustrate one of the most persistent themes in the canon, particularly in these three unfinished antitotalitarian plays: the conflict of good versus evil. The last two lines O'Neill wrote on the final page of his notes for *The Visit of Malatesta* are "To the Day! To the Night!," possibly suggesting the day-night antithesis of man's dual nature. Malatesta represented for O'Neill a Christ figure, a man who had spent more than fifty years of his life attempting to improve the lives of others, suffering deprivation of every kind; a man who was humble, joyous, generous, giving all that he possessed to the poor and working as a common artisan with his hands.

All his adult life through his anarchist activities, Malatesta sought to change government and society for the betterment of man. When he comes to America, he sees a political system rotting through corruption; in the city he visits, it extends from the mayor down to the cop on the beat. In the family he visits all the members are hopelessly flawed: Tony by adultery, Angelo by his violent criminal activities, May by sensuality, Francina by vicious spitefulness and jealousy, Rosa by greed and gluttony. He begins his campaign of reform, therefore, with the lowest stratum of society: the family. "As an Anarchist he believed laws made the criminal—now he knows laws are necessary—not State laws but the implacable laws within the family." Several times he speaks of the "happiness of the family." His goodness, his spirit untainted by evil, creates guilt and uneasiness, a restlessness within them; "his coming brings out and makes active all the longings for liberty, in its members vague dreams of the contented discontented who, for his coming, would remain that."

Malatesta sets out, as Hickey, viewed by some O'Neill scholars as a Christ figure, had done before him in *The Iceman Cometh*, to reform his friends and to banish their pipe dreams. He fails, as does Hickey, and for the same reasons: both men compromise their ideals. At the end of *The Iceman Cometh* Hickey pretends he had been insane to retain his own illusion that he loved the wife he murdered and to allow his friends to retain the cherished pipe dreams so necessary for their survival. Hickey is hopelessly flawed in his character, having committed adultery and murder and having led a self-indulgent, alcoholic life. On the other hand, Malatesta is described as the best of men, having lived a relatively flawless life before his visit to the Daniellos, where he becomes "shocked by the disregard for law: at all levels of society."

In the second and third acts Malatesta begins and implements his reform movement, but he has already experienced a "compromise with self," giving up his beautiful "Utopian dream" for the "unchanging simple things, family, love." It is Rosa who preys upon his weakness and devises the bed trick scheme that is to undo him, assuring Francina that "he wants to get married . . . but not as simple as that because he thinks he does not want anything so ordinary. He thinks he wishes to sleep with Society—human society—and they will have an only child called Utopia." Malatesta succumbs to the temptation of the solace of family life in the last unwritten scene of the play: "he agrees to marry Francina—and they have to find a job for him," a job as front man for the brewery, a position destined to erode Malatesta's value system.

On March 2, 1941, O'Neill explains why he must discontinue his work on *The Visit of Malatesta:* he had "lost grip on it," and he provides a possible cause: "the war perhaps." The dramatist considered the conflict between Hitler's fascists and the Allied forces as epitomizing the ultimate struggle between Good and Evil. The next day, March 3, he outlines *The Last Conquest;* the inner good-evil struggle of Malatesta is now waged in a spiritual conflict of opposites. The messianic, partially flawed Christ figure, Malatesta, is replaced in the new "spiritual propaganda play" by the actual figure of Christ Who engages in the never-ending battle with his ancient and ever-constant foe, Satan, for the soul of man enslaved now in a World State controlled by a Hitler-like dictator. Whereas *The Visit of Malatesta* shows the corruption of character by materialistic greed, *The Last Conquest* depicts the world of victors and vanquished that greed created and sustains. *The Visit of Malatesta* points the way to avoid such a conquest. O'Neill seemingly despairs of modern man's response to his warning that excessive attachment for material possessions can lead only to the enslavement depicted in *The Last Conquest.*

The Visit of Malatesta seems to have more viable stage potential than the other two plays in the loosely labeled antitotalitarian trilogy. The fragmentary bits of scenes could easily be sorted out and placed in logical order in appropriate acts. Descriptions of characters are so well defined in the early notes that one can envision the roles being played by specific stage actors. In contrast, *The Last Conquest* is so vast and sprawling in design that it could be staged only as a monumental religious pageant like *Lazarus Laughed. Blind Alley Guy* is considerably fragmented and badly flawed and conceived.

It is unfortunate that the "Malatesta comedy idea," as O'Neill once referred to it, was never completed, never staged. The play would have been O'Neill's mature venture into familial comedy. *Ah, Wilderness!,* his only completed full-length comedy, was written in 1933 in his middle period.

Daniello Bearing Freedom
Jan. '40[1]

Daniello[2]
The Visit of Malatesta

<u>Comedy</u>

Scene of play—small city—Tony's saloon and residence (upstairs)—time, around 1913

Tony Daniello
His wife
Elder daughter
Her husband
Their children
Elder son
Younger daughter
Younger son
Malatesta
Two old friends of Tony's who have also known the Daniellos abroad—shoemaker and truck gardener (a gardener on estate)
Big Jim Delehanty, policeman and friend of Tony's—also ardent Irish independence patriot
Connor, boss of city machine, also Irish patriot

Tony (50)—popular with Italians—political power—fat, prosperous, contented, benevolent husband and father—yet absurdly cherishes romantic past as young man in Italy when he was anarchist and friend of Malatesta—the great moment when he spent night in jail—likes to still imagine himself an anarchist—hero worship for Malatesta—his two pals also.

The Elder Son (25)—has all his father's practical side—an Italian-American realist—(Tony D. in appearance and nature)—his father's lieutenant in all practical affairs—as likable as he is—good son—admiration for father's dangerous romantic past—but affectionately amused, too.

Younger son (19)—all his father's idealistic revolutionary side.

Elder daughter (30)—the contented discontented—her satisfaction is dissatisfaction with her well-meaning, ineffectual husband whom she really loves with a fierce maternal possessiveness—she likes to complain this marriage was forced on her by parents because his family was supposed to be well-off, but truth is she was in love.

Her husband—within the family, he is regarded as a great practical mistake, although they all like him and appreciate he's done his best—to outsiders they excuse him as being a student.

Younger daughter—quite beautiful—the picture of big-eyed Italian female romantic sentimentalism.

Idea, Comedy   Feb. '40

Cesare Seeks Surcease[3]
The Visit of Malatesta

(Notes)

Scene	Small city, Connecticut—around 1923—Tony Daniello's saloon (residence upstairs)—and his beach cottage
Characters[4]	Tony Daniello (48) Rosa, his wife Francina (40) 1st cousin Rosa
Humbert assass. 1900	Angelo ⎱ two of seven surviving children out [Frankie] ⎰ of nine—five living away, N.Y., Chi- May ⎱ cago, Boston—Maria, Johnny, Al [Ralph Lombardo—(35)—Julietta's husband] Pete Gebardi, a head gardener on estate, old pal of Tony's, fellow immigrant, associate Anarchist days
Joe Genaro Dominic[5]	Gus Bascone, shoemaker, (ditto) bachelor Big Jim Delehanty, a cop, old friend Tony's, an Irish independence patriot Pat Connor, boss of city machine Cesare Malatesta (50)[6]
Tony	Fat, healthy, contented, prosperous, benevolent

husband and father of children who are all doing well or promise to do well (exept Julietta, who made a mistake in marrying the failure Lombardo)—Tony is popular and influential with Italian-American bourgeois, yet with an incongruous romantic idealistic side to him which cherishes the memory of his youthful Anarchist past in Italy when he was a friend of the leader, Malatesta—great moment of his life when he spent night in jail with him—likes to imagine he is still an Anarchist—he's not a conspirator and plotter—engages in secret meetings with his pals, Pete and Gus, both of whom are also content with life and proud of success—He is a good Catholic because he is but he explains this away on practical grounds.

Rosa   Hugely fat and healthy, mustache, immensely good-natured, affectionate, tolerant, matter-of-fact realist—adores Tony and children—is amused by his romantic dreams of radical past—she remembers them well as she knows all of group—was ardently for the free love, no sin aspect of liberty—the memory amuses her—she was pretty and stupid as May is now—Tony was her accepted lover and when she got pregnant she made him marry her—but she cheated on side, principally with Malatesta, and she is not sure but she thinks Julietta is his child.

Francina   Thin and temperamental—a lot of ham in her—self-dramatizes and delights in scenes and passionate outburst—imagines she threw her life away by mistaken love for unworthy object and married beneath her—likes to bring up all the men she thinks she could have married and their successful careers—the truth being she gave herself to Lombardo with deliberate calculation and intent to be pregnant and force him to marry her—at that time his people [were] rich wholesale grocers and he was college graduate—a fine match—but his people lost money and he is a book reader who is dead lost—but, although she pretends to despise him, she has come to love him with a fierce, maternal, protective passion, and her children,[7] too, and is not frustrated a bit.

Angelo His father's lieutenant in business—has taken over a lot of the active work—(Tony D. in appearance) as likable as father and mother—good practical head—married, three children—good son—is amused by father's romantic past, but also impressed and admires Malatesta (but as applied to Italy only).

May Beautiful Italian peasant type—dreamy eyes—sentimental, romantic—has many beaus whom she affects to disdain—they are all "Small town," there is no romance in them—she is a great reader of words—she dreams of marrying a millionaire, or a hero of one sort or another—the beau her parents favor is son of political boss.

Gus Bascone The shoemaker—wiry, small, round-shouldered with the face and ferocious mustache of a Sicilian Bandit[8]—a bachelor with bitter scorn for woman's suffrage—and a hatred for feet and factory shoes—only the artist can take this scorn of ugliness off feet by making beautiful shoes.

Pietro
Pete
  Gebardi Tall, spare, a raw-boned earthy peasant—and as a head gardener on millionaire (Standard Oil)[9] estate, he is an autocrat—he stands for no nonsense from his employer—he feels the gardens are his by right of love and conquest and his boss is an interloper who understands nothing (beefs about his employer or lady friends plucking flowers)—but on subject of labor, he is at one with boss—indignant—too highly paid, know

nothing—he is a dictator and tyrant on his preserves.

Story   Feb. '40

Malatesta, physically exhausted by years in prison, bewildered and a bit frightened by the world when he is released, disillusioned and embittered by his confreres in Anarchist leadership, some of whom abnormally, jealously regret his return for fear he will oust them but each scheming to use him to help oust rival, etc. etc.—He is afraid if he stays among them he will lose all faith in the Revolution. He also blames himself, wants to think his mind has been warped in prison. What he particularly hates is their readiness in plans for future to justify all the means of the tyranny they are fighting provided they use them for their ends. He finds himself confused, furious, continually quarreling. He wants to excuse them, blames himself. They have had bad leadership, goes off weakly on old tangent psychologically. They must be brought back. By him. But he is unfit now. He must have rest in entirely new atmosphere, get back health and mental calm, perspective, etc. He thinks of U. S. where Movement can hardly be said to exist—he remembers his old friend Tony and his old mistress, Francina,[10] and this latter's yearly invitation to visit—from letter he has caught atmosphere of untroubled, contented family home—all he has missed. So he leaves. The Italian government is glad to wish him on U. S.—and his comrades are glad to get rid of idealist.

The situation in the Daniello family is such that his coming brings out and makes active all the longings for liberty in its members, vague dreams of contented discontent which, but for his coming, would remain that.

Prosperity and comparative idleness have made Tony regret the lost anarchist ideals of free love—his eye has roved to a young gal, whom he knows he could get, and Francina has grown very fat—Julietta dreams of divorce, defiance of Catholic marriage, and a career on the stage with many rich men who would keep her in extravagances—"look at Duse."

Angelo is ambitious. Law-abiding (more or less). The progress in the vegetable end of the business is too slow. He has visions of becoming Artichoke King of the state, and if he hired assassins and terrorism by bombs is a short cut, why not?[11] Malatesta will approve of assassination and bombs, as a matter of principle, and of defiance of law. He is scornful of Father's objections—an old anarchist.

May is just generally lazily vain and rebellious. She doesn't like high school, the rule of father and mother at home is too strict, she doesn't want to marry and be bored, she doesn't want to have children and be tied down—she has idea of crusading for birth control and woman's rights because if she knew surely how not to get pregnant she could have a lot of fun—especially with an adventurous lover who had the courage to defy all the rules.

Mother's watchful concern over May in light of her own and Francina's experience with men—she knows what she really wants—but her concern is good-naturedly understanding and sympathetic, if highly realistic and cynical—her fear is May will give it away because she sees so much in May like her at the same age—she even points out to May she will get fat quick afterward, like she did. Her realistic attitudes highly shock her family.

Malatesta speaks English with British accent—very correctly—result of years of exile in England (after escape Italian prison) where he made living as tutor[12]—then he had sneaked back to Italy but had been arrested and sent to prison—but again escaped after years—to England—then got into U. S.—lecture—his first visit.[13]

He is tall, thin, handsome, romantic-looking, grey mustache, goatee, aristocratic, dressed well always in black—years in prison have left mark—outwardly unbroken, undaunted—inwardly tired, a bit bitter, disillusioned and hopeless about Utopia—lonely, too—longing for rest and a home—food, warmth, serenity, a wife, children, etc. He fights against meanness and disillusionment by bursts of passionate detestation of society, goes to extremes, used to believe there could be transition, almost bloodless, to ideal society because of man's essential goodness, but now he says there must be complete destruction first, past must be wiped out—those who resist must die, etc.—but then he sinks into exhausted depression—he feels he used to love man but now he despises him, and that is wrong, is a fault in him.

Angelo—his fear of anything that might bring publicity—it's poison—inconsequential remark—"I'd rather be pals with a chimpanzee than a reporter."

General Notes   Feb. '41

One of Malatesta's outbursts: "I used to believe man was good—now I know he is a dog, a beast, a swine!" Angelo: "Present company excepted, of course." Malatesta [becomes alert]: "Eh?" (Lamely) "Yes, of course."

The Shoemaker—always cursing feet and their ugliness—"Why did God make feet? (Then hastily) Only a manner of speaking. Naturally, there is no God. That is known, but if you needed more proof, you only need to look at feet. No God would create feet."

The everlasting argument between the Shoemaker and the Gardener—Is there a God? The Shoemaker denies, the Gardener says: "Yes—how can he be Anarchist if he believes in God."—Shoemaker: "You mean, the Church's God—a stained glass Pope of the bourgeois." Gardener: "I mean God of Poor, the Supreme Anarchist—when Revolution comes, we will take him away from bourgeois—Church, too—call by different names."

Delehanty joins in this argument: "All you have to do is look at the ocean and the stars." Shoemaker: "All right. I look at the ocean—a lot of water with some salt in it—if I had enough water and enough salt, I could make it myself. And I look at the stars and I see that they are only stars, and what good are they?—electric lights are better." Delehanty: "You're an ignorant wop. Napoleon looked at the stars once and he said they proved God." Shoemaker: "Napoleon? A crazy Corsican. Corsicans are all crazy. They will believe anything."

When Delehanty meets Malatesta—half soused: "As an old friend of my old friend, I'm glad to meet you. But I warn you I don't agree with anything you say, except bloody ruin to England and the freedom of Ireland, and I think all anarchists shouldn't be allowed in this country and those that are ought to be shot or in jail, and don't try strewing any books in this town, or I'll run you in as look at you, friend or no friend. So now I've warned you, here's my hand, and welcome to you, and sit down and let's have a drink on the house."

Farrell,[14] the boss, comes in—catches Delehanty who has to arrest someone, so he picks quiet, harmless stranger at the bar for disorderly conduct—followed him in to make sure.

Farrell sees vote in Malatesta—maybe several—when Malatesta denounces Capitalist system, he admires his soapboxing—he would be useful for Italian vote[15]—tells Daniello to make him see the light—vote for socialist ticket is wasted—no chance—leaving pats Malatesta on the shoulder: "You'll learn. Listen to Daniello. He'll put you wise. That socialist talk may get you something back home but there's nothing in it here. You'd starve to death. See you on the bandwagon."

Farrell comes to see Daniello regarding getting out Italian vote—but also about his son and May—good match—but says she won't accept him—(Resentfully): "What's matter? Doesn't she think he's good enough?" Daniello: "She doesn't think anyone in world [is] good enough except maybe a movie star." Farrell: "Well, you better get some sense in her head." Daniello: "You have a daughter." Farrell (At once gloomy): "I have, for my sins. She wants to be a nun."

Another perpetual quarrel between Shoemaker and Gardener—former insists Gardener's boss is an aristocrat and must be shot—Gardener likes boss who used to interfere with gardening: "I told him. You are a fool. Would I tell you how to run your copper mines, etc. The boss, he has brains. He says all right." Shoemaker: "He should be shot." Gardener: "He has brains, I tell you. He has millions, great success. He will never give you a chance to shoot him. The minute he sees anarchism marching he will join us."

They each tell him [Malatesta] how much money saved each month—once to go back to Italy—but now to buy house, land.

Delehanty says: "If anarchism comes, what good? No one believes in God or money any more. We'll all be no better than a lot of dirty animals."

Malatesta commenting on universal lawbreaking remarks bitterly: "In Italy the poor at least have to obey the laws." Delehanty: "This is a free country, where all have equal rights."

Concern of all about May—can she be married off before she's seduced?—like her mother once was—Shoemaker says: "I have never said it but I always suspected you, too, were her lover as well as Malatesta before she married Daniello." Gardener: "You. What do you mean, too? Do you dare mean to tell me you betrayed our friendship." Shoemaker: "Don't take out your knife. I have one, too. So long ago. And we believed in free love." Gardener: "As anarchists, we still believe." Remember about Francina[16]—a flame, etc.—they rave—then disillusioned—and now, a truck—2 ton—she would rather have a bowl of spaghetti than Casanova—the way of life—(Thoughts about old days).

Francina laments (about Malatesta's coming): "The nearer he gets, the fatter I feel."

Curtain on 1st (?) Act—Malatesta's speech—passionate and moving—tells of experience—reasons for coming—to recover my faith in the human spirit, in simple happiness, etc.—they solemnly approve: "You've come to the right place."

(Change idea about older daughter)—widow—still wears deep mourning—full of dramatic, tragic, uncontrollable grief—although truth is she did nothing but bitterly scorn her husband (his character the same)—now she makes romantic fantasy about him—a great poet, his aspirations stifled by her family's commercialism, etc.

From his friend, Daniello's, letters Malatesta has got idea of simple, happy family life—all he has sacrificed for the cause—he dreams of this in prison—and when he gets out and is disillusioned by own followers who are as anxious as Government to exile him, it becomes his idea of heaven to work at a humble job with his hands—at craft and forget men's greed for power—they are all sentimentally touched but at the same time disappointed—they excuse him, effect of jail, treachery of followers—he'll get over it—make a comeback—food is what he needs, Rosa thinks—friendship and good talk of the old days with a bottle of red wine is Daniello's opinion—a job to take his mind off is the son's opinion—a woman's love is the older daughter's opinion—and this gives them all an idea.

Francina makes a confidant of May because only sympathetic listener although she is exasperated by her stupidity—cow-like stupidity.

Connor and Daniello—about daughters—Connor: "Wants to become a nun." Tony: "In America?" Connor: "Of course. Where else?" Tony: "Then you shoulda worry. That is nothing."

My Francina,[17] she is a highbrow. She reads the National Geographic. She wants to be a nun in Tibeta. With the Chinks. And her a good Catholic. Can you beat it!" Connor sighs sympathetically: "If they only would, eh?" Tony: "Swella chance!" Connor: "Swell chance is right. She'd expect me to build a new convent for her and put it on the payroll. My other daughter married a bum. The only thing he can do is imitate John McCormick singing Mother Macree, and he can only do that when he's drunk. I've got him on the payroll as a construction engineer. He pulls the boss of a concrete union; [he works] whenever the foreman yells at him and tells him to and he's sober enough to listen. He's a promising lad, if you don't care about what you promise. Someday the newspapers will get on to him, and there'll be a great yell of throw the grafters out. They'll name me, of course, not him." Daniello again says: "Thatsa nothing. You don't know the half." Tells of Francina's marriage: "He reads books, so I make him bookkeeper, although I don't need books, and on my honor it's only fools who keep books—but I think books for giving good front—I warn him but when I look, first entry is case of scotch 55$—so I made him a waiter." (End conversation where they both become dutifully proud parents again.)

Rosa blames daughter's ardent romanticism on herself—sons have sense, take after father, but girl [is a] fool like she used to be—"men used to call me the angel of the barricades, the rose of the revolution—they said my spirit was a bright wind, the inner flame of freedom—and I believed them—I know now they meant I gave it away free."

Toward end, after Malatesta denounces them all and tries to beat it, both daughters say: "I am with child"—May because it strikes her as dramatic—Rosa boxes her ears. "Do you have to copy sister in everything?" Men of family very serious about this—son gets guns from behind the bar.

(One of reasons Malatesta is going is because he feels temptation of women—in honor.)

Malatesta is shocked by disregard for law—they explain [it is] easy in the old country because [there are] few [laws]—here [there are] so many [that] if all the laws were enforced everyone would always be in jail—every fool who can do nothing useful is elected to the legislation and gets a law passed—but this is a free country so no one pays any attention, not even the police.

Malatesta [is] astonished speakeasy [is] wide open—should think they'd have to close it down—Daniello remarks gloomily: "It wouldn't be shut long. The cops are too thirsty."[18]

General Notes   Feb. '41

Connor and Daniello—old pals—came up ladder together—both eager for the marriage of May and Michael—Connor worried—Michael can't get her to say yes, etc.—"Warn you as a friend she's getting talked about as a flirt"—Daniello shrugs: "Isa nothing. She bats the bug eyes, she walks and wiggles da prat. But isa nothing. Her mother keepa da eagle eye out. Sleeps in the same room witha da door locked. My Rosa knows all da tricks. Anyway, May [is] too lazy taka da trouble. If it was easy, I might worry, because she's lika cow, not wisa da game. But we all watch, make it too hard. She would have to use brains and she ain't gotta none. She would have to take trouble, and she's too lazy. She bats her bug eyes, she wiggles da prat, but da rest, it's too much trouble. So don't worry. She maka da good wife."

(He talks about May to cronies after Connor goes.)

Daniello tells Connor of Malatesta's coming—describes him enthusiastically but no mention of Anarchism—fought for liberty, etc.—Connor approves: "He can keep right on fighting for liberty over here. We can use him in a land where a thirsty man isn't allowed to take a drink. (They are drinking.)—Suppose you'll make him a guard on your trucks?"—Daniello indignant—tries to explain without explaining—idolatry: "Great, educated man—dreams—freedom for the world." Connor: "Well, like charity, it begins at home."—Daniello: "[He's a] great orator."—Connor interested—use him in election, etc.—Daniello gives up—then after Connor goes [he says] to shoemaker and gardener: "Wise guy but how could he understand?"—then discussion: "What's to be done with Connor when the Revolution comes?"—shoemaker the extremist says: "Must be shot."—Tony: "No, he's a good fellow—and controls the machine—will become an Anarchist—as we'll need his machine—against the counter-revolution—he is a good Republican party member because it pays, but when he sees Anarchism pays better—."

Delehanty's disillusionment and scorn for Malatesta—English accent—can't believe he ever did anything for freedom—besides he's a teetotaler—no revolution was ever started drinking water.

First scene alone between Malatesta and Rosa—she says: "I see wonder in your eyes, Cesare. And I know what you are wondering. You are wondering how any woman can be so fat and live." (She sighs) "Well, one pays for everything. I pay fat for wisdom." Malatesta: "Wisdom, Rosa?" Rosa: "Yes, the more I saw of life the more I was convinced that only the desire for food can be gratified without disillusionment—that is, if one has a good cook or is a good cook oneself, etc."

He says: "Should have married you, Rosa."—She says injuredly, amused: "You don't have to shut your eyes when you say it, Cesare. That is not polite. Marry me? Yes, that was the least you could have done, considering what I gave you—and all free, too!" Malatesta: "You forget we viewed marriage as slavery. You, above all. You were a flame, etc."—Rosa: "The angel of the barricades. I know. But even in the barricades, a woman does not lose all her common sense, she is wondering which of the comrades still alive would make a good husband." Malatesta blurts out: "Perhaps I suspected with reason your flame of freedom burnt too freely, and I was but one among many who enjoyed—." Rosa: "Not many. Only three, I swear to you."

General Notes   Feb. '41

Malatesta [is] disillusioned, bitter, sad, sick and weary—seeks surcease and sanctuary within the family—in jail, his broodings in solitary have turned back in nostalgic memory to his own family—with remorse, regret—for he had disregarded them—also regrets he hadn't married Rosa—spoiled youngest child of a shopkeeper, whose other children (two sons, two daughters) had kept to own class—brilliant student—their savings had sent him to the University—he had become assistant professor—great university career ahead of him[19]—then radicalism, arrest, flight to England—returns, conspiracy. Humbert's assassination, arrest, conviction.[20] Lipani Island—one brother has become important Fascist—he gets Cesare pardoned (to get rid of disgrace) on pledge he will abstain from political activities—he pledges because, of course, a pledge to tyrants doesn't count—then he starts to engage in underground activities—but finds old pals don't want him—fighting for the leadership, jealous—also afraid he will compromise them—then both Fascist police and his Anarchist pals warn him to get out of the country—24 hours or be liquidated[21]—both have it all fixed to smuggle him into U.S.

In jail, his spirits had still sternly rejected as weakness his longing for bourgeois family ties—but afterwards when comrades disown him, he gives in—and remembers Daniello—and Rosa—so what he finally demands is money enough to get him to the town in Connecticut—his compromise with self—that dream was beautiful, but only Utopian dream—not possible until man grows a soul—in a thousand years, perhaps—meanwhile, there are the unchanging simple things, family, love, honest toil, etc.

So when he is first alone with the three Anarchist cronies and Rosa, and they say, now we can talk (cop is present) at first he is afraid of cop—they and Daniello reassure him—then he says gently, no talk of politics, gentlemen—tells his experiences and resolve—after he leaves, they discuss worriedly—but reassure selves—temporary—or maybe testing us—Rosa says: "He wants to get married"—shoemaker (bachelor) taunts: "Yes, that will sure restore his love of liberty." Rosa says: "You asked me to marry you 47 times."—Daniello (laughs): "That many? I thought it was only 46. And to think I only asked you once." Rosa: "You never asked me at all. You were too timid. To you I was a second flame of freedom, etc." Daniello tells what he and his son have done for the poor—made them alky cookers[22]—their earnings now as compared with before—Malatesta asks the shoemaker and gardener how they are doing—each prosperous—they boast of savings, property—then guilty, complain—no better then slaves chained to back of Roman galley, like Ben Hur in movies.

"Francina's husband didn't drink," Angelo relates (to Connor?). "One drink makes him sick—I tried to get him drunk a couple of times. I was going to loan him the [word here is illegible] and tell him to beat her up—but he passed out and she beat him up—now she's repudiated."

Plot (in nutshell)   Feb. '41

Malatesta seeks surcease in the family—all he asks is to be accepted as one of them, forget the past—they welcome him but won't accept recanting—at least, men won't—they think he is being crazy—doesn't trust them—Rosa sees desire to be married—time he settled down.

He at once becomes the subject of all sorts of family intrigue—becomes bewildered and exasperated by contradictions—their American beliefs and activities.

Finally, the main family plot is to get him married to Francina—At end, they have made him into fiery Anarchist again—Malatesta: "The first thing is to destroy the family"—they agree enthusiastically—he is again helpless before their ability to ignore even the most blatant paradoxes between their supposed beliefs and their lives—and all of them so good-natured and kindly and likable he cannot hate or despise them.

The end is he agrees to marry Francina—and they have to find a job for him—"books is all he is good for—doesn't know how to make pineapples, can't shoot, too absent-minded to tend a still, he'd blow himself up or set the house on fire—no good at political work because English accent and because he can't seem to get an American system through his head—can't let him start a newspaper because [word is erased]—only thing [is] to keep books as a front—but afraid first entry he'll make will be 50 cases of Scotch at so much—yes, we'll have to hire one of the boys to be assistant and tell him what he is to enter—it will cut dough but what the hell, we're making plenty, and he's a good guy, we gotta look after him someway, now he's marrying into the family."

Scene in which Angelo tries to make clear to Malatesta how things are in the U.S. and how to act if you want to belong—Angelo: "You're an anarchist. Well, what of it. Only that's your business, see? You don't go round telling people what you believe. Who cares what you believe? You wouldn't go round shouting 'I'm a Baptist,' would you! They'd say, all right, what the hell, be a Baptist, etc."

Malatesta denies he had anything to do with the assassination of Humbert—terrorist group of fanatics—true anarchism never justifies bloodshed—Angelo disgusted: "You mean to say you wasn't the brain behind bumping off Humbert. Well, for Christ sake, don't tell Pop that. (Then he thinks with relief) Oh, I get it. You don't trust me. Well, no hard feelings. You're wise, at that. Don't never say nothing. And don't never know nothing, that's the right way."

But at very end when in consultation Angelo, father, two cronies [talk] about Malatesta's future. Angelo says disgustedly: "Do you know, I don't believe that guy had a damned thing to do with bumping off King Humbert."—his father and cronies turn on him ferociously.

Act One   Feb. [17] '41

Speakeasy in back of grocery store—night (crowd's worries let out).

Tony and Angelo—Tony about to leave and meet train—Angelo's attitude toward father [is] one of tolerant kidding, amused affection—Tony gloats over profits—Angelo: "Yeah, but we'll do better"—Angelo's plans—then talk of Malatesta—Tony has been meeting all trains since Malatesta's letter a week ago—Angelo: "Take a cot with you, use at station"—Angelo practical about Malatesta—job for him—if he can make pineapples—"Must have guts—if he's not stir-crazy, etc." Tony indignant—[son] doesn't understand—Malatesta [is] a great revolutionist, etc.—Angelo says: "He's an anarchist, against laws, especially unjust law like Prohibition"—but his father is encouraged to tell again story of great moment in his life when he, Rosa, Bascone, Gebardi belonged to anarchist band in Italy—darkly mysterious about parts of it as some thing that even now it is not safe to reveal to even family—Angelo amusedly bored: "I know—heard story ten thousand times—but you forget when you've a skinful of wine with Gebardi and Bascone—you tell a lot more—King Humbert got bumped off—and you sure all pushed—you and Gebardi and Bascone released and told to get out of Italy—Malatesta sent to jail as brain that planned it—well, what of it—guys get bumped here every day and hardly get names in papers." Daniello: "But a king with a whole army and fun's fun!" Angelo: "A king gets plugged same as anyone else—and that Wop army ain't no good—and fool cops, we know they can be fixed"—Tony gives up disgustedly—but demands respect for Malatesta—Angelo agrees: "Seems he must be a right guy. I'm all for him."

Incident of knock on door—peeps back—Angelo recognizes but sends away—private club—only for friends of family—go around to my place on Front Street[23]—wide open.

Connor comes—business?—Connor: "No only friendly visit." He jokes: "Where are the Red conspirators?" Tony with superior voice: "Have become bourgeois"—Connor (amused) "I see. You're the only genuine article"—then he talks of May and son—Tony, the fond father, assures him everything [is] all right—then hopelessly: "Anyway what can I do? She'd do opposite"—then discussion of family troubles—which concentrate finally on Francina and her grief—only 1st cousin of Rosa, too—Angelo cynical: "Don't take Sherlock to tell what's the matter with her—needs a guy"—Tony shocked: "Don't talk like that. She's your mother's first cousin—been like an aunt to you—very religious woman"—Angelo: "I got a system to beat her—don't listen—think of something else"—Tony again says: "Everything all right with May—good girl—you can trust my wife, Rosa—she knows all the tricks—sleeps in the same room—she keeps her good"—Connor worried because his son [is] using it as an excuse to get tanked up.

Tony goes—scene with Connor and Angelo—discuss Malatesta—Connor asks if [it is] true Malatesta [was] brain of King Humbert killing—he's heard Tony, Bascone, and Gebardi whispering surreptitiously about it when full of red wine—"Hear 'em in the next state"—Angelo clams up: "Don't know nothing"—Connor says: "Needn't be cagey with me—no use for kings—and none of my business what happened in Italy long ago, except I wish it had been king of England"—but warns him [he should get] no notion to bump off President—have to stop that even if he is a Republican[24]—Angelo gives his advice about Malatesta—they discuss future—Angelo: "Speaking of business I'm glad you added a proposition—brewery—need beer as front, etc."[25] Connor impressed: "Who'd run it?"—Angelo: "I would, get someone to front for me—some respectable guy"— Connor starts to go—reverts to May—Angelo full of brotherly contempt: "Paul's[26] a right guy—tell [him] for me, forget it, get another doll. May's a dumb broad. If I was him I wouldn't marry her for a million bucks—Sure, she's pretty, I guess. Everyone can't be wrong, even if I can't see it."

May, Rosa enter—May: "Where's Poppa, etc." Angelo: "Where's the Black Death?"—his nickname for Francina—May: "Went upstairs to weep"—Angelo: "If husband was in the room [he would have] murdered her."—May kids [mentions her] old boy friend Morroni—Connor "Aha! So that's it"—Rosa jokes: "I had many beaux—I was like May, only with brains. I was a passionate flame, men said, and my heart was full of dreams to free everyone in the world from tyranny—all the men, I mean. I don't remember thinking of women, etc."—Connor rebukes May about son—May bats her eyes: "If he was more like his father, I'd marry him tonight"—Connor is calmed—then under spell: "She's dynamite"—Then Rosa tells all about daughters with extreme frankness—Connor gets up to go.

Bascone, Gebardi enter—arguing about movies from radical standpoint—capitalist propaganda poisons minds of people—May embraces them—[their] reaction [is] the same as Connor's—"Worse than an infernal machine in the house"—Rosa shrugs: "As busy as I am with her to chaperone, what harm? She has fun, and you have been lying to yourselves how your passion would embrace her, if you were young, etc."—Connor goes.

Talk about Malatesta—Bascone and Giebardi [are] full of romantic mystery—stupid of Tony to think Malatesta would come openly on a train—Italian secret police will be following, U.S. sent police looking for him—he will be in disguise, etc.—Rosa full of memories—has been feeling fatter and fatter since she knew he was coming—May [is] frankly curious: "Is he very handsome? What did he look like?"—Rosa describes—May enthusiastic—Rosa: "But, of course, he has changed—like me." May: "Were you very much in love with him, Mom?"—Rosa: "Never loved anyone but your father."

Delehanty comes in—hiding outside until Connor left: "Grand man, is Pat, but unreasonable at times"—Angelo derisive: "Yes, he thinks a cop ought to be sober sometimes and walk a beat instead of sitting in a ginmill and being God's gift to bourgeois, etc."—good natured banter, kidding.

Francina comes in—deep mourning—sits down casting gloom—everyone irritated, but constrained to passify—urge drink, food—finally Angelo makes remark that gets under her skin—she flares up into acid fury—blasts one after another—ends up by fit of tears—Francina: "Never respects my grief"—no one is amused but Rosa and May—May says: "She needs a man, don't she, Mom." Rosa: "Sush! Don't talk like that." May: "Why not? You're always telling her that"—Francina goes on: "Yes, May, your mother thinks love is like a dish of spaghetti, when one is gone, you just help yourself to another"—Rosa: "Well, there is something in that." Francina: "Bah! All you think of is food. Look how fat you are! At least, I have kept my figure"—her hopes Malatesta will come—someone to talk to who still dreams of freedom, who is not a slave to food and money and hooch and shoes and the dirt of gardens and graft, etc.

Tony returns—disappointed: "No one got off the train but a little man with glasses and a beard"—others: "But he might have grown a beard"—Tony: "Nonsense, that disguise is for the funny papers, would make him stand out like a lighthouse, etc."—all let down, start to go to bed when there is a knock—no one pays much attention—some drunk—Angelo opens peephole—truculent: "Go on, Bum. This ain't no public speak. This is our house, see. What? You're—— Well, for Christ sake! Oh, come in, come in. We're all expecting you."

Malatesta enters—all taken aback by his appearance—black beard[27] and mustache, dark glasses—little thin man, stoop-shouldered, frail. Well dressed entirely in black—he at once recognizes Tony, then Bascone and Gebardi—his eager warmth and relief—their reserve and suspicion—"Maybe he's a Federal agent"—Angelo says: "Suppose you take off those cheeters and let us have a look"—Malatesta bewildered—takes off glasses, explaining about eyes—then they recognize—vociferous warmth and apology—"Of course, glasses and beard are a disguise"—Suddenly Malatesta sees Delehanty and starts—bitter reproach: "So, my supposed good old friends, you betray me like all the others. You have the police waiting"—now it is they who are bewildered—then they laugh—wonderful joke—"Delehanty [is an] old friend"—kid about him which Delehanty takes with a good-natured grin and retorts [after he] shakes hand in warm welcome: "I'm all for you when it comes to Ireland and bloody destruction to tyrants. But mind you, I part with you when it comes to denying God and the Roman Catholic church."—this last bewilderment is too much for Malatesta—he begins to crumple up—explaining weakly: "No money, nothing to eat"—faints—consternation—solicitude—get him to bed—Francina takes command—Rosa [goes] to kitchen—Tony picks up Malatesta—light as a feather—goes upstairs, leaving Delehanty and Angelo—Delehanty says: "Well, got to get back on beat"—takes another drink—Angelo says resentingly: "Imagine his passing out after taking a slant at you. Well, at that, it ain't so surprising."

Act Two   Feb. '41

Following morning—dining room of house upstairs—Rosa, Francina and May—Malatesta has been served breakfast in bed—by all three.

Francina [is] indignant about May's flirtatiousness—rebukes Rosa for improper training of daughter, etc.—Francina and May go out to market—Malatesta comes in—has heard them go—scene between him and Rosa—he wears raincoat as a dressing gown, she [is] in a dirty old wrapper—memories of the old flaming romance—scene breaks up when he hears someone coming upstairs—goes to shave, finish dressing—Rosa reflects: "He should never have shaved."

Tony, Bascone and Gebardi come up. Bascone and Gebardi have declared holiday to celebrate Malatesta's arrival—Bascone: "Gebardi lies to boss—he laughs, says: 'Don't get too drunk.'"

Angelo comes—then Francina and May return—family council and argument on Malatesta's future.

Malatesta comes back—his story and explanations—his ideal, return to the family, simple things, etc.—their relief and disappointment—"You've come to the right place" etc.—May bats her eyes, etc.

Finally Francina says: "Now that's settled, get out of here, all you men—go downstairs if you want to get drunk"—strict housekeeper, broken routine has ruined day for her—but she shows calculating soft spot for Malatesta—at very end, he apologetically but firmly condemns drinking—capitalist poison to dull the minds of people, etc.—amazement!—then hastily catches self—"Old habit, I forgot I am done with all that cant"—puts it differently—"For the happiness of family. Alcohol corrupts love and respect within the family."

They all agree with him that Utopia is impossible until man outgrows his base greed—his spiritual immaturity—and develops a soul: "No Movement can do it—they lead to greed for power—each man and woman strives within himself or herself to conquer own natures—from the ape, etc."—they solemnly agree—he goes on: "One thing we can all do—give up the poison, alcohol."

A Probie!

General notes (cont.)	Feb. '41

Connor—one of pet beefs (beside family) is mayor of town is giving him trouble—"A good guy but dumb—goes to banquets, gets skinful and talks—don't know nothing but what I told him to say during campaign—'I pledge my word of honor to clean house and throw the rascals out'—told him that's the wrong line now—he's become a disturbing element—makes himself unpopular—people at peace now, don't like being bothered—I try to make him see it—I tell him, 'Dave, you talk too much—you'd think you elected yourself—I elected you—and it don't make sense now we're in, that throw the rascals out stuff'—I tell him: 'For Christ's sake, be reasonable, how're you going to throw yourself out?'—that stopped him—but only for a minute—then he pulls an oldie on me—'But I ain't a rascal'—can you beat it?"

Angelo's final conclusion about Malatesta's position in anarchist movement (after he believes he had nothing to do with bumping off King Humbert)—"He was a front they pushed out to make them look like harmless nuts—a dope"—and then he gets idea that's the way to use him now—front and dope for brewery.

Before Malatesta's arrival—their reactions to his coming—Tony, Bascone and Gebardi delighted—like old days—we can all sit in here and drink good wine and talk of the Revolution—but uneasy lest Malatesta start anything in this country—worry for their business—rationalize—besides, time is not ripe—everything prosperous—no discontent—he will listen to us—

knows we know conditions—time to lie low—make plans for day—when we are all poor and starving, etc.

Angelo is worried that Malatesta may be recognized: "Big story in papers—of course, nobody gives a damn what happened in Italy over twenty years ago, or who bumped off King Humbert—most of them think all kings should be bumped off anyway—but they read he's staying with us—and then reds read—and then everyone begins to think about speakeasy and how much money we make—and everyone gets mad—they're not making so much—and then they write letters to complain, etc.—and the next thing there's a padlock on the speak, and I have to make another plan, and there's new profits to pay, and a lot of trouble, and the big shot in the city lets me know if I can't keep this town in line, I'll move in someone who can"—etc.—but Angelo is game: "Malatesta is father's old pal—we stick by him."

They think Malatesta has escaped (he got life)—truth is [words "in papers" are erased but faintly visible].

Act Three   Feb. '41

A month later—Malatesta [is] going strong on the reform of the family—fully recovered in health now, full of energy and immensely talkative—his manner persuasive but firmly dictatorial—and whenever he gets under any of their skins so that they turn on him, he immediately blames himself and his previous experience—out of touch with humanity, has become awkward and tactless—so finally it is they who feel in the wrong—because they see he is quite sincere in this.

Francina has become his ally in this Puritan movement—she has pointed out the failings of members of the family which he must reform—and she particularly implants the idea of herself as the poor relation, the humiliated drudge, the defenseless widow—she changes her tune about dead husband—quits hero worship of his memory when she sees this displeases Malatesta—he suggests husband was perhaps weak—she agrees—he suggests she stop wearing mourning—points out that one of the things which prevents growth of the soul is man's enslavement to past, to the dead—she agrees—all the time she is shrewd and calculating underneath—and firmly blackmails each member of the family she discovers disobeying his edicts.

The Visit of Malatesta · 33

He has the whole household in subjection and severity [if they are] disobeying his laws—Rosa's acting—drinking of others—selling of drinks—urges abandonment of everything but innocent growing, close to simple things of earth—but run at small profit, just enough to support family.

One person he gets nowhere with is May—he rebukes her flirting—extols the beauty of innocence and virginity—duty as future wife and mother of family—but May simply bats her eyes, wiggles and giggles—and he becomes aroused—Francina interrupts scene—for a moment angry and jealous, drives May off—then when Malatesta kisses her hand coldly, as caring less to her, she shrewdly sees her advantage—afterwards encourages May.

He insists Bascone should marry, and that Gebardi become reconciled with his wife—he thinks it is their duty to give greedy savings to help educate men to see Prohibition is salvation of family—They assemble in the backroom—only sneak in when sure he is not there—saw with Delehanty—he hints that lecturers are needed to go forth spread the gospel of deliverance from alcohol—his change of viewpoint about law—as Anarchist believed laws made criminal—now he knows laws are necessary—not State laws but implacable laws within the family.

Angelo tries persuasive argument—Malatesta gently points out he twists things around, makes end justify means, should have been a Jesuit—Angelo: "Me, a Jesuit!"

Angelo finally calls in Connor for advice and help—it is Connor who suggests front man for brewery—but Francina would put him wise—Connor says: "That's easy. Buy her off"—Angelo: "You don't know her. She'd keep raising the ante, etc."—Rosa joins the conspiracy—suggests marrying off Francina to Malatesta—gets rid of both—Angelo eager: "Kill two birds with one shot" but he is doubtful "if you bring her into it, she'll hold out for a million—and how will you get him to want to marry her?"—Rosa says leave it to her: "I know a lot about men and a lot about women, too. There is no fool like an old fool, as your father knows, and as I might know if I wasn't too fat, and they are both old fools. And there is no fool like a young fool, and of all young fools our May is the most stupid"—Connor: "Where's May come into it?"—Rosa: "As bait to catch a sucker. She is so stupid she will never know."

Change plot so Rosa (the realist who loves diamond rings and food) becomes the brain behind all the plot to get rid of Malatesta and Francina.

She is the only one who realizes Malatesta is telling the truth about himself—all others think it's a stall.

He has grown a beard in prison—they think it's a disguise—but bad one—rumors soon circulate in town (due to Bascone's and Gebardi's mysterious hints) he is an anarchist—(Gebardi gives him a job "close to the earth"—his boss laughs: "Looks like an anarchist in movies. Where'd you get him?"—No good at job and Gebardi thinks best to advise him to quit).

Rosa and Francina close—but both see through the other.

Francina against Malatesta at first, but mothers while scolding him—Rosa convinces her he means what he says about family—Francina says: "Then he wants to get married?"—Rosa says: "Yes, but not as simple as that because he thinks he does not want anything so ordinary. He thinks he wishes to sleep with Society—human society—and they will have an only child called Utopia."

Rosa tells Francina: "I cannot tell the men the truth about him, because they are not like us, they need romance in their lives, and so they believe what they want to believe and what they read in newspapers and in books or see in movies—I do not know but I would bet all the songs about love in a calm cottage and heaven's rainbow, etc. are made by men. A woman would write songs about love in a castle that had two autos and a hundred diamond rings." It is Rosa who points out, when Francina complains about May flirting with Malatesta, that it is a good thing to make him wake up: "She will say a stupid thing to hurt him and he will bounce back from her and you will catch him—you have kept your figure although you eat as much as I do"—Francina: "I do not eat as much as you do. No one does. That is impossible."

Malatesta gets so he hates to see Rosa—wants to get out of sight—nothing against her—always feels deep affection—but she is a symbol of death of all his dreams—she used to be a slender flame, etc.—Francina tells him: "Yes, she is very fat and lazy. I tell her, if you would be like me and not eat so much and be active, you would keep your figure"—(and Rosa tells him this: "[Francina has a] figure like May's—she does not dress to show it off—she is modest—but I assure you if you saw her taking a bath, you would be surprised.")

When finally men are desperate about what to do with Malatesta to get rid of him, Rosa talks to each and says she will fix it—to Bascone and Gebardi, each of whom has given him a job—Gebardi gets rid of him by saying he's had to cut down—but Bascone has no excuse—her price is a diamond ring—but she will let them off easy—from both, not from each—she tells husband the same—and Angelo and Connor, assures each—she has already got promise from Francina if she gets him to marry her—(Rosa wants to get rid of him, too, because he makes her feel too fat)—she now holds up Delehanty for promise to buy her each week a two-pound box of chocolate creams.

She tells them her scheme will get rid of not only Malatesta but Francina—(she wants to get rid of Francina, too, because she eats so much—yet doesn't get fat, etc.)—she says: "I will get them married"—they are all indignant—"Fine scheme!—have them here forever!"—"Wait. There is the brewery. It will appeal to his idealism, to make restitution for the passion of the family." "But that's only a front." "He will never know. He sees only what he wishes to see." "But Francina will know." "Yes, you will have to buy her off. She wants to marry him so it can be done cheaply—a cut of the present [take]—and we would have to support them, if you didn't, etc."—"And this will solve the problem of his scandal—resign as an anarchist—Probies will think he is a moral citizen and those who know the brewery is Malatesta's real love will esteem him as a patriot who believes in Democratic freedom"—"He will be fine front for the brewery—and you can get him to lecture in churches on family prohibition—he loves to talk"—they say: "Whole scheme depends on marriage and he may be a damned fool but he is not such a fool as to marry her—no one is!"—Rosa says: "That is where I am the brain. I will fix it"—Connor: "Well, it's true anything on earth can be fixed if you know the ropes."—Rosa: "I know his ropes and they are very honorable. Listen. Here is the scheme. You will have to help" (she whispers)—they listen with a few protests—Angelo: "But he won't go to her room. What would he go for? Christ, even after twenty years in the can, nobody would fall for—" (Whispers)—Connor: "I don't like May being dragged into it. She's going to marry my son"—Rosa: "She will not be dragged. Haven't I taken care of her?"—they all reassure Connor—Rosa says: "I have brought her up to be a good happy wife. She is so stupid she will never suspect anything. And when she knows Francina is to be married, she will want to be. She is like that. She never does anything for herself. She imitates." (Whispers) Rosa says: "And you will have your knife [to Tony] and Angelo will have his sawed off shotgun. Malatesta always hated violence and force."[28]

After meeting breaks up, scene between Rosa and May—May has listened—Rosa gets May to write a note—but first May holds mother up for a diamond ring: "I listened at the keyhole"—Rosa admiring but annoyed: "Remember it is smart to be stupid but very stupid to be too smart"—May: "Shall I sign [my] name?"—Rosa: "Well, thank God, you are not smart—but remember never sign name—except to property deed."

Francina objects to May scheme—Rosa says: "Bah! What do you care how you hook him. Once you have him you will make him forget May"—Francina: "Yes, since I have seen him shaved, I know I can make a good, faithful husband of him. He has a chin like my first husband—a very beautiful chin. I think—stronger than my first but not too much stronger."

Objections—"But Francina will say she didn't write the note." Rosa: "No, she will not."

Delehanty's remark about Malatesta's accent: "Did he go to Harvard?" (his prejudice against Harvard) "No." Delehanty: "He sounds like a Harvard wop to me."

Francina: "Passion Rose of the Revolution."—final curtain, reporter interviewing her—story of life—"They called me the Passion Rose of the Revolution."—they all burst out laughing.[29]

Scene Malatesta and Francina—She tells of Tony's affair with girl—wise to his pals giving him an alibi[30]—Rosa: "She tells him '[Tony], You are as handsome as (name hero), as strong as a stallion and younger than any of the young men. I love you passionately and when I lie in bed without you I dream of you and moan and tear the pillow slips with my teeth longing for you, and so will you give me a hundred dollars to buy silk stockings and a few other little things I need to make myself more beautiful so I can keep your love.' So Tony gives her the hundred because she proved she loves him so passionately. She is stupid that one, but not a fool. Now me, I was very intelligent at her age, but what a fool I was. I always gave it away. Of course, then—the excuse that none of you had anything. I suppose you still have nothing, Pado?"—Malatesta shocked—Rosa: "No, no, I was not making hints for I am much too fat, and you are old and should husband your strength (she insists on tucking a shawl around him)—and anyway I love only Tony and desire no revenge because I understand and forgive him. After all, if some handsome young man should say to me: 'You are as beautiful as Venus with Mary Pickford's smile and I die of longing for your love and dream of you and moan not able to sleep and tear my sheets to shreds with my teeth, and how about giving me two hundred?' I might give it to him."

Francina is always eating—garlic and slabs of cheese and red wine—Tony complains to his pals and cop, excusing his philandering—Tony: "I love Francina and no woman could ever take her place in my heart, but how can you desire passionately one so fat she should be in a circus, and she is always eating" (as he talks he eats).

She approves of affair before marriage—romantic background—sharing—all for love, etc.—she is very anxious May should be seduced—Rosa: "But one cannot advise her openly. I would have brought them up in the true Revolutionary spirit, where one can desire such things freely, but Tony would not allow it. He said. 'This is America and they must be brought up as good Americans.' I said: 'Don't you think Americans make children before [marriage]?' He said: 'No, they are a very cold people who think first of making money.' "

She does not let Tony know she suspects his affair—would spoil it for him—romantic intrigue—sweet assignation—makes him feel a young anarchist again—"I refuse to believe children's warnings, or friends—they think I am very stupid."

Beeg—lika—justa come—can't speaka—by jeez—fina place—what's you want—les—aina-she's (it) thisa—peacha no price—so what the hell—if we dona gotta—thasa good—thissa—Santa Maria—no, and no!—donna lie!—troub' (trouble)—betta (better)—she's a spoiled (is)—I no gotta work—[31]

To the Day!
To the Night!

·2·
THE LAST CONQUEST

Introduction

A first reading of *The Last Conquest* will inevitably raise the question why Eugene O'Neill, in his last creative years, when he was in bad health and frequently in pain, would attempt to write a work of such monumental scope. What needed to be said in this play that had been left unsaid in others in the past?

A first step toward answering this question is to look at the author's initial idea for the work written on August 30, 1940: "Christ-Devil on the Mountain play (Duality of Man's psyche—opposites—with application [to] present world crisis)." The dimensions of the work then become more apparent. The Good-Evil struggle, man's lower nature engaged in deadly combat with his higher nature, had been fought in a number of plays previously in the canon. O'Neill produced a memorable gallery of central characters who were hopelessly split: Dion Brown in *The Great God Brown,* Reuben Light in *Dynamo,* John Loving in *Days Without End.* The dramatist had a new and more specific goal in mind beyond the depiction of the battle on an individual level. The phrase "with application to present world crisis" indicates clearly his intention: to explore and depict the Good-Evil political split among nations that he perceived in the early 1940s. To represent the two clashing forces, he foregoes utilizing mere mortals and uses supernatural powers in a divine/profane split as opposing combatants. The actual field of battle is, as O'Neill points out, "Man's psyche," but he refers to universal Man rather than to a specific individual. What he contemplates here is a morality play, a political as well as a spiritual propaganda work.

The Last Conquest is set in a futuristic totalitarian state peopled by mindless robot slaves besotted by greed and self indulgence, who had, eons earlier, tired of the responsibilities of being free, of values that seemed archaic. A series of dictators had so ravaged "the already sick and faithless souls of men" that they paved the way for "world-wide spiritual exhaustion and the acceptance of the new Salvation and the Divine Tyrant Redeemer principles in a Holy and Indivisible World State." Obviously, the balance between the Good-Evil supernatural beings has been shattered. In former times, when it seemed as though the world was so besotted with evil that good had been thoroughly eclipsed, some turn of events occurred to restore the balance. Currently in the twisted world O'Neill portrays, Evil (Satan, the force claiming this World State as his domain) seeks an even greater distorted control and plans to wage "a last campaign of Evil to stamp out even the unconscious memory of God in Man's spirit." When Satan, the Minister of Spiritual Affairs, presents his plan to the puppet "Super Elite" leaders of the World State, he explains that man had, at one time, indulged in "fantasies about Evil and Good, flesh and spirit, the eternal opposites in his nature, which waged a battle for . . . his immortal soul." To Satan, Christ is, as he remarks, still "alive as man—in war with me."

Actually, Satan has a secret secondary reason for instigating his plan. He has grown bored after many centuries of the one-sided struggle, of unmitigated evil. The soul of man has become a pigsty in which he is condemned to live. He desires two things: Christ's help to restore men's pride, "to make them live again the conflict of Good and Evil—the eternal opposites," and a release from man, a negotiated exile to a refuge in the blessed isles. He even begs Christ's mercy to "take the doom of final victory from me."

The Last Conquest is, in essence, a two-character play. The two are identified as Christ and the Devil in the early 1940 notes, as "The Man" and "The Magician" in the original scenario dated March 1941, and in the later notes as Christ and Satan. All the other characters in the March 1941 version are "life-size marionettes (or dwarf-ventriloquist dummies)." In the first scenario Christ is depicted as alive and is the one responsible for renewing the ancient conflict that disturbs and rouses Satan from his exile among sinners.

Satan is, undoubtedly, one of the most complex characters

O'Neill ever conceived. On one hand, he is proud and boastful, reminding Christ of his earlier state before his fall: "I was once known as Lucifer." His tragedy is that he *knows* what he has lost. This part of him wants to persist in the temptation and ruination of man, but his job has been made too easy. Unintelligible, brute slave man still has the possibility of gaining the paradise lost to him. In these periods Satan is filled with giant despair and sinks deeper into the sty of the psyche of man, whom he no longer needs to tempt ("There is nothing left of the soul in man to fight") and for whom he feels nothing but deep contempt. Man, as Satan describes him, clutches his vices lovingly to his bosom and seeks only the warmth and safety of the evil one's place, indulging in "females and wine," as does Satan, and "wallowing in the warm mud." In these periods Satan identifies himself with man and laments the fact that he has "too much of man's flesh."

On the other hand, Christ has to encourage Satan at times to continue the eternal charade in which they are engaged. The tempter is weary of his seemingly endless centuries-old assignment. He longs for some sort of pardon and a million years of solitude far from mankind. One of the strangest aspects about *The Last Conquest* is the loving bond that seems to exist between Christ and Satan throughout the centuries. Christ treats his adversary with great dignity, compassion, pity, and the spirit of brotherhood. Satan, in turn, adores Christ in the purist sense of the word. He has numerous moments when he demonstrates empathy with Christ, and he is deeply disturbed by the excruciating pain that Christ endures during the crucifixion scene in the play. He begs Christ to let him take his place on the cross, at first compromising, saying he will use fake nails to create the illusion of crucifixion but later willing to endure the actual agony. His great worry is that Christ will die without hope, without some sign that the hearts of men have been moved, a sign of possible transformation and regeneration. Several times Satan expresses a desire to halt the series of events leading up to and including the crucifixion.

Religious purists, especially those devotees of the "fire and brimstone Old Testament God," will perhaps scorn O'Neill's humanized, modernized Satan. What O'Neill is subtly conveying is the concept that God's mercy is so bountiful, so all-embracing and universal that even *the* cardinal sinner of all time, when truly repentant, may experience some faint, reflected rays of clemency. Some may find it ironic that a significant end-product of O'Neill's years of philosophical reflections should be a character such as Satan, one of the last he is to conceive. One can certainly deduce a kind of humorous bravado in O'Neill, a touch of mockery here from a man long ago exposed for so many of his early school years to the rigorous doctrines about hellfire and punishment by Catholic teachers. There is nothing too terrorizing about his Satan, a creature who is worried about the lack of reporters covering the stadium event in Scene Two because he wants to be able to show his news clippings to neighbors and relatives.

The dummy-dictator, called the Savior of the World in later scenes, is actually a puppet in the early notes. Later in the Prologue he "seems to be a living man" but is diminutive. He is completely under the control of Satan and is a shadowy reflection of him. He is the "apotheosis of man emptied of the spirit"; he epitomizes the worst vices of mankind; he is cruel, petulant, selfish, deceitful, and vindictive. Wisely, Satan had his age stopped at seven—"age of playing slaves and soldiers." He behaves ludicrously, and O'Neill, in this Don Quixote-Sancho Panza duo, must have slyly had in mind the partnership of Hitler and the buffoon-like Mussolini. Referring to the dummy, Satan remarks at one point in the play: "The theologians of Alexandria would have had a great time rationalizing that nut." Described as a "symbol of the modern world spirit," the dictator has been instilled "with only the cunning" Satan has given him. Strangely, however, they have a symbiotic relationship. Not only does this "leader" know what Satan allows him to know but he also has insights at times into the mind of Satan, a feat that does not seem too amazing when it is recalled the two are nothing more and nothing less than a ventriloquist and his dummy.

O'Neill makes no attempt at any point in the play to characterize Christ. But, as he progresses in the development of the play through the various sets of notes, he succeeds eventually in creating an aura about this figure that lends credibility to the concept that one is in the presence of a divine being. In the early February 7, 1941, notes, when Christ is simply called "The Man," he appears to be more human than divine, treating the Magician with "affectionate brotherliness." Wisely, O'Neill does not assign him too many utterances and gives him a mode of speech "as in the Testament whenever possible—with simplicity." O'Neill makes no attempt to find appropriate parables at points in the play where the author indicates they are to be used.

Rather than have Christ draw Satan back, as originally planned, to resume once again the ancient confrontation, O'Neill has Satan in the April 1942 Prologue attempt to recreate the presence of Christ in the wooden statue he carves, the face, in particular, being a remarkable likeness: "It is the face of Christ, the Man of sorrows face gentle, infinitely pitying and sad." In the eight-scene scenario of November 1942, O'Neill depicts Christ as more divine than human. Christ, in fact, infuses the statue. The author had tried previously in plays to portray a Christ figure; Lazarus in *Lazarus Laughed* and Cesare Malatesta in *The Visit of Malatesta* are fairly successful attempts. Had the dramatist completed *The Last Conquest* he would have at last succeeded.

O'Neill envisions *The Last Conquest* as a theatrical pageant, but he seems determined not to make the same mistakes he made in *Marco Millions* and *Lazarus Laughed*. In his first August 30 notation, he states he wants to create a "pure poetic form." Fortunately, he abandons this scheme, although some aspects of it might have appeared in the final version of the play; the author was capable of making tremendous transformations as he created, with great discrepancies at times between scenario drafts and completed plays. One *Lazarus*-like device he prudently discards is the April 1942 plan to use masks. For example, the Minister of Propaganda, "a living midget," was to wear a mask that would be a "replica of faces of the carved ones of the other members of the Council."

For the full-scale production of this massive reenactment of scenes leading up to and concluding with the crucifixion, Satan plans to enlist the aid of a slave theatre director and state actors who specialize in character parts. In his pride he plans to assume all the major roles in the play-within-a-play: "I will be director of the drama, ringmaster of the circus, leader of the orchestra." He will also, of course, play the leading role. In the March 1941 notes, though weary from the repetition, he prepares for his role "like an old actor making up the part he has played many times." His voice grows stronger and "revived by the approach of the curtain," he talks and "sits on the box and makes up the conventional Mephisto face." He displays an "actor's joy at the size of the audience." O'Neill's early experiences as an aid and observer during his theatrical father's road tours and his later apprenticeship during the production of his own early plays serve him well when he envisions the technical problems of staging *The Last Conquest*. To solve any sound problems in Scene One on the vast Mount of Temptation, he says: this part "is microphone—loud speaker stuff." For the night scenes Satan plans to "arrange for a thousand spotlights." The setting is, in a number of scenes, understandably flexible. The curtain will rise on a vast cyclorama. To be depicted are "Jerusalem, Ancient Rome, and megalopolitan capitals of civilization." In Scene Five, the Garden of Gethsemane, the stage is to look like an "outdoor Greek theatre." The setting described most minutely is the majestic Hall of Black Mirrors, which has an "obvious theatrical atmosphere." Scenic designers were to provide the "varied ranks of marionettes" as "part of the settings—background, dramatic and moving and changing."

O'Neill apparently cannot resist the use of mechanical devices, which proved to be so disastrous in *Dynamo*. In a last version of Scene Two, included in the procession that enters the stadium are "baby tanks (life size) followed by a truck load of puppet apostles." There is an "ass (life size)" with Christ on it, "his feet dragging on the ground (no saddle or stirrups)." Earlier in the notes O'Neill had contemplated using a "merry-go-round ass on wheels." Later in Scene Four, in the Hall of Last Suppers, after the Savior futilely attempts to stab Christ in the back and sees blood but no physical reaction from him (Satan later explains this is a "very old theatrical trick—bladder of blood"), he runs to the Statue of the State Goddess, exclaims "Mommy," and "flings his arms about her." Immediately "the arms begin to close on him with mechanical jabs." He is rescued by Satan, who reminds him of the numerous times previously when the Savior had used the button to kill his victims.

The dramatist planned an extensive use of music in *The Last Conquest;* stage musicians, for example, are to perform at the Last Supper. In some fragmentary thoughts jotted down in the November 1942 notes, the author writes the word "End," by which he presumably means the end of the play. The word is followed by "blaring of bands as people are marched home—

hymn to a murdered prop." If the "murdered prop" refers to the wooden carved statue of Christ, newly crucified on Calvary, it suggests an idea O'Neill used before in *The Great God Brown,* where the mask of Dion is treated as a living entity. When Dion's wife Margaret enters the home of William Brown, she disregards the body of the just-killed Brown, lovingly picks up Dion's "mask and kisses it heartbrokenly." Music recurs again in Scene Three, the Interior of the Temple: "Hymn—choir of pimps—the Whore's Weasel [is] sung." (The origin of this choice ditty is unknown.) Perhaps the most dramatic and effective use of music is at the end of the play when it is played and "turns into a hymn of Thanksgiving." By this time the palace and Savior have been destroyed and the hymn of thanks appropriately changes to glorious Easter music, symbolizing the resurrection of these dead souls who have been kept so long in captivity.

Ibsen's response when questioned why he wrote *A Doll's House,* "for its ending," can also be applied to *The Last Conquest.* On one level, that of modern man, O'Neill's "hopeless hope" is that man would somehow overcome his lower base nature, his enslavement to materialism and apathy about the misery of others, and allow his higher nature to triumph. On a second level, the international political one, O'Neill strikes a blow against totalitarian governments and their sadistic, cruel leaders. The author, through his many references to the monstrous Nazis and despotic World State, leaves a lasting reminder of the desperate war that is being waged between the forces of Good and Evil. On the third and final level, O'Neill attempts to encourage a spiritual awakening and an awareness of the benevolence of a Supreme Being in our lives.

A personal "dark night of the soul" experienced by the author perhaps explains why he was creatively stymied and unable to complete this play. On November 19, 1942, he notes in his Work Diary: "develop some inner struggle about it that has held it up." The following day he adds: "I think the inner conflict is because it is at its final curtain a declaration of faith by one who is faithless—like D[ays]. W[ithout]. E[nd].—a hope for faith instead of faith—and also a futile feeling that no one will see the truth, not even the author." He does continue with the play, however, trying to be "the objective dramatist," for nearly another month of intensive work. He seemed to have an obsession to finish this play.

O'Neill spent more working days on *The Last Conquest* than on the other two unfinished plays combined, writing ten sets of notes for it, dating from August 30, 1940, to December 13, 1942. Three days later, on December 16, he wrote to his friend Dudley Nichols and said: "*The Last Conquest* remains for the most part in scenario, although it constantly haunts me." Nichols maintains that as late as 1948, five years after the dramatist had ceased to write, he was still deeply absorbed in this "projected work of immense scope." Nichols adds: "To me it is tragic that he was never able to complete this magnificent project." What does remain, however, are the extensive notes. When one keeps in mind O'Neill's creative genius and his theatrical skills, it seems certain that *The Last Conquest,* had it ever been completed, would have been one of O'Neill's most memorable plays.

The 13th Apostle*
First notes on idea

Aug. 30, 1940[1]

"Straw For The Drowning"

Curtains or
  Presents a Straw
    More Than Straw

Idea

Christ-Devil on the Mountain play (Duality of Man's psyche—opposites—with application present world crisis)
Poetic pure form

Psychological point—duality of man—Christ and Satan as the opposites—renunciation vs possession—he that gaineth his life shall lose it vs greed for power—humility vs pride—the believer in the soul of man vs the condemned materialist and self-styled

---

*For many drafts O'Neill used this as a working title.

realist who can see only the cunning animal with intelligence as real—the stultification in latter attitude because it is self-justification which conceals self-loathing.

The inevitable conclusion of temptation scene—which is attempt by Devil to force his values on Christ, to make him sell self, to prove there is no soul, to take possession of it—Satan's insecurity in face of Christ's denial—humiliation of Christ's understanding, pity, and love—and feeling he is himself tempted to renounce, longing—hatred and revenge—must be tortured—body's pain will force him to abjure faith—torture, tells what he will do to him—Judas betrayal which is natural means to end and symbol of man's soul always for sale—crown of thorns (Christ's amusement: "So you have denied already your crown is of thorns") beating, etc.—and if he doesn't abjure, crucifixion—death as answer—as Christ points out: "suicide of the spirit."

(The Devil assumes many characters in play—Judas—High Priest—Pontius Pilate—Peter (3 denials)—centurian at crucifixion who puts sign on cross: "Hail, King of the Spirit"—who calls up: "Saves them—let's see you save self"—who commands soldiers to dice for clothes of the spirit—who insists Christ wants water and then gives him vinegar.)

Last supper scene.

Entrance to Jerusalem scene—Devil has arranged burlesque of Caesar's triumph—an ass, etc.—people jump at chance for fiesta, carnival, drunk—Devil tells them, never mind if you don't understand what he's getting at—you do understand food, etc.

Pilate scene—the Devil is denouncing High Priest and Pilate—then goes to balcony and calls to crowd: "Let us crucify him" and they yell back.

The crucifixion on same mountain top.

Crucifixion—crowds revengeful, sadism gradually turns to horror and pity—Devil watches this: "They are becoming sentimental. He has taken too long to die"—sends his secret police into the crowd—whisper of spies among them—then each will be afraid to open mouth—for they always suspect each other—and rightly—order them to go home and not listen to the news—(Radio broadcast of crucifixion?).

Devil says: "I shall build a chalet here—for meditation on the nature of man—on his selfishness, his stupidity, etc., etc.—his adoration of power—his envy of the courage of the cross.

Finally he sends everyone away: "You are a long time dying, Brother. Not considerate—when you know how much I desire peace."

Propaganda For   Aug. 31, '40
"More Than Straw For The Drowning"[2]

Notes (cont.)

Scene—Dialogue in the Night—first temptation scene reversed—it is the unseen (?) man on the cross who tempts the Devil with all the peace of the spirit of renunciation—pride stands in [his] way: "Better to rule in hell than to serve in heaven"—the amused answer is: "But think of the terrible pride of renouncing pride—the pride it takes to be meek and humble without the compulsion of fear—the power that needs only power over oneself to be all powerful—etc."

End of this scene—dying words: "Into Thy hands I commend my spirit"—Devil's words: "My hands? I have washed my hands of the spirit. What the hell would I do with your spirit? I make my own."—at end, envy, longing for death: "Let me take your place—go down and try to save them if you like—I wash my hands of them—they disgust me—I hate them"—he stays to be sure no propagandist takes the body away so he can claim a miraculous ascent of the spirit to Heaven.

Dawn coming—Devil still haranging—his voice cracked—annoyed with self—talking to the dead, talking aloud to myself (frightendly): "No, I don't mean that!"—sees figure on cross dimly—satisfied: "You're still there! It's finished"—more of the immense crowd gathering on the plain below—ordered to put cotton in ears, pads on eyes, and pull covers over heads—stay in homes with blinds drawn, undress, put lights out, go to bed (This in other scene)—Devil angry at first—then sees it's good thing for them to see for themselves.

Light comes—uneasiness—unfamiliar—and yet reminds me. Sun now has risen—figure on cross is he—and he has on Christ's clothes—Devil stunned—if not he—who?—I've seen him before many times—who?—It is I!—no, this is another of

His fake miracles—a trick—easy to explain, the hand is quicker than the eye—memories—the Indian rope trick—hypnotism—growing noise from the crowd, of joy, of release—he is overwhelmed—they are coming—he hides behind cross—tries to explain change of clothes—any means to be justified—(he puts on clothes)—then notices they have all stopped—awe and reverence—"good, they are kneeling"—"Well, I intended to make them make me a god, so much the better"—"the fools, they always mistake a change in the face that is in their mob for freedom—I am willing to play that game or any game"—"I do not believe it. I will never believe it. It could not be for them that he would be I and I he—they have all lifted their heads—they are staring at me—I know that helpless look—I put it there—God, how I pity them and love them—they really mean so well!"—(Horrified at self) "What's that I said? Suppose they heard? They would laugh with derision at me for trusting them—they would crucify me—slaves seek only a master—I must speak to them—show them that just because I have changed my clothes and possessed him, too, as I possess the world, it does not mean change"—He begins to speak—"Listen, My Brethren, do not kneel. I am as the least of you. I am the Son of Man." (He stops bewildered: "What? What am I saying? But I seem to mean it"—and "Hail, Son of Man"—he goes on to preach Sermon on the Mount (?)—or combination of Christ's speeches).

At the end—his kneeling humility and release—"I am the Resurrection and the Life" etc.

His speech to the crowd—an attempt at old dictator mob-moving harangue—in asides, disgust with its lies—his horror that he had begun to believe them himself—Christ's words keep breaking through—his confused remittance—possessed—but joy in it, too—getting rid of self, freedom—finally, his speech becomes Sermon on the Mount.

Mountain in play is mount of temptation, of Sermon, Mount of Olives (Garden of Gethsemane?), Zarathustra's film on high mountain catches my last solitude.

Mode of speech—Christ as in the Testament whenever possible—with simplicity—Devil with a dictator's—executive orders in practical matters—in spiritual issues with confusion.

"The 13th Disciple"[3] Feb. 7, '41

<u>Christ-Satan and duality of Man play</u>
(notes)

Disciples—Christian clergy of all time—each representing different epochs down to present day.

The city—Jerusalem but also ancient Rome and capitals of today—megalopolitan capitals of all civilizations at similar periods in decline of cultures and the advent of Savior.

Crowds, minor speechless characters—all done with lifesize marionettes which are used by scenic designer as part of the settings—background, dramatic and movable and changing.

The Mountain of Temptation of opening scene overlooks city and surrounding plain, the country which exists for the city—no meaning beyond this—the mountain top is also the Garden of Gethsemane—and the Mount of Calvary.

Satan is the 13th Disciple—invisible except by Christ, his opposite.[4](?) (He is not Judas, as indicated previously, but the corrupt realist in Judas—is Judas but isn't—denying the spirit, as Judas' flesh was betrayed and sold his spirit for the realistic value of 30 pieces of silver.)

Satan: "The Son of Man? I am Man. I disinherit you. I deny you" (this thrice). Christ throughout gently but commandingly asserts brotherhood, identity.

Satan (last scene) in bitter despair—sitting bound at the foot of the cross: "Is there never an escape from this eternal cycle of recurrence in which victory is defeat?—this everlasting suicide—the triumph of Death—Yes, I am King Death—must go down to my subjects, the Living Dead—or the unborn—strange hallucination of theirs to imagine they have been born and are alive in this realistic viewpoint, I suppose."

Sounds of multitude approaching—"cannot face them" (turns away—drop curtain vista rim—varied ranks of marionettes behind, hands raised in hail salute as he stares at them—his disgusted reflections on their natures—then pity in his contempt—his devious gestures of saluting them): "Hail My slaves! I mean, my loyal subjects. The last great victory is won."

The 13th Apostle March '41
Notes

Garden of Eden—The Magician in final plea of anguish: "Let me take your place—change clothes—they will never know—all they see is the uniform."

There is from the first a secret gladness that The Man has come back on the Magician's part—Magician sees The Man—senses this is immediately devious—is glad, yes, because there will be final meeting—an end—can return back to sty—let men destroy—The Man will be reborn—"Don't stare at me. What other means could I dream?"

1st Scene—Magician mentions exceptions—savior of dreaming man, etc.—wonder—then disparages.

Signal—salute of cannon on death—Magician to Dummy: "Afraid men misunderstand the signal—He is reborn in them."

The 13th Apostle

(Original Scenario) March '41

Scenes

Scene One—A mountain top—dark, dawn, sunrise
Scene Two—The city—Reviewing stand in the Great Square—the same morning
Scene Three—In the Temple of the State—that afternoon
Scene Four—Banquet hall in the palace—that evening
Scene Five—The Garden of Gethsemane (use what Gethsemane means)—that night—dawn
Scene Six—Inside the Palace of Justice—morning of same day
Scene Seven—Calvary—sunset, dark, nightfall of same day
Scene Eight—Calvary—dark, dawn, sunrise following morning

All the scenes of this drama are laid in a secret place deep within the duality of Man's soul—an ancient battlefield of the Spirit, haunted by memories of murder and birth, of greed and sacrifice, of loathing and aspirations, which dwell in the Past Everlasting, the deathless Symbols of Fate and Salvation.

The time is the Future, which is the Present, which is the Past.

<u>Characters</u>

The Man, Son of the Spirit
Satan, the Great, a Magician
Caesar
The Twelve Apostles, Soldiers, Guards,
 Police, Priests, People

[The play takes place within the haunted soul of man where lives in everlasting life the symbol of truth.]*

March '41

(Original Scenario)
The 13th Apostle
<u>Characters</u>

The Man
The Magician
All other characters are life size marionettes (or dwarf-ventriloquist dummies)[5]

Scene One—The mountain top—just before dawn—they come up—identical robes—Magician exhausted—big box on shoulders—box of tricks—dialogue in which the Magician reveals his weariness—the same old drama—longs for an end—for peace—so many times before—so many times again—the Magician: "How long?"—The Man: "Until they see"—The Magician: (Contemptuously): "They are mine. They will never see. You will throw your life away again"—The Man: "I am the Life and Resurrection. I have many lives"—The Magician: "You are a fool (Revengefully) You force this on me, remember? You're driving me up here! I was comfortable lying in my sty among the sinners. I now wish for a simple life—no questions where, how, when do we rest"—About advantages of sty—food, females, drinking and eating, the safety of the sty when you shut out horizons, and thrive in man's need—in which to his bidding to gestures for physical companionship and dreams of food and females.

(Grumbling) The Magician: "Why couldn't you have a contented Realist choose? Why remind me I am an old ruin? Why

---

*O'Neill crossed out this line in brackets.

make me play all these parts again? Do you need to be reminded that I always win? The wounds on your hands and feet have hardly healed since the last time. When will you give up this hopeless salvation dream of yours? Even if I did this a thousand times, they could never see your truth. If they saw they would not remember. They remember only what they should forget. They never learn. When will you stop kidding yourself and stop loving them? They don't want love. It humiliates them. It makes them suspicious. When you love them, they think you must be either a liar or a lunatic or both. Personally, I think you are both—and a masochist to boot. I suspect your eagerness for crucifixion." The Man: "Of course, you are a Realist?", etc.

All through this introductory scene in the dark before dawn. The Man's attitude is one of gentle, affectionate brotherliness—seeking to inspire courage for this battle—pitying—at the last the Magician pleads to have the chalice removed—in the name of truth, their identity—how long?—he is weary, bitter—The Man tells him it must be, over and over, until they are—chides him gently—The Man: "Your courage is low in the dark—when it grows light you will see only the form of things as they are—you will see what is real—you will not be haunted by the truth." (Helps him to his feet) "Come, my Brother, Get up. It is not proper for a King's victim, a manifestation of Caesar, the power behind all thrones and behind the altars of all man-made gods to be so depressed." The Magician: "Don't forget I had a hand in making you a God," etc.—The Man points out dawn and sunrise—like a curtain (Curtain rises on cyclorama) Magician says: "Yes. Curtain is about to go up. The Tragedy Begins. I am tired of always being cast as the villain in this piece—as Satan," etc. The Man says: "Do you think I like always to be the Sacrifice in vain—but someday it will not be in vain."

As it begins to get light, the Magician rises from the box, hurriedly but wearily (like an old actor making up for part he has played many times), takes off robe, takes uniform from box, puts on black uniform, Minister of Foreign Affairs, medals, honors—rebukes The Man. Magician: "You always play in your old robes—no wonder no one believes that you have anything to do with the present—or think your worlds have any meaning in present world"—The Man: "That is what they must learn—that there is no present, that years may pass, etc. but in the spirit, Time stands still. Until man begins to live in Truth, there is no present, much less a future, but only the Past's stupid repetitions." The Magician: "I know. Only concession you will make is to one common speech of the day in story they can understand! You mean so they can hear you. They do not want to understand—now less than they ever did. They will attempt to distort your words to justify any greed and constantly forget what they do not wish to remember. They will reduce your voice to a rising and falling pulpit sing-song in abandoned churches on Sunday morning—They only believe in Gods who are manifestly tested and pronounced free from adulteration, mechanized, streamlined, and economically determined. These wise men will see in you the result of a beshrewed gland or a manic depression. They will defame you by explanation until dust settles on your words and you are a madman guided by superstition. They will allot you a number of the sick and insane, so they can hold you in contempt and love you as a brother."

As light grows, the Magician's voice has grown stronger, of derision—like an old actor revived by the approach of the curtain—he talks—he sits on the box and makes up the conventional Mephisto face—then as the sun [is] about to rise, he mocks again—pleads—Magician: "Give it up—they are only worth contempt—they should be destroyed—let them destroy each other—but chance has fled—they have reached the point where others questioning this would believe not only that the end justifies the means but that the end is the death of the spirit and [they] will be forced to believe that, too, and act accordingly—give it up—let's get drunk—Baudelaire—nothing but wine to be drunk—that [is] in the sty because it induces efficiency of the workers."

But The Man insists the spirit [is] still there—tells a story—The Man: "A man sees a stranger drowning, jumps in, with last strength pushes stranger on a rock—[he] drowns"—The Magician dismisses: "You and your parables!" The Man tells other stories—tracing man.

Magician pleads for [him]self: "I am You—You are The

Man—I am The Man—etc." The Man pitying: "But [it] must be."

The Magician bitterly antagonistic—strong, defiant, threatening—boastful: "Only giving you a last chance—warn you this time it is really to death—without the publicity of resurrection—for even gods can live on earth only in the soul of man—and I have killed that soul—this time I will have the final victory."

Magician remembers cynically—he would not believe such a thing could be done without a notice to the reporter—he could not imagine that even after death he could not show his clipping book to the neighbors and his major relations—it was a mere reaction to an ancient conditioning of proper conduct—"I am sure a Psalm could explain it—[a few words unclear] Many a day a hare or a rabbit leaps a long distance—anyway these are but exceptions which prove the contrary"—The Man replies: "If only a hare happened in two thousand years, it would give me hope, it would prove that spirit still lived in man, not all mind—it would prove man is the final victory."

Then memories of the sun rising—The Magician: "A little modern religious ceremony connected with this—different from your time—not so different either—Caesar again—but Tiberius had a mind and this little man has only the cunning I gave him—dictator dummy—crown and seals—Son of God, Son of State he erected, he the God Father of his own divinity—theologians of Alexandria would have had a great time rationalizing that nut as they did with your simplicity—transforming truth into a system for keeping power."

He makes the Dummy summon the sun to a new day—The Magician: "You see, he dislikes the past, while he imitates it—etc."

In the first part the Magician is sad Christ has a victory—but even a god can die when no hope [is] alive in the soul of man.

Magician: "The Dummy is my most interesting creation—he is really great in one thing—no one has ever transferred a greater contempt for himself into a contempt for man—I told him the secret that this is the sign of the great secret self-contempt—that he could take advantage of this and make himself its symbol and it must aim toward self-destruction, to longing for death and to love of murder as the means to death—when you know your own life is contemptible and means nothing, why then you see that your neighbor's life is worthless, and murdering him is a good deed."

The temptation soon begins—wariness again—The Magician: "Must we go through this again—they all know it by heart—churches—but they will not hear or understand the meaning now, any more than they ever did—much less—I think they have always considered you a fool because you did not accept—well, I know it is our fate to go through with it—(to dummy) Come on! Speak up, little Man. Prove to him the soul has no value when you can sell it, that selling it is the only way to prove it exists in the world of realism—make him your best offer"—The Dummy: "Yes, Father"—Dummy speaks arrogantly—offers The Man the spiritual leadership of New Order: "Work under me—have them contented—tell them Heaven on Earth has arrived—church property will not be taxed—tell them any lies you like—bigger the better—as I know—but don't tell them you are the Son of God—because they think that I [am]—and, as a matter of fact, I have flashes of insight when it is revealed to me that I [am]—why not?—Alexander the Great, Caesar, Pharoahs, etc.—sometimes alone, I design temples, etc.—(cynically amused) You are a fool—the Great Fool—but I can see you, I mind you—you died once to save them—you should have let them die to save you—you don't know them—but I do—they are beneath contempt—they would feel most at home if they were forced to live underground in sewers with the rats—they are slaves—they love slavery—the security of a prison cell—etc."—(his harangue of contempt becomes hysterical—spirit is for the elite, the powerful, those liberated from scruples, those who dare to face reality, etc.).

Magician says: "They hear your voice, O Caesar, O Little Man—multitudes [are] coming up the mountain." Dummy says: "Take me away. I cannot be seen consorting with a Jew,[6] even if he is only the ghost of a dead Jew" (to The Man) "Quick! Your answer! Don't let your being a Jew bother you. I have had a family tree manufactured for you which shows you are, like me, the son of an Aryan emigrant to Palestine—I will have it so when you die there will be a place for you in Vahalla—not the highest place, of course."

Dummy: "New Trinity for New Day—The State—I am the State, the Father and its Son—you have come down to proclaim the Kingdom of Heaven is now arrived here on earth—you will be head of my church—numerous churches—and do not worry about subalterns—I will have them beheaded."

The Man refuses—with contemptuous pity—The Dummy begins to sputter furious threats: "I will have companions rended as I have [them] beheaded." Magician shuts him up, hand over mouth—Magician: "There—there—you anticipate—it is not time for that yet. There is no point in this. We must go through it all."

Tramp of marching feet—Magician [is] cynical—goose step up a mountain side—(disgust)—Magician: "Pah! What scum! Don't want them here"—he makes dummy say: "Halt"—sound stops—mockingly to the Man—Magician: "Would you like to address them, Brother? I have warned you the spirit in them is stone dead."

The Man—Sermon on the Mount—a vast silence.

Magician: "You see? Well, this scene is over, thank God." (To Dummy) "Send them back to their barracks, Little Man, and give them a slogan to cheer them on their way, the stupider and more strident the better"—the Dummy screams: "Comrades, Brothers, Chosen People! Forward! Out the Past! To the New Day! To the New Order! You have nothing to lose but Liberty! Forward in the name of the State! I promise you that never will there be peace on earth! But just the future must be destroyed! There must be nothing left in the spirit but the desire for death! etc. March!" (Sound of tramping feet receding)

Magician (cynically): "One of my best efforts, see, Little Man? It is insipid they accept it without question. It fills their empty bellies and minds with expectation and pride" (Wearily, puts dummy away in box, puts box on shoulder—to the Man): "Come on Brother. To the next scene (Hopefully) That is, when you see now how hopeless it is, and that I have men already—as final as complete victory—the last time you had some chance—[you] actually accomplished something—but times have changed—no chance now—etc. (Pleadingly) Please give it up! I do not like the role of judge and executioner. You are no danger to me now. Give them up. There is nothing you can do. And nothing further I need do because now they will destroy themselves—come with me to my sty—we will wallow in the warm mud, and ruminate about the good old days before my head grew too large for my hat and I was cast down from heaven to tempt these fools who never needed much tempting—about time my punishment were over—it has been dull."

The Man refuses—Magician: "I think you must be a masochist, Brother."

<u>Change in foregoing</u> Magician in mocking irony—says before he takes dummy from the box: "I must get final instructions from my master, my adored leader"—holding dummy up, he introduces him and explains him—"[He is] the final perfect expression of the highest low desire in the heart of every man—my masterpiece—the lust for power—the fear of liberty—the slave's ambition to askew liberty by owning slaves—you had better beware of this little monster—as formidable as a machine—no manners about him—he is a realist—he faces men as they are and uses them accordingly—he sees they are still beasts if you but scratch their surfaces, and he is a shrewd and relentless scratcher—he sees they are weak, cowardly and brutal, etc."

Magician asks dummy humbly for instructions—Dummy tells him how to swindle The Man into a bargain—promise anything—etc. when Magician repeats The Man's refusal to him, he flies into rage, threats—(What he wants stopped at once is preaching: "What shall it profit")—Magician: "Dangerous—the fools, I know them—they will believe any lie however incredible if it flatters their vanity—they might begin to believe again they have souls—that is bad—you cannot have a soul, etc." Dummy recovers from rage, cannot believe refusal: "You haven't found his price—or you haven't brought enough pressure—try ridicule—make a fool of him—corrupt his disciples—get them to betray him—show him his cause is hopeless, that my hand is everywhere."

What dummy wants The Man to do—admit the Father God is the State—preach new truth consistent with man's and nature—source of Christ's teachings.

Magician explains the dummy: "Not our ruler but mind who lives now in their lands, and records in the making in other lands—these little men are but symbols of modern world spirit, etc."

Beginning of Scene (and throughout)—the part the Realist Magician insists upon, that he is the real Son of Man—Magician: "You can remain the Son of God, if you like—means nothing—God is dead—we no longer believe in him. Therefore he cannot exist."

Scene Two—(Triumphant entry into the Holy City)—Reviewing stand, in sports arena?—Leader's platform—Statue of the State above the Throne with Dummy—Dummy staff grouped around—lines of dummy troops—painted drop rows of spectators, all in gesture of salute—bands, flags with sickles, hammers, swastikas, etc.

Magician dressed in uniform of chief of secret police—makes his report—national holiday—New Feast Of All Fools—carnival—proclamation in your name that there must be joy—laughter is heard as he passes each spot—band before him and after him so he cannot be heard if he tries to speak.

Sound of raucous mob laughter rises in louder and louder gusts—parade enters—tank with dummy driver—with merry-go-round ass on wheels—The Man is seated on the ass—Leader laughs and all laugh—procession stops before Leader—Magician says: "Invite him up to sit with you. They will think that the biggest joke of all"—He does so—The Man comes up with dignity—the Magician taunts him ironically: "A triumph!"—The Man starts to speak—the Leader is frightened: "Order band to play"—Magician says: "Your word is the only law, of course, but I advise letting him speak—they will not understand—they will only remember they have been ordered to laugh"—The Man starts the parable of   [O'Neill leaves blanks here]—interrupted by laughter, more and more.

Scene Three—The Temple of the State—Immense Idol of Moloch (which Leader has designed, statue from Flaubert—with added touches I suggested—Liberty as evil demon under foot—or the soul)—Magician now in priestly robes—High Priest of Bureaucratic Priesthood—immense newly established church—trouble it is expanding so rapidly there will soon be more priests than congregation, as the Magician explains—He is taking The Man on tour of the city—to show him how desperate his cause is—Magician: "I suggested to Leader you should be allowed complete freedom, within certain limitations, of course (The Man is in chains)—as he could say afterwards he gave you every chance—deigned to take you around in person—a great honor."

The altar of temple is a slave block—the place a market—Magician explains: "We do not use money any more. Human lives are the only recognized legal tender—a life's work for the State."

The Leader explains new mythology: "I am the son of Moloch. I am also his Father and Brother. This is impossible to understand unless you are one of the elite, an adept of the New Mysticism and Council Order. I had no father. I am my own father. In the beginning, I was. I was the Beginning. I am Man."—Magician chiding: "Now, now, my Little Master. That is all a little vague. You need not explain to this Man what ingenuity there is in man to see? the truth in absurd theological implications. He knows. They are like monkeys with a ball of twine. If they accepted simple truths they would have to live by them, etc."

(Magician, when Leader says: "I am the State": "They all say the same stupidities these little men—but it's truth now.")

Magician to The Man: "Where is your whip to drive money changers out of the temple—or do you believe with them that these belong in this temple—that now, at last, man has found a faith which is in harmony with his true aspirations."—he explains the system of living sacrifice—Magician: "The old who are worthless to the State—a ceremony—and all—satisfied—you would be impressed at eagerness of sacrifice—[they] are glad to die—and they do not expect heaven in another life—if you told them they would live again, they would scream with horror and cry for mercy."

Again The Man Speaks—starts a parable—Magician says: "I am sorry but only the Priesthood can make speeches here—[you must] submit speeches—I know—perhaps I could get the Leader to give you a speech permit—I would tell him the truth, that no one would listen—if knew I would curse what you just said."

(Magician to The Man: "A very foolish statement has been attributed to you: 'Give unto Caesar [the things that are Caesar's and to God the things that are God's]'—it works out in the end—as now—that Caesar gets all because he makes himself God—with my help and advice.")

Scene Four—The Last Suppers—An immense banquet hall in the Leader's palace—the windows all barred—at the suggestion of the Magician, this mob banquet is given in honor of The Man—to prove to the world the Leader's generous broadmindedness and continuing desire for friendly relations and cooperation, in spite of the rebuffs he has received to his kindly advances—The Man and his Disciples are in no sense prisoners but guests—however, the Magician warns: "The Leader's patience has worn thin—this is The Man's last chance to join in establishing the new order, the Kingdom of Heaven on earth—at the termination of the banquet, an ultimatum will be delivered—the Leader's patience is exhausted—he is the soul of kindness but he can also be terrible to them who would willfully distrust him in his divine mission to save mankind."

This is all explained in a speech of welcome delivered by the Magician after The Man and Disciples are driven in by the guards and iron prison gates to the banquet room locked behind them—all are in chains—He explains his own presence there—chief of secret police—Magician: "Naturally, I have to be here to see nothing is said or done which would endanger the worship of the State, or disturb the public peace. However, that is mere formality. I know whatever you say or do, O False and Self-Deluded Son of Man, is not at all dangerous or has any meaning now. Your words are empty proverbs. So tell any little parable you like. In fact, you must feel completely free. Be merry, eat and drink, for tomorrow—You can even perform any miracles you like, here in privacy, although this is a great concession because my Little Master, on my advice, has let the people believe he is the only miracle worker. I may give you an example of it later on because in such matters I always act for him as a humble guest."

He recognizes the Apostles—greets them with mocking good fellowship—like old times—Thomas—jeers at Peter about crowing cocks—better put cotton in ears this time, or you will become a realist—buttered side of the bread—finally to Judas: "You look out of place—no impractical answer—a realist—an immoral determinist—the soul has value only insofar as you can sell it," etc.

Magician apologizes: "Doing all the talking—a habit I've learned from my adored Master—he prefers his own voice even to the agonized screams of the maimed and tortured—he would like to have all the tongues of men torn out so he would be the only voice, but I have advised him the time is not quite right for such a move, yet"—Magician sits down, opening banquet—Magician: "There is no wine of course (except for me, here—it is night again—the night air is bad for realism—it is better to be drunk when meeting ghosts)—I remembered that, etc. My Master wishes you to have every opportunity."

The Man changes water into wine—etc.—the Magician rouses himself from gloomy, dejected mood: "Wait, I was waiting for this. I will cap your miracle with two—I mean my Master will. Won't you, Little Man?—by mystic realistic power of the State"—Dummy: "I am the State"—Magician: "That was water—now wine—I admit it—a good trick—a lot of commercial possibilities—but watch—Come on, Little Man"—Dummy speaks: "I am willing to sacrifice lives of a million men—now taste—wine [is changed] into blood, you see—after that the second is easy—One must not be afraid—taste again—water—blood [is changed] into water—a very impressive miracle—it has had a great success with the public—I think even now of your Apostles."

The Man speaks pityingly: "The miracle of Circe"—Magician laughs: "No, do not disparage her"—[I have a] soft spot for her—as a realist—as I see it, what she really did was simply to give a mirror to man and make him see himself—and immediately he began to grunt with gratitude and relief at being freed from the curious obligation of pretending to be something higher."

The Man speaks (Last Supper scene)

At end, before delivering ultimatum, the Magician, drunk now, speaks as if only he and Christ were there—persuades, pleads—then delivers ultimatum—Magician: "[I will] give you a night to think it over—go in the Garden—beautiful night, learn again how sweet it is to be alive—etc.—in the morning, arrest—you will get a fair trial in my court—my Master has appointed me special judge."

Magician has them taken out—because no appetite—Magician: "But I know one who has a thirst"—sits down with Dummy, drinking—finally his disgust—spits in Dummy's face—Magician: "That is what I think of my victory."

Scene Five—Garden of Gethsemane—night before dawn—The Man alone, praying—Magician comes in leading Judas on a chain—two guards follow—then he stops, impressed—sends Judas and the guards away.

The Magician points out the beauty of nature, the sweetness of life—Magician: "[I have] got the Leader to make a last offer—I will take you away—you will disappear—there is a place called the Blessed Isles[7]—no one knows but me—I often go there to recoup my strength when the stupidity of man gnaws like a madness at my brain—no man has ever lived there—there is sky and sea, etc.—beach—for philosophy—to a sufficient distance, men are annoying, etc.—of course, you would agree to stay there until old age puts a natural end to this life of yours on earth"—The Man: "No."

Scene in which he pleads with The Man to take away the chalice from his lips—his doom and punishment to see only the ugliness and greed of men, their stupidity and madness—to tempt them to self-destruction—Magician: "[It is] so easy, they are so weak and greedy—yet I have grown to know them so well, I feel one of them, I pity them—(he tells an incident or two he has seen proving men's fineness—similar to The Man in Scene One)—behind their lowest cowardice there hides a heroism which is ashamed of itself—from my long association with them. I have become as one of them. I am the Son of Man, too—You know it well—You and I are the opposites within men—within each man—in eternal conflict—but now, at last, I feel that I have won—so I pray that the Inevitable Purpose, in which you and I are one, should have mercy and take this doom of this final victory from me, which I was condemned to win—I am afraid from this death tomorrow there will be no resurrection for you, Brother, on this earth—and I would not murder you—you understand, not really murder.

The Magician is crushed and in anguish—The Man comforts and rallies him with smiling pity—The Man: "These are night thoughts and when day comes your courage will return—your exultation in victory—you have become too much a man—a daylight recluse whom the night fills with awe and bewilderment and humility—you have explained the stars in daylight, but behold when the night comes, they are still there. You have not explained them away and all is confusion and awe again and anxious longing to pray—And do not feel crushed by victory—I can release you from that doom—You have become too shallow a realist—you see only the surface—Look out: I warn you many a commander has gone down to defeat because his self-confidence mistakes a plan of the battle for battle itself—and there is an old wisdom which says it is darkest just before the dawn—we will get tired of pretending they are only monkeys—there is no boredom so deep and real as the boredom of animals"—Magician: "I am not bored. I keep thinking of the cross"—The Man: "So will they think of it again—when it is time. I am thinking of a cross too—the cross on which they have nailed themselves from which I would deliver them."

Dawn of dawn—the Magician wearily, hopelessly rouses [him]self—Magician: "Well I suppose we might as well go on"—he calls guards to bring back Judas—betrayal scene—pieces of silver—Judas: "Do not forgive me, Master, or I shall have to hang myself."

Irish sunrise—the magician greets it—taunting triumph about Judas—Magician: "I told you they will all sell their souls"—The Man: "The eleven others did not"—Magician: "Bah, I only needed one and chose the one with the greatest envy and the simplest price, money. The others all have their prices, if I wished to take the trouble to denounce them"—then puts The Man under arrest—will bring him before the judge.

Scene Six—Courtroom—The Magician as the Judge—robes—his conference with the secret police—Magician: "Have my orders, or rather the Leader's orders, been carried out? You have gathered a great crowd outside? Good. You have made them understand they are to shout as instructed when the signal is given? Good. Caesar thinks it admirable for propaganda purposes that it is the will of his people and he obeys that will. A little democratic pretense comes in handy now and then—when one wishes to wash our hands."

(Statue of State (Nordic Kali) behind Judge's stand—Magician has placed Dummy on [or between knees]—beneath Kali's feet is the blond Goddess crushed figure of Justice.)

Prisoner [is] brought in—scene as in New Testament up to "What is truth?"—Magician: "But you need not answer. I know what you would say: A thing of the spirit. A simple thing. Proud become humble. Humble become proud. Love one another. All men are brothers. The Golden Rule. Such outworn mystic moral nonsense. The truth is there is no truth. But there are facts. Such as, there is no God but the State. The Golden Rule is dead. We no longer believe in gold because we haven't any. The Golden Rule was a luxury for those who had the gold and security to practice it. But they always felt the security of their neighbor would be a shift from them and endanger their security. They thought even too much was not quite enough for safety, etc.—I am afraid you have no place in a realistic world. In fact, my judgment on you is that your very existence is an act of treason against the State. So (The signal is given—the mob shouts: "Crucify him!")—the Magician says mockingly: "You hear? The voice of your loving brothers. Which is the voice of the people and so of the State, and so of Caesar. It is finished."

Scene Seven—Calvary—sunset—background sky and semicircle of the People (Fools front rank) whose ranks cover the slopes of Calvary, leaving only a small cleared space at the very summit, in the middle of which is the Cross, with the Crucified unseen, facing rear—Magician dressed now in old medieval black costume of executioner with a black mask cover for upper part of face—Dummy sits on ground with back propped against the foot of the Cross, facing front—several soldiers of Dummy's special guard (Death's Head) in black uniform—the rank of the People (Fools) composed equally of men and women—civilian clothes like ugly efficient uniforms, shapeless, shoddy, men's one pattern, women's another, but very little difference. All women carry baby in arms. Their faces, turned upward to the Cross, are expressionless and blank, and incurious, as if they watched with automatic obedience something they had been ordered to watch—observe it dispassionately, without pity, without the enjoyment of cruelty, like people to whom torture has become a commonplace incident, who are pitiless because they have been disciplined to crush all natural feeling in themselves, to express nothing but prescribed emotions with prescribed gestures at a word of command.

Magician in savage, jeering words of having come to the end—job finished or nearly is—Magician: "He takes longer to die this time"—realistic reasons for this—Magician: "Crucifixion is a lost art—when he fell down dragging Cross up here, I offered to have him shot but he refused—I explained to my Little Master that public spectacles may be dangerous"—(with angry disgust for the people) "but I need not [have] been worried. Look at their faces. There is not spirit enough in all these millions to furnish a lama with a soul! As I ought to know, for it was I who tempted them to get rid of their hampering superstitions as the first step toward the New Clean Viewing of Mankind"—but the Magician's mood is forced, emotionally assertive, nervous and hectic—he is really participating in this torture of this Man on the Cross and he prays for the mercy of death to end it.

A groan from The Man—the Magician (torturedly): "Let him die! Why can't you let him die? Father of Man why have you forsaken Him"—(a voice from the Cross calls with gentle reproach to the multitude.) The Man: "O Son of Man, Brothers of Mine in the Spirit, why have you forsaken me?"—a vague stir from the ranks, a dumb puzzled look sweeps over their faces as if their minds were touched fleetingly by a ghost of long-forgotten memory—The Magician forgets his role for a moment—is exaltant: "They heard! They felt!" etc.—then in savage denial—Magician: "The Dogs! They forgot their orders! They dared to feel! (Addressing them) I ordered you whenever he spoke to laugh. Laugh! (Mechanical laughter)—a sick laugh. I must give them a good joke (to Cross) You must be getting thirsty up there. Would you like a little wine?" The Man: "Yes, I am thirsty to drink again from the deep well of the spirit—in the soul of man." Magician: "A dried up well, Brother—an exploded myth! But lives now for you. Sorry I have to serve [it] in a sponge but you could hardly drink from a bottle, eh? (to crowd) Laugh! A joke! Can't you see the point? And here's another point. It is vinegar not wine (Guards with whip beat)— So laugh! (Mechanical laughter)—Is that the best you can do? Wait!" He snatches up the Dummy. Immediately the crowd automatically salutes: "Hail, Caesar!" All eyes [are] turned to him. Magician chuckles: "My Little Man, but valuable you are, now what passes for their minds are conditioned to you— Pavlov—the dog's mouth can be made to salivate with hunger at the sound of an empty bell as if it were a cornucopia stuffed with meat. Speak to them, my dear Son. Fill their empty minds with strident nonsense they will match and with threats"— Dummy shrieks egotisms and threats of destruction. A mighty chorus: "Hail, Caesar!"—Magician (savagely putting Dummy back) "Fools! And I hoped a moment ago you were remembering—(savage denial) Hoped? I mean suspected—foolishly suspected a danger, a hidden spirit of treachery—of sedition— they don't know where to look now—they would all like to go down like sheep, forgetting that impulse, afraid of it. They must not be allowed to forget"—he picks up Dummy—makes him give order to keep eyes on Cross till Man is dead no matter if it takes all night—example of what happens to blasphemer against the State—all eyes on Cross—Magician chuckles— sneering at Dummy: "You fool! In the night the soul may chance to awake—chance to dream—and turn from watching the fate of things outside to the truth within (Tensely—to The Man on Cross) You must not die. You must survive the night no matter what torture—I promise to share it—I have to share it— (forcefully) He looks as if He were dying now. Yes, I feel his soul at his lips."

[Man on Cross: "Father, into your hands I commend my spirit."—Magician (frightenedly): "He is dying. They must not know. If I can keep them here. Keep them from hearing his last groans. (He raves at Dummy again) Say anything, Little Man, so long as it is hard and nonsensical. Tell them you are God!"— Dummy speaks: "Why, they hardly looked at you. It is]*

---

*O'Neill crosses out this paragraph.

Magician calls pleadingly to The Man on the Cross: "Courage! You must have seen how for a moment your spirit in them [is] dimly awakened—You cannot desert them now—in the dark I will give you a sponge with wine, not vinegar—and if you are too weak to speak, I will speak for you—I am a practiced ventriloquist, as you have seen—in the dark they will never suspect—I am a good mimic, too—I know your voice by heart and your truth—I suppose you think I will speak in mockery—no, I mean I will speak as if I were you—I suppose you wonder why I do this?—I confess I wonder myself (Defiantly)—You suspect that through long association with men, I have become as one of them, that I pity them, that I regret having accomplished my mission of destruction too well, that I feel this final victory over you as self-defeat, that I would not have you die without hope (Jeeringly)—Perhaps you think I even admire your sacrifice and love you as a brother? (With an unconvincing countenance)—Well, it is none of these things. Bah! You know me. I have my magician's vanity. I love to deceive fools. I am proud of my box of tricks. It amuses me to play jokes on men and see their silly eyes bewildered and impressed—I love to confound their sluggish minds with paradoxes—I love my power over them—and what greater paradox than to speak for you? (Change to pleading)—But you must not die until—I would not have you die without hope (Looks up)—He does not answer—he is dead—they must not know—I must speak for him—quick—what shall I say?" (He speaks in exact imitation of The Man's voice.)

Scene Eight—Night before dawn—The Magician's parable of the Siamese Twins—the duality of Man—the opposites—nature of the opposites—Magician: "Although born of the same mother and linked together, individually, they were as different as night is unto day—the Realist was the stronger outwardly—became dominant physically—but could never make the other admit his value—he grows to hate him with a deadly hatred—becomes a great power in the world while his brother remains a failure, content to be powerless, not desiring any possessions except the freedom of his soul, etc.—the dominant one explains his brother who must always be with him, as his attendant slave, his jester, his mad fool—denies brotherhood—mocks him before multitudes and orders them to laugh at everything he says, even at the very sight of him—but at the same time, [he] knows [he is] always with him, cannot help suspecting that perhaps the laughter is at him—as he becomes more powerful, a conqueror in wars, a great general, a dictator, he hates more and more—finally he makes the people proclaim him the Emperor of the World—plans a great coronation ceremony in which he will crown himself—tries first to be free of the twin—calls in all the best surgeons but they confess [operation] probably would be fatal—as a realist he dreads death above everything, etc.—so [he] has to have a gorgeous robe made for the twin, too, in which twin looks like a fool—so put out at the ceremony—that night he cannot sleep—the twin sleeping peacefully beside him infuriates him—he thinks if he was dead the surgeons could remove him from me without danger—so he strangles him—and in the morning the attendants find that a terrible miracle has been accomplished—in the great royal bed there is only the one figure, that of the Great Emperor, who during the night had committed suicide."

The Magician introduces the parable—"[I] give you this parable so you may each regard your own spirit in the mirror of the night undistracted by the glittering mirage of appearances."

At the end of the parable there is dead silence—then a gasp of horror, then a rising murmur of vague understanding from the crowd which develops into a cry of joyous freedom which turns to a hymn of Thanksgiving (Easter music).

In pain between verses the Magician says: "The dawn is coming—time I died for him—after a few words of farewell from Him to them"—He speaks for The Man: "O Sons of Man, Brothers on the Cross! Why have you forsaken me? (Silence)—I am the Spirit within each of you, the free spirit, the soul, the secret longing for self-sacrifice, etc., the divine simple good in you which though it be crushed for a time is forever unconquerable. I am the Resurrection and the Life in you, and whosoever, etc.—shall never die."—Chorus of Multitude ("We promise! It shall never die!")—Magician: "Farewell! Into your hands I commend my spirit." (Magician gives this like dying speech.)

Dawn—followed swiftly by sunrise—crowd eyes figure on Cross, arms outstretched to Him, faces exultant—the Magician returns to type—puts on military cloak dripping with medals—cynical, jeering tone: "The blessed day again after the dreams and confessions of the night. Now we can see again what we really are. (Addresses the crowd) My master desires that you return to your barracks now. Good Slaves. The Man is dead. We hope it has been an object lesson to you. So may old traits perish who deny the Godhead of the State and the divinity of its only Son, our beloved Leader. You may go home I say! (Crowds don't hear) What's matter with you! There is nothing so impelling about a crucifixion you should stand and gape forever. (To guards) Drive them away!" (Soldiers don't hear) Magician addresses the Dummy jeeringly: "Why, a great change seems to have come over your revelers, My Little Master. Your subjects seem to have forgotten they are slaves. I can read even a brooding, joyous resolution in their faces. I would not rebuke them now, if I were you. I would not remind them you are the Son of God. I would not even let them see me, if I were you. They seem to be in a mood of new realism where they might even revile you—To be brutally frank, I think you had better hide—(picks up Dummy and hides under cloak)—we had better go into exile for a while—(Grumbles). In a single night, all our good work has been undone—I shall have to start my conspiracy all over again—just when I thought the final victory was in my grasp—just when I had dreams of being allowed to retire—Campfire—well, take heart, it will be more exciting—my tempting had become a silly pretense—there was nothing left alive in them to tempt—(Looks at the crowd again)—Yes, now there will be something to fight—a million glorious defeats for me to make me respect man again (Mockingly)—Yes, Yes, Little Man. We are going. I can feel you clinging to me like a frightened monkey. I hear your teeth chattering." (He starts off the hill down right. No one looks at him. About to walk between the ranks of people, right in front, he stops to gaze back at the figure on the Cross—in tone of affectionate mockery)—"Forgive me, Master, if I do not show proper respect for the dead. You know that I know you are not dead. (With rueful loving complaint)—A sorry pass you have brought me to! A merry trick to play on me to use me and my manhood and my worst pity for my fellow men to win the game again—to make of me a 13th Apostle! But I warn you this isn't the end. We will play this drama out again and yet again! I still have a trick or two. I know this weakness. So don't think this is a final victory (Gloomily)—I wish to God it was!" (He slides abruptly off through the crowd that remains unaware of him.)

Further notes made before writing 1st draft of Prologue

April '41

The 13th Apostle
Notes

[1st Scene—establishment of Satan-Christ (or Lucifer-Christ)—the eternal opposites within the dual nature of Man—twin brothers, the Son of Man—also of the Spirit of the Universe, the Great Soul of Life.]*

The whole action of the play takes place within the Soul of Man where truth exists as Symbol in eternal duality.

The night of Lucifer's fall restated—he fell through pride, rebellions, jealousy, greed for power—and he was exiled to the earth—his revenge is to attempt to make men, who are sons of God, His creations, into his sons—that is, by instilling his rebellion and jealousy and pride and greed into them to make them so proud of themselves they will make Man into a God—with one man a symbol (God doesn't become Man, Man becomes God)—almost murdered in the old days when rulers assumed divinity—then you came and my plan seemed upset for a while—your simple words of Truth *seemed* to heal the world—the symbol of your crucifixion in the flesh seemed to reveal to them that they had a spirit—I say "seemed." You know as well as I it was but seeming—etc.

The blind alley into which materialism (put into their nature by Lucifer—naught is there but what you see. By your seeing, you create it. Naught exists outside you with any value except what you bestow upon it—beauty of nature is in your eye, etc.)

---
*O'Neill draws a wavy line through this paragraph, thus eliminating it from this manuscript.

has led them—scarcity amidst plenty, etc.—tried to win by praying to the State—they don't see that a little simple charity, kindness, thoughtfulness would conquer all this—and with recognition of brotherhood of identity—a little remembrance of your simple truth—a little virtue—a little reality in what they call Christianity, take your name in vain—rallying self: "But, of course, it is I who does not let them see it—Or who did not let them—for, in a way, joke is on me—by following my tempting they have denied me, too—there is no evil, they say—irrational prejudice—so I have left them alone, seeing this last cynical weakness doomed them without positive effect on my part—so I have been dying in sty—etc.—pity for men."

"Soon among men's word came a Rationalism for Rationalism's sake—a truth in selling becomes a slogan of the future and manuscript, until meaning in it lost all meaning—We no longer believe in such nonsense. We believe but [it] is only for many a pain's sake—the joy of work for work's sake without ambitious motive, that is worthless—a dangerous lie—and so, to live for life's sake, to be good for the sake of God, is nonsense—it does not jibe with economic determinism—it is even presumptuous to say I am a Man anymore. We believe a man is a beast of the State"—Christ says gently: "We?"—a pause—then Lucifer confesses: "I feel they are brothers—I can even pity them"—but his pity leads to seek for their annihilation—"give Man death and let the poor mad fool be released from himself and sleep at last in peace."

"Denying the simple truth of good, he becomes lost in a maze of scientific fact, which he soon forgets was the creation of his mind aided by a few instruments he had invented—he soon made science into the law of a God which was himself—the more explained, the more was left unexplained—I helped him to convince himself at the same time of his honor—he multiplied his paradoxes and perplexities and called them knowledge—and mistook knowledge for wisdom—bewildered, longing for the simplicity of meaning again, he found the simplicity of evil—which demands nothing but appetite and greed—he is no Son of God now—God is his son."

In as far as possible, Christ's speeches are confined to His words in the Gospel—Lucifer's speech varies—sometimes resembling Zarathustra (in his night scenes) sometimes (in his different roles of diplomat, etc.) descending to a coarse cynical colloquialism.

Lucifer explains why all takes place in two days: "We do believe in speed for speed's sake. Thus we have found memory for self-respect. Having lost a goal, and a purpose termed a goal, one cannot admit it. One must keep the illusions. And so speech and more speed. Flying through air at 300 miles per hour, we must believe one is going somewhere for some purpose, etc.—This I put into their minds—perhaps I hoped that someday, soaring through space at terrific speed like an aimless count bound for nowhere, saving time which, being saved, one stares at helplessly, wondering how to insert it—man might suddenly see himself reflected in speed or in a mirror, and laugh, and laughing die, a laughing suicide: You hoped that men might die through your lies—but we have lost our sense of honor, too, as people do, who adoring no God, just adore themselves—so humbly salute the ridiculous—we erect monuments to it which would resemble primitive stone—immense public buildings like temples in which the State squats on an altar—we are all suspicious—laughter is forbidden—for who knows what one is laughing at?—so we have commandeered and regimented its use—for appropriate occasions—you will hear it—it is now in the service of the State—public festivals are ordered in which at a signal the mob laughs at the Spirit—I pointed out to Caesar that this is a safe ventilation for an old superstitious longing."

The dummy—blank face, primitive carving, eye sockets without eyes, an enormous mouth—crowned with wreath like Caesar—Satan explains him derisively—"the Son of Man, Father of the State, but only son of the State, too—the mythology of his enigma is still obscure, we have not quite made up our minds yet—Servant and Master, Leader and Led—all we are sure of is that there is divinity in him—he is the apotheosis of man emptied of spirit, the quintessence of the real—he is the Truth with no moral nonsense about it—he is I in everyman—the part of him which is mine—the part which now becomes the whole."

The Great Illusion—the Magician has fostered in the minds of men—the illusion of relativity, of knowledge through service of data as the means to Truth, of the demonstrated fact as the truth, of the oppositions as the good.

Play against State worship—self-adoration of man in lowest image.

Notes made between writing 1st draft of
Prologue and 2nd draft*

Carefree—flickering shadows—soldiers around campfire—crowd in chains—
among last words—Satan says [he] can go on with battle because he thinks to bring others to see the future—when men will no longer be bound on the wheel of past stupidities—when you and I can at last be reconciled within the soul of Man—

<u>Scene One</u>
(Fragment 1st Scene—original conception with Prologue)

Scene: The summit of a mountain in the darkest hour before dawn four days later. At first, nothing can be seen except a background of sky in which stars are beginning to recede and grow dim. Against this, the summit is a deeper darkness, sloping steeply upward a few feet from left and right and rear to a small flat span on top. Near the edge of this, right-front a boulder forms a natural seat.

There is a sound of someone climbing and the Magician appears, outlined against the sky, struggling about on all fours as he manages the last few feet to the summit. He cannot be seen clearly but it is apparent he carries the limp figure of Christ over right shoulder, as one carries a fainting or wounded man. Also, under his left arm is a smaller figure, like a ventriloquist's dummy. He stops beside the boulder and puts the smaller figure, on top of it—then lowers the figure of Christ from his shoulder and carries it in his arms a few paces away to the edge of the summit at rear and, as in the Prologue, fixes it in a standing position, facing the eastern sky at rear.

The Magician (stands back from the figure. He is breathing heavily from his climb—sardonically): "There. The stage is set for what I choose as the most effective opening episode for our

---

*All notes made in late May and June 1941 on the first Prologue are missing. O'Neill appears to have made corrections on this draft and destroyed the marked copy after completing the second draft.

stupendous revival—the great legendary Temptation scene. It never really happened, of course. I know you too well. I was not such an imbecile as to waste time trying to tempt an absurd fanatic with bribes that had no value for him. (A threat in his tone) But never mind. This time it will happen for all our modern world to see—and hear. What a simpleton you will prove yourself in its eyes! Yes, the most effective opening scene I could possibly have chosen. It creates the right sardonic mood at the very start. The hero is at once revealed as a fool. (He pauses scanning the eastern sky.) No sign of dawn yet. We are early. I wanted to arrive here before our audience of citizens of the World State assembles on the slopes and the great plane beneath. I hate the mental stench of the crowd! I loathe the filthy touch of the Mob! (He pauses again. A faint far-off groundswell of sound is heard rising from the plain as if an immense multitude miles away.) Listen. They are assembling now. (Sardonically) You can never say I did not provide you with an audience. I doubt if there will be a single absentee. At my suggestion, Our Savior, the True Son of Man, issued an edict prescribing the death penalty for any citizen who did not attend with all his family. (He turns away.) Well, let us rest until it is time for the curtain to rise." (He comes back to the boulder and sits on it, placing the Dummy he had left there on the ground beside the boulder; its back propped against it, facing front, as he faces left.)

"I confess I am tired. I have grown unused to climbing mountains, living as a man among men. I am not what I once was. To much of man's flesh has clung to my spirit, too much of his weakness to my strength, too much of his shameless senility to my pride. The contagion from long contact with the sickness of men's lives (with disdainful disquiet). Bah! There have been times lately when I have felt as sick as if I had become a man, subject to Time and changes, conscious of growing old. There have been times when I have caught myself secretly longing, like him, for the peace of death—(With bitter self-mockery). I, once known as Lucifer, the Eternal Rebel, the Defier of God and Fate, the Prince of Pride! (Then rallying himself) Bah! These are night thoughts pondered by memories of the past and the disease of dreams. The truth is, I have grown soft with a conqueror's surfeit after the final victory. (His voice rises tauntingly) And you know that is not boasting. I *have* won! O Brother in Man, My Opposite and Enemy, You are dead! Our long duel within what Man used to call his soul is finished! You no longer exist there! He has driven you out! He has killed you! (He adds grimly in a lower tone.) As you will see clearly demonstrated within the next two days. (He pauses—then disgustedly) What imbecility to talk to a wooden puppet I made as if it possessed life! He himself would never dare to return to earth. He sees men as they are now. Better to pretend he has forgotten them as they have forgotten him. Or perhaps he has forgotten them. I would not blame him. Often now, I wish I could forget."

Notes for revision of Prologue

June '41

Keep dummies cut—or any hint by Magician that figures not alive—also details of plan except make fool of Christ—figure has already heard plan—okay depends on figure of Christ and demonstration—answer to dejection.

Cut on Pygmalion and Galatea[8]—coming in Scene One—cut any comment of Goddess as Magician's masterwork—he attributes to Savior—flattery—great artist as well as great everything else—ironic comment—becomes the creation of what one creates—then sees application to himself and figure of Christ—(collaboration in Goddess—I did the manual labor of cutting wood but yours was the inspiration, the great conception, etc.).

Cut out any talk in which Magician identifies himself as Satan.

Cut out direct address to Christ at end—or most of it.

New—Magician says: "I will be director of the drama, ringmaster of the circus, leader of the orchestra."

New—Magician says: "We will make him admit—as a free confession—that he has made mistake, is a fool."

The Savior of the World is a real living character—small man, not over five feet—our narrator, mystic egomaniac—a fanatic hysteric—Satan uses him as perfect instrument for a stronger will—dictator kept more saving rationality and common sense, which made them confirm divinity—that is, couldn't believe it themselves although they longed to and [Magician] encouraged belief in mob—but this one really believed it, believed in myth of his divine origin—perfect Trickery for Satan.

Minister of Propaganda also living—a dwarf—double for lifelike characters in later scenes.

<u>Scene One</u>
<u>Notes</u>   June '41

Magician catches himself talking as if Christ [were] alive—Magician: "Memory resists you—barely alive in soul of man turned into a sty—let's pretend—need someone to talk to—can't understand me any more—no evil when no good life."

Magician's bitter disgust with man because of loss of pride: "I did not mean that! That is not me. Nor you—your humility springs from a great pride that not even death could make you quit or retreat. Now all [is] gained. Victors have a fear of each other—all retreat—faith in himself is for sale at bargain prices."

Magician's triumphant boast: "I alone am left in the heart of Man—I have conquered—I alone am the Son of Man—I am God! (Then he is disdainful.) Talk like my Little Master—creature of created—you understand, I mean I am the God of Man."

His feeling of being lowered and corrupted by men—evil corrupted to meanness—etc. "I have become a man." His self-questioning—Magician: "Why did I bring you back? I exaggerated situation—no memory of you at all—no spirit left—no causes"—reasons he'd like to believe—Magician: "To finally humiliate you myself—my own memory of you—then to demand of your Father who is just that I have worked out my punishment—done my duty—fair fight—hell in hearts of men—want to be released—Blessed Isles—commute my sentence to perpetual exile—I have lived thousands of years in men, continually in the company of his thought—now I want to be alone for a million years to dream and forget."

But he imparts this as sole reason—perhaps pity for man, as a man—perhaps a hope.

Story of drowned youth: "Kissed him as if he was my son—no religion or hope hereafter—but pride in himself that encompassed fear of death—your pride and mine."

Unimpressed by soldier's courage—privation—suspects—

mob psychology—backed by glory—hero—the best is to die in a room alone, calumniated, as a token of years of torture as a token of faith man has a spirit which can be damned.

Had to bring Savior along because of ceremony making sun rise.

Notes   July '41

Magician starts ventriloquist dialogue—to pass time, amuse self, practice—Magician: "[I] know so well what He would say"—goes on for a time—then suddenly a voice comes from the figure—Magician [is] taken aback—then tauntingly triumphant: "[I] knew you must accept this challenge—satisfaction—this will be final victory indeed!"

Christ tells him: "You have become entirely Man"—proud denial—Christ: "You called me to come. I came in answer to your prayer." denial—Christ: "Do not be afraid. I accept this drama as you have planned it, O Son of Modern Man. I will be your puppet—say nothing you do not wish me to say—save you a little ventriloquism, that is all—all you have to do is give me the cue."

Christ points out: "You think you have won because, having become Man, you think in terms of time, you see only the present, etc."

Magician reminds Christ of understanding often at first coming—men had been given truth, everything done to reveal clearly what was good and evil—free will—up to them—if Magician made them finally desire destruction and death—if he wins, then his desire of living in the hell of the hearts of men, should be commuted to exile—(this is one of the reasons he gives for calling Christ back—wants release from men).

Christ says [He] will never speak except at night alone with the Magician—otherwise remain as puppet with words put into mouth—Magician says: "I will play fair—only your own words." Christ: "But you promised I would deny my faith on the cross." Magician: "Don't you remember saying: 'Father! Why hast Thou forsaken me?'"—pause—Christ: "Yes, for that moment I was all man." Magician: "Yes, Yes, and that is what his spirit cries now to a deaf heaven!" Christ: "You seem to regret you have made him deaf."

Magician in a revealing moment confesses his victory is without satisfaction—disgust rather than pride—because not the kind of victory he wanted—man not recreated in image of his spirit—not the proud, defiant, irascible rabble who is evil and noble, who refuses all compromise or evasion—he has become the base hypocrite who stoops to any lie, measures, degradation to gain power or security—Magician: "And I have done the same—anything for victory—I sometimes think he has corrupted me more than I have him."

(Christ: "I see why you called me back—to save from thyself, O Man.")

Magician gives Ruler of World as an example—believes nothing—even when safely adoring his own divinity something within him surfaces: "There is no God."

Set plans (as originally conceived)
(with Prologue added later)*

The 13th Apostle (or The Last Campaign)
Notes—fresh angle approach   April '42

Savior of the World is a living character—small man—(at times this makes him feel inferior, hates Magician's height, threatens to have his legs amputated—then Magician soothes him by reminding him his predecessors [were] all small men. Alexander, Frederick the Great, Robespierre, Napoleon, Buddha [were] probably small—Confucius, etc.)—lives in trance of self-worship—hysterical outbursts—and a childlike dependent quality at other times—Satan is Daddy—an absolutely immoral, ruthless, primitive savage child with no taboos but many superstitious terrors.

In Prologue, he is all mystic trance self-adoration state—staring at face in black marble table top.

In Scene One, the voice of Christ—acknowledges [He] has come back—is in image—accepts challenge and exact condi-

---

*In his Work Diary on July 4, 1941, O'Neill states: "drawing sets for scenes." He drew a scene for the Prologue and for each of the eight scenes. On July 7, he notes that he has "gone dead" on the play and "will put aside, try something else." He did not resume work on this manuscript until April 4, 1942, nearly a year later.

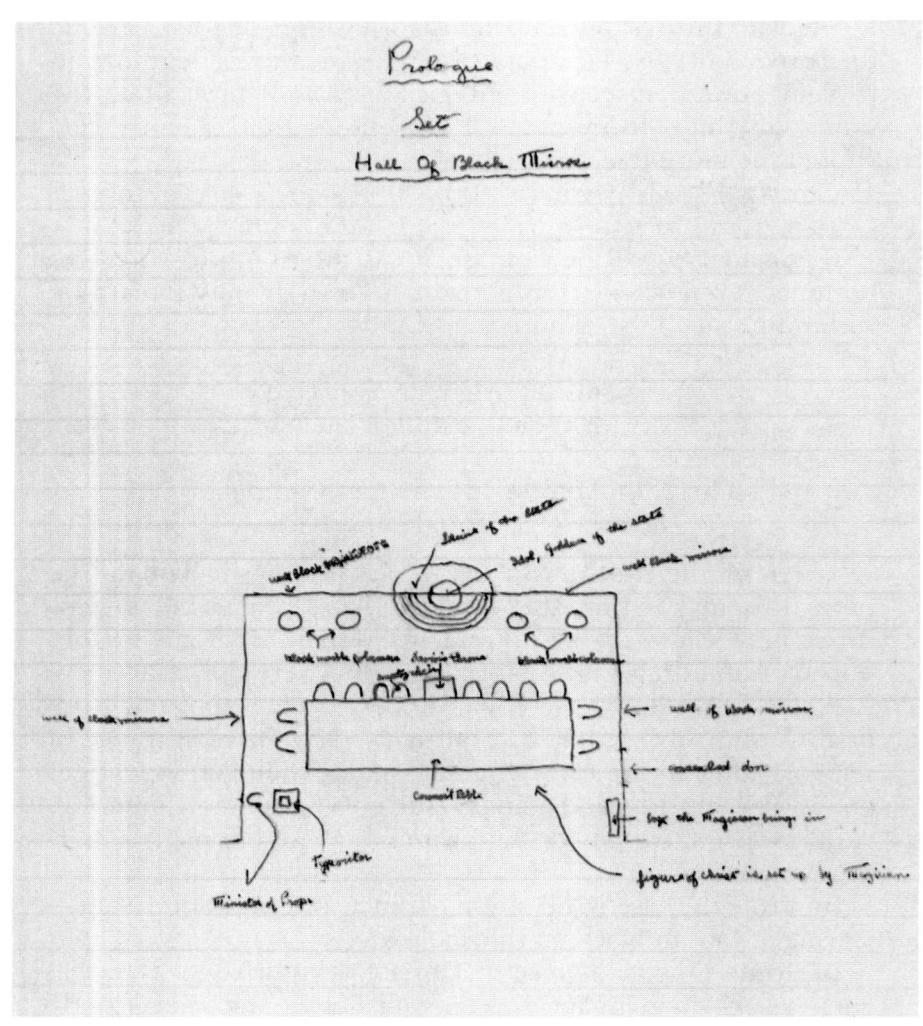

Prologue: Hall of Black Mirrors. (Courtesy Yale Collection of American Literature, Beinecke Rare Book and Manuscript Library)

Scene Four: The Hall of Last Suppers. (Courtesy Yale Collection of American Literature, Beinecke Rare Book and Manuscript Library)

Scene Five: The Garden of Sadism. (Courtesy Yale Collection of American Literature, Beinecke Rare Book and Manuscript Library)

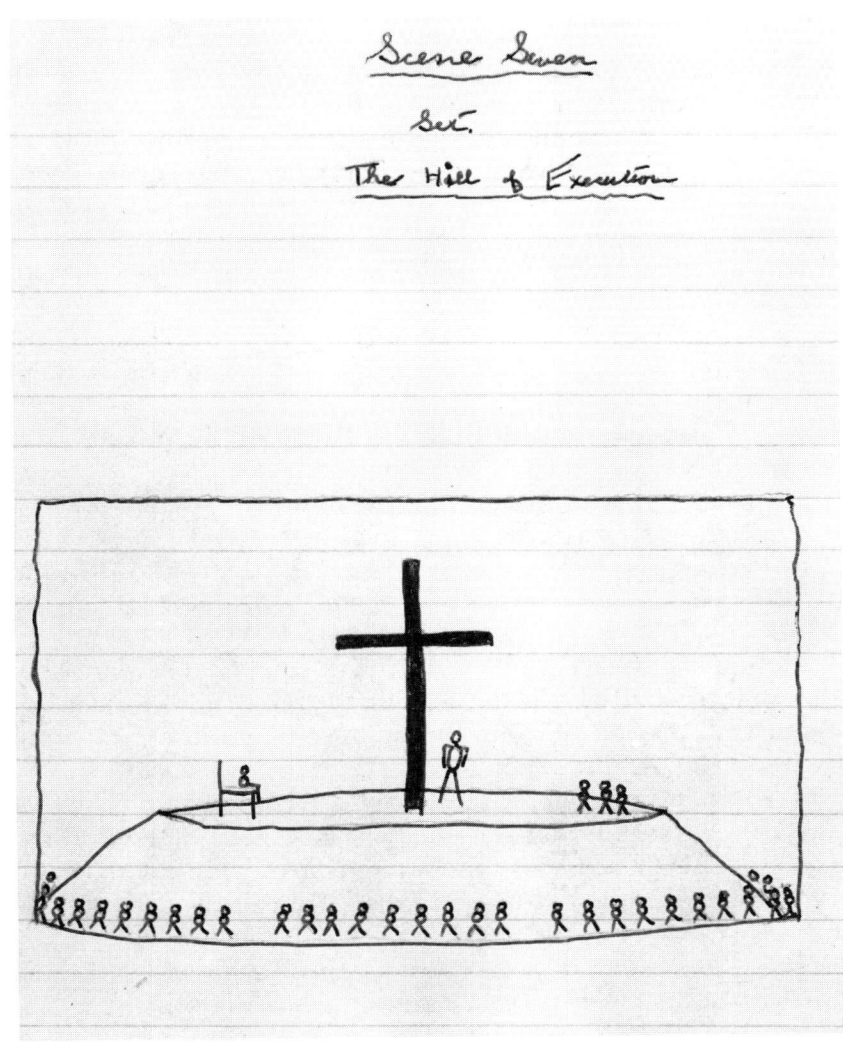

Scene Seven: The Hill of Execution. (Courtesy Yale Collection of American Literature, Beinecke Rare Book and Manuscript Library)

tions as laid down by Satan—Satan: "You think you can win that way? foolish"—Christ: "It is not for Me to win. It is for Man to win through Me, seeing himself in My image."

Savior of the World—asleep at first, Magician worrying—[Savior] wakes from nightmare—frightened of this dark child—frightened of heights—of mountains—of Nature—alternately furious at and clinging to Magician—takes back consent to Last Campaign—wants to go home to Mother State—weeps—is petrified when Christ speaks until Magician reassures him it is ventriloquism.

At dawn change to games, conjurer?

In stadium scene, jealous of Magician, drawing whip—Magician: "Give me the whip."

In temple scene, jealous of State—Savior of the World: "I am the State—My mother is an old bitch."

Supper scene—his miracle—blood to water.

Garden—dwarf as Judas?

Courtroom—Satan as Pilate: "What is truth?"—Savior of the World breaks in hysterically as Satan prompts: "I am the Truth."

Mount—Christ: "I am the soul, the spirit of God in Man. I am the Son of Man who is the Son of God and not of Satan, of Good and not of Evil. I am the Resurrection and the Life and who so believeth in Me, etc."

Toward end—Savior of the World to Magician: "That's what I've always wanted, Daddy."—Magician: "What?"—Savior of the World: "To be crucified. Without pain, of course. And naturally, I mustn't die. And not to save others. That's absurd. To increase my own power and glory."—Magician: "You are indeed the perfect son of slave man." Savior of the World: "To make my fools of slaves believe I can easily do what any other god has ever done and do it better. You must arrange it for me. I command you. You are a magician. I know you can fix it with a few cunning illusions—it can be done effectively with no inconvenience to me"—Magician: "I am afraid I have already arranged it, Majesty—as your subjects are arranging it—perhaps not quite as you wish."

[Masks—The Minister of Propaganda (a living midget) wears one which is a replica of faces of the carved wooden ones of other members of Council (Prologue). In following scenes, wherever the midget plays the role, or doubles in another, he wears a mask.]*

The Savior of the World—his face that of ideal hypnotic subject—or ideal actor's face—without character of its own except an infantile self-absorption, a vague, day-dreaming self-adoration—a vehicular face which must be possessed by a role, which is negative in itself, but capable of expressing intense emotion when possessed by a part.

The Savior of the World is expert ventriloquist and hypnotist—learned from Satan—but now claims he is much better at it than Satan and even that it was he who taught it to Satan in order to make him a more useful servant—it is Satan who speaks for the Minister of Propaganda, etc.

Prologue—add no more East—inferior yellow races crushed—only West now—[in] all material

<u>The Last Conquest</u>
[A Fantastic Pageant Dealing
With the Recurrence of
an Ancient Duality in a
Possible Realistic Future]†
Once upon a time in that spiral of the past
we call the future

<u>Characters</u>
The Savior of the World
The Members of His Supreme Council, thirteen in number, composed of the chiefs of His army, navy and air force, and the various Ministers of His cabinet, including
The Black Magician, His Minister of Spiritual Affairs and Superstitions

<u>Scenes</u>
Prologue: The Hall of Black Mirrors in the Savior's Palace on a night in the Future

---

*O'Neill has crossed out this paragraph, indicating the elimination of this idea for the use of masks.

†O'Neill drew diagonal lines through these four lines in brackets, indicating their elimination.

Scene One: An ancient legendary mountain top—a little before dawn four days later
Scene Two: The Great Stadium in the Capital of the World—morning of the same day
Scene Three: Interior of the Temple of the State that afternoon
Scene Four: The Hall of the Last Supper in the Savior's Palace—that evening
Scene Five: The Garden of Sadism in the grounds of the Palace—a little before dawn of the following day
Scene Six: Courtroom in the Temple of Justice—later the same morning
Scene Seven: Summit of the Hill of Execution—sunset of the same day
Scene Eight: The same—a little before dawn, the following morning

<u>Prologue</u>*

Scene: The Hall of Black Mirrors in the palace of His Divine Imperial Majesty, the Savior of the World. This is His favorite room in which He holds all important secret conclaves with His Council of State. It is long and narrow, with a lofty domed ceiling of black marble and a black marble floor. The side walls, left and right, are lined solidly with high black mirrors. In the end wall, at rear, is a shrine of the Divine Dark Mother, the Goddess of the State, flanked on either side by two marble columns. Three steps lead up to a curved recess in which the idol of the Goddess stands on a high altar. But as this part of the room is in deep shadow, one cannot see any details of the shrine. There is merely an impression of a black figure, bigger than life-size, seated on a throne, outlined against the back of the shrine, which, although dark in color, is lighter than the prevailing black of the room.

The room has a heavy somber grandiosity. In spite of an obvious theatrical atmosphere, a quality of being designed and staged to awe and oppress, it possesses also its own appalling

---

*On April 14, 1942, O'Neill notes in his Work Diary: "start rewriting the Prologue." On the seventh day following this notation, he describes his work on the Prologue as "rewriting" or "revising," words that must certainly apply to his reshaping the missing 1941 Prologue.

sincerity as a reflection of perverted will-to-power and morbid distortion of spirit. It has the semblance of a crypt devoted to an oblique self-worship—an adoration with black mirrors because in them the self-beholder's will to self-deception can instill the darkened ghostly image with whatever life it needs to assume as the true life.

The only light in this room comes from a metal desklamp on the conclave table at center, and from a small spotlight, concealed in the ceiling, directed so it falls on the throne of the Savior of the World.

This ebony table, heavy and ornately carved, is set lengthwise across the room, with the ebony throne of the Savior of the World placed at its middle, at rear, facing front, flanked on either side by four chairs, similar to the throne but smaller and not so heavily overladen with carved ornament. At each end of the table are two more chairs. At left, front, of the conclave table, by the wall, is another of these chairs, front, right, drawn up to a small metal typewriting table with a typewriter on it.

All the chairs except the one at the Savior's right, that of the Minister of Spiritual Affairs who is still absent, are occupied by members of the Council—the heads of important ministries, the Chief of Staff of the Army, Grand Admiral of the Navy, the Commander of the Air Force, etc. The chair at the typewriting table is occupied by the Minister of Propaganda.

These members of the Council, who comprise the Super Elite class of the World State, do not appear to be living men. They are too small, for one thing—no larger than a ventriloquist's dummy. Their chairs are made with raised seats like children's high chairs so that they can sit mechanically at the table. And their faces and bodies have a wooden quality, all the faces carved imitations of each other—emotionless faces, coldly intelligent, insensitive, capable, ruthlessly determined. Every member wears the uniform of his exalted rank, the chest adorned with rows of medals.

His Divine Imperial Majesty, the Savior of the World, seems to be a living man, although because of the mystic trance He is now in, it is difficult to tell. Contrasted with members of his conclave, He appears large and powerful, but in reality He is a small man not over four feet in height, with a middle-aged paunchy body. By deliberate intention to heighten the contrast between Himself and them, the uniform He wears is simple, without a medal or stars or ornament of any kind. He sits with one elbow on the table, a hand supporting His head. His pale face is frozen in an expression of soft inner contemplation, a bit staged for effect like everything else in this Hall of Black Mirrors, a bit self-consciously pop-eyed but like the room, there is a frightening sincerity about Him. He is genuinely lost in a gloating monomaniacal sense of His own divine superiority and low ignobility of all other men. His large pale greenish-blue eyes are still and glassy. Then in a touch of the antic in his face—an antic fox—something of a burrowed weasel, too, of an immutable bug, of an ultra modern Narcissus who realistically adores his own reflection in a cesspool. Although he is middle-aged, he still possesses a depraved and deprived adolescence, a youthful cruelty, an immature imperviousness to the sight of sorrow and pain. Above all, he has the quality of a medium, a hypnotic subject, a fanatic who is empty and lifeless when not possessed by his fanaticism, an actor who is a starring vehicle for the part he plays.[9]

There is no physical resemblance between him and any of the dictators of totalitarian nations, like Hitler of Germany, who has preceded him and whose realistic wars, although they met temporary material defeat in the end, triumphed in principle and so ravaged and maimed and tortured the already sick and faithless souls of men, that they paved the way for final, worldwide, spiritual exhaustion and the acceptance of the new Salvation and the Divine Tyrant Redeemer principle in a Holy and Indivisible World State. The Savior of the World owes much to these men, who spiritual heir He is, but of course He can never admit He owes His power to anything but His own Divine Genius and He has decreed that no memory of these men must ever be spoken or written.

For a moment after the curtain rises, there is silence. The members of the Conclave sit unduly erect, shoulders squared, arms stiffly at their sides, hands beneath the table, eyes staring straight before them. It is as if they dared not glance at their Savior, having learned that he who looks upon God is apt to be assassinated.

A door concealed in the mirror at right, front, opens and the Magician, Minister of Spiritual Affairs, enters. A tall man, over six feet, he appears a giant in contrast with the dwarf figures at the table. The Hall of Black Mirrors fits him. It becomes at once his room. The black uniform he wears is, like those of all his colleagues, adorned with rows of medals, stars and crown. It fits tightly and displays his immensely powerful frame—broad shoulders, great chest, slim waist and hips, muscular long legs and arms. Under his arm he carries without effort, as if it were a toy, a coffin-shaped box, painted white, about six feet long.

His body is like that of a young athlete in his prime, but his swarthy face is marred by deep lines and his hair is iron grey. It is a face which has the quality of being molded in bronze. A hawk's face with a big aquiline nose, piercing dark eyes which seem always fixed on the peaks of a far-off mountain, a jutting angular jaw, a thin-lipped, flexible orator's mouth, a broad intellectual forehead. A face that is like a symbolic mask of the spirit of evil, implacable pride, and yet has a mocking trace in its expression of the conscious mountebank and charlatan. A tragic face too—or perhaps it is merely bored and weary—bored by victories and wary of times.[10]

He lowers the coffin-like box to the floor, then clicks his heels and raises an arm in the ancient Roman salute,[11] his eyes on the Savior, his expression servile. He speaks and his tone is self-depreciating and deferential—a strange, resonant, persuasive and insinuating voice which continually hints at a double meaning.

The Magician: "Hail, O Divine Master of Manhood, and Savior of the World! (The Savior does not move but without any change in his trance-like expression his eyes turn and fix themselves on the Magician's eyes. The Magician does not seem to notice there has been no acknowledgement of his salutation. He comes to the empty chair on the Savior's right—apologetically) I crave your august pardon for my tardiness, Master. (He bows with formal, grave politeness to the figures seated around the table) And I also beg the indulgence of my eminent colleagues of the Conclave. (As if he heard them grant this indulgence, he sits down and turns to the Savior whose eyes remain always fixed on him, his manner familiar and yet deferential and subservient) My excuse for being late, O Master, is that I had to put a few final touches to my work before I dared bring it here for Your sublime approval, as You commended me to do."

The Savior (in a vague whisper, as if groping for a cue): "I? (He stares in the Magician's eyes—then suddenly with strident arrogance) Yes, I. I alone command!"

The Magician (bows his head humbly): "And I obey, Lord. (He indicates the white box) It is there. It is done. Well done, too. I flatter myself, considering it is no easy task to create a living likeness, working entirely from memory. (He pauses, as if suddenly confronting some image in his mind, and his face for a second becomes cruel and sneering and insolent—then matter-of-factly) But before I show it to you, O Divine Master, I think it would be well to explain to my colleagues the plan I suggested to you for this new campaign of conquest—(His voice grows oratorical) Your last conquest which will assure Your final, absolute dominion over the minds of every man, woman and child in your vast empires of the World! (Then quietly) It is imperative that everyone here possess a thorough realistic understanding of the purpose of this plan since each must take some part in it. (He turns deferentially to the Savior) May I speak for you, Master?"

The Savior (in a whisper as before—gropingly): "Speak? (Then as the Magician stares into his stare—stridently, in a rising tone that seems to strive for escape and comforting release in a high note of hysteria) Yes! You may speak. But it is I alone who speak! I give the Word and I am the Word! I am the End and the Beginning! I am the Son and the Father of the State! I am the State! I am the Divine Son of Man, the Superman, the Inspirer of Peace on Earth, the Savior of Mankind. I am the Son of God. And I am God!" (His mouth closes on an exhausted, piercing quaver. There is a pause. It is as if He and all the other figures were waiting mechanically for the inevitable, organized roar of hysterical acclaim from millions of throats.)

The Magician (with servile flattery): "Who dares deny it, Lord? You are adored throughout the world, as the One True Living God, the Divine Son of the Omnipotent State, which is the All-In-One and One-In-All. (He moves reverentially to the side of the shrine, at rear—then turns to the members of the Conclave) You heard our Savior command me to speak. So I advise you to listen carefully, forgetting for the moment the little murderous hates and jealousies of each other's power which naturally exist between us. I need not remind you of the fate awaiting those who are inattentive to our Master's words. They die, of course, that is, the fortunate ones do.

(He leans over the table, his manner suavely business-like, resembling that of a Chairman of the Board explaining a new campaign to the directors) "As Minister of Spiritual Affairs, it is my duty, as you know, to maintain constant surveillance over the thoughts, and particularly the dreams, of men. For I must admit they still do dream. No method has yet been derived to rid them of that ancient weakness. Nor would it be wise world policy to do so, because my investigations have shown that almost invariably men's dreams nowadays are merely harmless visions of requited minor greeds which seem to keep their hopes and ambitions realistically occupied. For example, take what I have found to be the most typical dream. A man sees himself in imagination as a superior and successful citizen of the State because he has contrived by low cunning to own one more pig than his neighbor possesses. Naturally, I encourage such dreams for so long as a man can believe one more pig than his neighbor has meaning, he is his neighbor's slave, and his own slave and the slave of that pig and freedom remains a vacant word to him—a word which he does not mind being forbidden to utter. (He smiles deprecatingly) Perhaps you feel my argument a trifle abstract and mystical, Fellow Members of the Super Elite. I know what deplorable realists you all are. But the point I am leading up to is that while such dreams are useful and wholesome there is a morbid factor that men can still dream of the future at all. It proves that spirit still exists in them unconsciously now, of course. But it is dangerous because deep within it, a certain faint memory lies dormant. Now there is no reason, generally speaking, to forbid men to remember, because they are incapable of relating the past to the present, or of ever realizing the truth which our Divine Master (he bows to the Figure of the Savior) has understood so thoroughly, that there is no present nor future but simply the past marching on with an imbecile's doggedness, to meet its eternal recurrences in Time (He smiles deprecatingly again) I fear you must find that a trifle abstruse, too. (Briskly) To the point then.

"The dominant memory I have detected in men is concerned with an old legend, a tale of Divine Savior God of Ancient Times who became a son of Man because of his love and pity for mankind, that he might sacrifice himself and suffer and die in order to save them from evil and awaken the good in them that they might live as brothers, loving one another, and so transform our world of greedy hates and lust for possession into the Blessed Kingdom of Peace on earth. (He speaks this last as if, in spite of himself, he seems moved. He is abruptly conscious of this himself and continues quickly in a sneering tone) A stupid superstitious folk tale, of course, incredibly irrational and unscientific. It dates back to the age of man's mental infancy when he indulged himself in childish moral fantasies about Evil and Good, flesh and spirit, the eternal opposites in his nature which waged a battle for the final salvation or destruction of a ghostly supposition he called his immortal soul. (Ironically apologetic) You are impatient with such nonsense I see, Gentlemen of the Super Elite. Remember that was long ago. Of course, we enlightened ones of the world today know by experience there is but one nature in man. He is an animal with a brain governed by his belly and his sexual organs, and one word, Greed, explains him and all his hopes and fears.

(He pauses—then in a blunt business-like tone again) "I pointed out to our Divine Master the dangerous element in this legend of a rival son of God who had been crucified for disturbing the power of Ancient Rome. According to this legend, on the third day he rose from the dead. Now you will agree, Gentlemen, that it is imperative for the safety of the State that men must believe in the absolute finality of death. Otherwise, Our Savior's great potent weapon, the terror of death, is taken from him. The skull, grinning an idiot's mocking leer at the possessions of life, is a realistic symbol of our Master's power which must be ever present in the consciousness of every loyal, obedient subject. If death were not the end, if men should ever believe again that they had souls, who would fear him? And without fear where—? (He pauses) I think I need not dwell on that dread possibility, Gentlemen. I can trust you to imagine where you would be.

"But the greatest danger in this old legend is a prophecy that this ancient Redeemer will appear a second time on earth. Obviously this is a grave potential threat to Our Master's absolute power because so long as men can remember, no matter how dimly and subconsciously, the faintest dream of a return of the spirit, they have not been completely conquered. They are not then hopelessly contented slaves, the ideal citizens of the World State, which Our Master, having in mind their future welfare and happiness, is determined they must be. Hence the need for this last campaign of destructive conquest which I have suggested to Our Lord and for which I now seek the final approval and the command to proceed—after he has seen my work (He indicates the box) I think it admirable to attack it now. It would be unwise to run the risk of waiting until men's unconscious dreams gather strength and become at last a conscious hope—or even worse, a seditious prayer.

"We must anticipate the enemy and drive the issue into the open where it can be dealt with realistically. We must bring this old Savior back on earth ourselves, now while men are totally unprepared to receive him. We must ourselves create this enemy, so to speak, in order to destroy him—produce his second coming, stage it as a gigantic theatrical pageant, an enormous farce which he will be compelled to repeat his former salvational career on earth for the amusement of all our loyal subjects assembled in the immense circle of the world by our Savior's command to witness the absurd spectacle. (His face has hardened with a cruel sneering revengefulness. He laughs) Now you do see the point, Gentlemen. As my colleague the Minister of Propaganda (he bows to this figure at the small table) knows so well, there is no destroyer like derision. A burst of jeering laughter can annihilate where too strained harshness would fail. One stupid sneer on a man or woman's lips is worth more than ten tanks when the foe is the spirit. We will purge the memory of this former Savior from men's minds forever by making them laugh at him. We will provide him with carefully picked followers, Apostles and Disciples, recruited from the actors in our State Theatre whose specialty is farcical character parts. Our Divine Lord will greet his appearance with apparent tolerance, as one treats the senile in their second childhood who mutter in mumbling dreams of the brave things they did in a past that is forgotten. Of course, in the end, we will be forced reluctantly to crucify him, not because Our Divine Master condescends to regard him as a rival, nor because the childish doctrine he preaches constitutes the highest danger to the World State but simply because under the law of our enlightened realistic State, the mentally disabled are executed.

(He pauses, smiling cruelly) "You see, Gentlemen, I honestly believe this is the most astute of all the plans I have ever suggested to Our Divine Master to increase and stabilize His power. (In a sinister joking tone) I am afraid once this last campaign is successfully accomplished, Our Blessed Savior will find Himself, as a matter of realistic fact, in the position Alexander the Great fancied he was in. There will be nothing left to conquer. Even the necessity of any other Son of God but Him will have vanished from the souls of men in an enormous gob of jeering laughter. (He pauses, glancing around at the ministers of the Conclave) I see there is a natural, practical question in your minds, Brethren of the Super Elite. How can I find anyone to act out the role of the old Savior of legend? Who could look the part and speak the lines well enough to dismiss the image in men's memories. (His tone changing to that of a sly stage magician boasting of his tricks) A simple matter, I assure you, gentlemen—that is, for one who has had my vast experience in creating illusion and disillusion. I think I may say without boasting, that I am adroit in all the artifices of a magician. Such as hypnotism. (His eyes turn to the Savior) Our Divine Master will bear witness—But no, I am sure He has never deigned to notice. (He looks at the ministers of the Conclave) I am an expert ventriloquist, too, as all of you are aware. But no, I am sure that is the last thing any of you would suspect. (He pauses, a veiled gleam of derision in his eyes—then briskly practical.) However, I shall soon convince you by a little practical demonstration that this matter of creating the old Savior can be safely left entirely in my hands.

(He turns to the Savior of the World) "With your gracious

permission, Majesty. (He goes quickly to the coffin-like box he had brought with him and throws open the lid. He bends and lifts a life-size man's figure out of it. This figure dressed in a white robe is so cunningly contrived with flexible joints that as it lies in the Magician's arms, it seems like a living man who has fainted or had just died. The Magician pits its sandalled feet on the floor and straightens its body to an upright position. Then, by using a joined steel rod concealed beneath the robe as a support, he fixes the figure firmly in a natural standing position, arms at its sides, at right of the right end of the council table. At first the face of the figure cannot be seen because the Magician who is much taller is between it and the audience. At last he steps back) There. But we need more light for you to appreciate my masterpiece. [(We still cannot see the face, The Magician speaks) There Divine Emperor of the World and Gentlemen. Is it not well contrived to swindle the foolish mob? But wait, you must have a good look at the face.]* (He strides to the wall and pushes a button which sends the light of a concealed spotlight in the ceiling full on the figure's face. It is the face of Christ, the man of sorrow's face, gentle, infinitely pitying and sad—a piece of wood carving executed by an artist who has worked with genius. The Magician declaims tauntingly) Behold the first Son of Man, the former Savior of Mankind. He who failed so pitiably in conquering the souls of men where You O Divine One (He bows servilely to the Savior of the World) have so gloriously succeeded! (The Savior of the World, half awakened from His mystic trance, lifts glazed eyes to stare for a second, arrogantly contemptuous at the carved image of Christ's face. The Magician also stares at it with a taunting hatred—sneeringly) He who died in vain, a false prophet whose words have turned to dust!

"I can remember some years ago, there still remained a few among the aged who quoted his foolish seditious parables—secretly, to themselves at night, behind in their bedrooms in the dark. But finally his word exhortations became so meaningless in our great realistic World State that even those senile ones

---

*These lines in brackets have been crossed out by the author, thus eliminating them from the Prologue.

locked in their own bedrooms after dark stopped quoting him for fear they would start laughing at their own folly. (A strange bitter irony has crept into his voice—almost a tone of pity. As if he were suddenly conscious of this, he changes tone abruptly and becomes the objective satisfied craftsman) Well? How do you like his face, Master—and Gentlemen? It is a fine piece of wood carving, if I do say so myself. (Sneeringly) It is what was once in the abolished past considered to be a noble face. I wished, above all, to achieve that effect, because it is the essence of our purpose that men must jeer and laugh with sneers at him, recognizing an old nobility. After that, there will be nothing to fear from any obedience we please. To make the ignoble obviously noble and the noble inevitably silly is the supreme function of our modern state. (He pauses—sneeringly again staring at the face of Christ) The face is remarkably lifelike, too, don't you think, Gentlemen? Would you not swear he is about to speak? Well, perhaps he is. Listen." (He bends his head down to the figure, and a voice does indeed seem to come from Christ's lips, a voice in no way like the Magician's but pitying and pleading.) The figure of Christ: "Love ye one another."

[(There is a moment's pause. For a moment even the Magician seems taken aback by the success of his ventriloquist trick, while the Savior of the World awakes from his trance to stare at the carved face of Christ.)

The Magician: "There! You see how easy it will be to make him appear alive to the simple mob. I will be his voice. (Mockingly) And I will deal honorably by him, too, I swear it. I will never make him say anything but what he said before. It will be the most gratifying irony of all, to use his own words to make him a fool! (He quotes jeeringly) 'Love ye one another!' Who could dream such sentimental idiocy would ever be uttered in this room amongst us! Is there one here who does not hate and fear each of his fellows? Which is as it should be amongst Supermen! There is nothing like hate to goad ambition on to frenetic conquest. Love, as I have heard, is content with so little! (Abruptly changing to a curt, matter-of-fact tone) There is no need for any further demonstration, I trust? I am confident you must appreciate the full significance of my plan—and the certainty of its success. Has any member of the Conclave any question? Or Suggestion? No? Good. (To the figure at the head of the table) And You, O Divine Son of Man and of the State? Are you content? May I give the command in Your name to start this last campaign?" (He bends deferentially as if he thought the Leader might want to whisper in his ear.)

The Savior of the World (arrogantly): "You may give the command. In My Name. In the Name of God. (His voice again reaching longingly for hysteria) I am Destruction. I am the Son of Death. And I am Death!"]*

The Savior of the World [(After this half awakens from his trance, staring blinkingly at the crucified face of Christ)]† (With amazed incredulity): "What? I thought I heard him say: 'Love one another.'" (He suddenly bursts into a shrill cackle of insane laughter which stops as abruptly as it started.)

The Magician (sneeringly): "His very words, Master. I happened to remember them. I knew you would be amused. (Jeering) 'Love ye one another.' Who could dream such sentimental idiocy would ever find utterance in this room among us? Is there a single one here who does not hate and fear each and all of his followers? Which is as it should be amongst Supermen. There is nothing like hate and fear to goad ambition on to further conquest. They inspire the inevitable Will to Power. Love, as I have heard, is abject and humbly content with little— a slave's ignoble emotion, aspiring to nothing beyond itself. (Abruptly he becomes the boastful showman again.) Well Master, and Gentlemen, my colleagues, I hope I have proved by that little demonstration how easily I can make my masterpiece appear alive to the stupid mob. I will be his voice (Sneeringly) and deal honorably by him, too, I swear it, for I shall never make him say anything but what he said before. It will be the most gratifying irony of all, with his own words to prove him a fool. (Briskly again) Well, there is no need for any further demonstration, I trust? Has any member of the Conclave a suggestion to offer? No? Good. (To the Savior of the World)

---

*O'Neill indicates that these three paragraphs in brackets are crossed out.

†These words of the stage directions in brackets have also been eliminated from the play.

And You O Divine Son and Father of the Omnipotent State? Are You satisfied?"

The Savior of the World (still staring at the face of Christ): "So it was only one of your tricks? I do not like to be deceived. (Bursting into shrill hysterical fury) Those who deceive me, die! Remember, Magician, I am the Son of Death, too. And I am Death!"

The Magician (humbly): "That is indeed the very soul of truth, O Master. (Slyly flattering and suggesting) But I know you are merely pretending you were deceived—out of the infinite kindness of your heart—as to compliment my skill. As a God, you see all and know all. You cannot be deceived."

The Savior of the World (quickly): "Yes. Of course. I was not deceived. I merely wished to compliment you. You are a clever and useful tool. I am satisfied. You may start My last conquest at once."

The Magician (bowing low with exaggerated obeisance): "Thank you, O Divine One. (This in a music-like tone) The first thing to be done is to prepare minds for his second coming. We must give it the widest possible publicity. (He turns to Minister of Propaganda) That, of course, is your work, Minister of Propaganda, but I shall be only too happy to assist you. Tomorrow you must have every newspaper announce to the world that a man has appeared who claims he is Christ, the Redeemer of ancient folklore. They will say he is being questioned by the Secret Police, but, at our Master's order, is being treated with kindness. He is thought to be suffering from hallucinations. The next day you will announce that after due investigation it appears the man's claims are valid and he is indeed Christ. You will say to the world at our Divine Master's supreme magnaminity that he has not ordered this false Savior of superstitions to be executed at once. On the contrary, Our Master has had him brought to the palace and will interview him. On the third day, you will announce that Our Master, after talking with the man, is so extremely amused by his half-witted conceits that He thinks they may prove equally diverting to the people. Therefore, Our Divine Master decrees a world wide holiday, a Festival of All Fools, in which the quaint fanatics from the Age of Ignorance will be allowed to repeat—under total supervision, of course—certain impressively ridiculous incidents which were once believed to have actually occurred during his former salvationist career on earth, the first incident to be exhibited promptly at dawn on the following day. Is that all clear, My Esteemed Colleague?" (He bends over the figure of the Minister of Propaganda. The figure's mouth opens and shuts like a manipulated dummy's.)

Minister of Propaganda (in a voice which shrilly imitates his Master's): "Perfectly—another little job of befuddling the joker mob. You flatter them, Excellency, when you refer to their minds. I am their minds."

The Magician: "Yes. You and I. That is only too true. Come, then. We will have the Conclave. There is much for us to do. (He picks up the Minister of Propaganda, holding him as a ventriloquist holds a dummy. He bows to the Savior of the World.) You will forgive me, O Supreme Savior of Mankind, the Goddess of the State. (He nods toward the shrine at rear—then adds with an undercurrent of inner amusement.) Your Celestial Daughter, too, for You gave birth to Her at the same moment She gave birth to You. Truly this is the greatest of all Holy Mysteries—as sacredly involved as the adventures of Iris and Osiris—and yet it is a demonstrated modern realistic fact. (The Savior of the World is not listening; he has relapsed into his Narcissus trance. The Magician glances at the figure of Christ.) I will leave my masterpiece here. This is the best hiding place until we need him for the first scene.

"But before I light the shrine of Our Great Mother, and the presence of the Goddess is made manifest for your intent prayers, I must change his position a little. He was a distinct individualist, as I remember. He must be made to kneel before the Omnipotent State. (He strides to the figure and manipulates it into a kneeling position with head humbly bowed.) There. Now he looks more like a living fact." (He goes to the wall at left and presses a button in the mirror. A flood of glaring light from concealed overhead lighting illuminates the shrine at rear and reveals the idol of the Goddess of the State seated on a golden throne. She is made of steel, the body all a polished blue-black, the face an enameled glistening white, framed by a mop of thick, coarse blond hair. With the exception of her belly which is obscenely fat, gorged and distorted, she is frightfully emaciated. Her arms and legs are thin as one dying of famine. Her big breasts hang down flatly like deflated rubber bags. Her face is so drawn and famished one can almost see the skull beneath. Her enormous protruding china-blue eyes glare with ferocious insatiable hunger; her bloody tongue is thrust out from between big sharp fang-like teeth and pallid thick lips. [Kali]* The black Mother Goddess of Death and Destruction except that this idol is blond. She is hideous and appalling. There are touches about her which indicate her creator owes more than a little of his inspiration to Hindu idols, of Kali, the black Mother Goddess of Destruction and Death. She wears a necklace of skulls and is girdled with snakes,[12] for example. Perched on one thigh, supported by her arm, is a statue of the Savior of the World, wearing the same surprisingly simple uniform. Crushed beneath her big, manly fist is a female figure in a Grecian robe, presumably the old discredited Goddess of Liberty, the torch dropping from her hand.)

The Magician regards this monstrous Idol of the State with an objective ironic appreciation. He speaks as if to himself: "Not as excellently done as my latest masterpiece—but nevertheless well done. A faithful image of man's permanent longing for the security of suicide. Our Gentle Lady of Cannibalism! (He smiles, then abruptly clicks his heels and raises his arm in salute to the Savior of the World—solemnly) Hail, Lord of Mankind! I respectfully bid You and Your Celestial Mother and Daughter good night. (He bows to the figures around the table) Gentlemen of the Super Elite, my colleagues, good night. (His eyes turn to the bowed head of the bending figure of Christ—a sneer on his lips but something of pity in his voice) And to you, good night, Image of my conquered Enemy and Opposition within the soul of Man." (He opens the door, a secret one in mirror, and goes out with the figure of the Minister of Propaganda perched dummy-wise on his arm. The door closes behind him. For a moment the picture remains of the Goddess of the State, the Savior of the World lost in his glassy-eyed mystic trance, the wooden puppet figures of His Conclave, and the kneeling image of Christ.)

---

*O'Neill erased this word in brackets.

The Last Conquest
Notes [Aug. 20, 1942]*

Scene One—after the sun rises at the command of the Savior (all this past part is microphone—loud speaker stuff from top of boulder, the Mount of Temptation having been so arranged.)

Temptation speech written by Magician, memorized by the Savior—offer to share power—discussion of power—"You will have, etc.—but, of course, a bargain—in return you must give up your silly idea of the duality of man's nature—that he is composed of the opposites of flesh and spirit—good and evil—obviously this is stupid—he is only flesh—his mind is matter inspired by electric currents, etc."

Answer: "What would it profit a man to gain the whole world and lose his own soul?"[13]

Magician (aside to crowd) "He thinks that Man—that is—each of you has a soul. (Laughter) He nobly refuses to exchange nothing for everything" (Laughter).

Magician at start explains to people—a spectacle to amuse you but also it contains a lesson for your edification.

Imperialism has reached final expression where even the homeland of the State is treated as a conquered colony.

Scene One—dialogue in dark with himself—"ostensible purpose to destroy man's last secret hope (unconscious)—then the race will perish in complete indifference of will to live—they will adore and pray longingly to Goddess of Our Lady of Death—but I suspect myself—too much man—do I too, as man, unconsciously hope—then it must be pride—or my occupation gone—to desire the already damned—I am sick with their sickness—one of spirit and pride—ah, for healthy proud men again who would defy the Prince of Evil?—who would have the Spirit of God in them—the courage to fight—ah, for some Ancient Enemy—the joy of battle and rebellion"—then he laughs cynically—"The Devil was sick—the Devil a saint would be, etc."

Satan (in weariness-bound aspect in his darkness dialogue with Christ): "Man is sick, sick from what I have done to him,

---

*The first entry O'Neill made in his Work Diary after the notation of June 19, 1942, "finish 2nd draft Prologue," is dated August 20. The next day he states: "idea story—start outline but fade out."

but also sick of himself. And I am sick of him, but also sick of myself, what he has made me, of the image of me he has created, of me as man. For my tragedy is I am not a Son of God like you who for a brief 33 years lived as a man, but a Crown of Evil whose only kingdom is man's soul."

General—as introduction, presented instances of man's sympathy with Christ appear—Satan appears outwardly worried and concerned. Satan: "More dim than I thought. It all goes to show you cannot kill what is in the innate heart of men—always exceptions to rule even in collective state"—but secretly he is pleased—and Savior of the World guesses that—as Satan says: "penalty for possession of his mind, he has true intuitions about mine."

The Last Conquest   Nov. '42
Notes

Satan (the Magician) can only make Christ come to life as he plays upon the subconscious memory of the people of the World until the memory becomes conscious—the figure then comes slowly to life—at Satan's goading the people become reawakened (pity, love, understanding, consciousness of good and evil, etc.)

1st time—Mount of Temptation—after Satan makes Christ refuse offer—a pause—the people do not come in on cue—Leader outraged—Magician apologizes—their sense of humor killed or murdered—forgotten how to laugh—Minister of Propaganda's fault—should have realized their brains so dull, forget instructions—most subject peoples cannot read—Then Christ himself says: "No"—Magician ironically satisfied—Leader appalled—Magician says he did it to cue you to speak—Leader says unprepared, has to rehearse—Magician says: "Then I will speak for you—simply make your mouth move"—Magician points out joke to people: [Christ was] "offered the world for nothing—for an old supposition called the soul which is an old superstition—denunciated in modern world"—points it up, laughs: "He is a fool"—then roar of laughter.

End—blaring of bands as people are marched home—hymn to a murdered prop—a demi-God which symbolizes that any end justifies any means—on his birthday—procession of

Madmen and State to adore his altar—as Magician explained to Christ as he leads him away: "So you came to life, did you? You thought their silence meant hope? Don't be a fool, etc.—But I am glad—something to fight against."

Prologue—change Satan to immense corpulent figure—the Leader, boy-like hermaphrodite but not fairy, sexless.

Scene One—Satan's talk, often he hypnotizes the Leader to sleep and [he will] not bother him when he talks to figure of Christ. First taunts it for not daring to come and accept challenges and merit the defeat—then in telling wearily of men's decadence he mentions death of democracy—men grew tired of the responsibility of living free with no higher law than the criminal code to define the use of freedom—their spirits corrupt and fat—the goddess of Liberty a fat woman in a circus—democracy with a paunch and bad heart and impotent.

Satan's confession—"[I have] become man, an individual like them—a soul—and now are all slaves—failed in my plans—did not want to destroy them—I want a world of rebels whose pride would shake their fists defiantly at the sky, at you, at all gods, who would say [they] are chosen to be damned rather than saved—they have mistaken a cheap cynicism for evil—what am I?—a Prince of Evil Pride is the thing for them—to keep my hold on them, I had to compromise, become man with them, become a Prince of Realistic Cynicism, etc."

Satan: "Why I dared you to return from the dead—for you were dead in their souls, where alone you could live, their great disgust for themselves—the soul cannot breathe in it—you have lost your dwelling place—so have I—I meant only in their outer consciousness—not a reason for existence there—the brutality and bloody cruelty exists automatically—a custom—a natural aspect of human nature—accepted without thought by obedient slaves of the State—there is no conflict—all is relative—no good nor evil—they are all spiritually dead—a fine thing for me to be—a fat corpse ruling the brains of corpses—I am a pathetic fat man, a gorged physical cannibal king, who vomits the carrion human flesh, which is all he has left to eat—He, Satan, whose proud fate and doom it was to conspire and turn the Sons of God into the Enemies of God!

"That is why I have dared you to come back—to help me

restore their pride, to make them live again the conflict of Good and Evil—the eternal opposites—You and I—the last and most perfect symbols of Ancient Truth—the truth in the *Bhagavad Gita*,[14] etc.—to save my pride—now a God is judged by his enemy—think of a God defeated by a crafty old fat man—think of Satan with no good in himself for his evil to overcome."

Then he grows merely pitiful—Satan: "No, don't come back—you are right—they are not worth it—they want and build bigger and better machines—what for?—why, in order to tire them, to keep busy, etc.

"Then find Faust—a striving of figure—or is it wasteful imagination—Are you then, Jesus?"—no answer.

First light of dawn—sound of multitude gathering—Satan coaches Leader—eager to make the sun rise—Satan: "I know you love that little game, but don't forget something more important this a.m.—have you learned all the lines I wrote for you." Leader: "Yes, letter perfect—but if I should forget you will prompt." Satan: "Of course." Leader's actor joy at size of the audience, etc.—then doubt—Leader: "Suppose he accepts my offer of world dominion with me and Goddess of State—You will have to kill him for me." Satan: "It is only a coarse image. Even if he were alive he would refuse your offer." Leader looks on figure curiously: "Must be awful idiot. Why would he refuse? What for?" Satan: "That you could never understand—I mean a crazed brain's believing, etc."

General—in each scene where Goddess of State idol is shown she is portrayed in another aspect: Prologue, Our Mother of Destruction and Death—Scene Two, Our Mother of Victory (War and Conquest)—Scene Three, Mother of Bureaucracy (and Fertility, Fecundity)—Scene Four, Our Mother of Gluttony (Cannibalism)—Scene Six, Mount of Olives, Our Mother of Earth (Nature)—Scene Seven, Our Mother of Law (Justice under feet)—Scene Eight, Our Mother of Sacrifice.

(In mob scenes, Satan via Propaganda Minister and his Slave Theatre director has mob ask Christ certain questions at times from Testament which Christ answers.)

Scene Two—triumphal entry of Christ into city, ending in the stadium of the Chosen Superior Race—Hearing shouts of laughter growing nearer, Leader grows restless and curious—mad at Satan—Leader: "You are giving him all the applause while I sit here like a dummy mocked by one hundred thousand silences"—Satan says: "Make a speech. You can always raise them to hysteria"—Leader: "But [I] don't know a speech. You haven't prepared one. What can I talk about? There is nothing left to talk about." Satan: "Talk about yourself, your divinity and divine origin—your mystic birth." Leader (pitiably): "I am tired of talking about myself—almost. There is nothing left to say." Satan: "Why, you can compare yourself with him, your efficiency as Savior of Mankind as Prince of Peace—spoil his entrance—tell them how Superior a Son of God you are"—Leader: "Will you prompt me. I will make the motions until your words inspire me. Anything to make my elite look alive. They had me dreaming I was Emperor of the Dead." Satan gives him a ringmaster's whip: "Your most potent scepter."

Leader descends to the arena. Magician attending him—limps to the pedestal of idol which extends around statue—applause—Savior cracks whip for silence—makes his speech—at first, amusing humiliation of Christ as blockhead, glorification of self—all his claims in old days proved false—did he ever seize power, attract warrior followers in conquests?—Caesar thought him a fool—etc.—finally he goes on to say, an intuition came to him, prompted by the cynical remark of a wise recluse of ancient days—Leader: "If God did not exist, it would be advisable to invent one. Well, there was no question I existed and I am a God and the only Son of God, as you all know. (A pause—then led by their leaders in each section, roar of applause) I did not mean to invest myself, but there must be a hierarchy even among gods. So in a mystic trance I conceived my mother who is therefore my daughter too—the Goddess of the State. There is a dangerous subversive heresy growing among some of my subjects—the false doctrine that She gave birth to me. That must cease. I hereby order it to cease under pain of death. It is impossible to imagine that what I created should take precedence over me. Without me, she is powerless. Watch how I lash the old bitch." (He turns and strokes the statue—a dead silence) He asks the Magician: "Make them applaud." Magician speaks cunningly: "Our Master, the Savior of the World, was only demonstrating to you that even in Divine Families there are misunderstandings and women must be kept in their places." (A roar of laughing approval. He speaks to the Savior in a whisper) Magician: "A dead switch for public morals to wash the family linen in public. The public still cherishes its memorial Mammy songs." Savior: "But you made me—" Satan: "I suggest you make up and kiss her." Savior does so. (Rise of curtain)

Then Satan says: "And now I will direct these sounds. Luckily the false prophet procession approaches. Hear the well organized laughter. It gives me a chance." He speaks like a jeering barker: "Gentlemen and women, the pageant of the superstitious past approaches. In a moment. The false Son of God of legend will return among you in power and glory, to judge the living and the dead as He promised. You will take particular note of his power and glory with his army." He takes ringmaster's whip and cracks it—procession enters—baby tanks (life size) followed by a truck load of puppet apostles—pole in the middle of the truck, ropes from it to each man—ass (life size) on which with Christ on it, his feet dragging on ground (no saddle or stirrups)—roar of jeering laughter from stadium, chorused shouts of "Where is your kingdom."

Savior and Satan come down with mocking respect—notice blood on feet—Leader awed and amazed—real blood—Satan laughs it off: "You don't appreciate my imaginative arts. But suppose I did make him die. So much more spirit for you when crucifixion"—leads Christ up steps to royal box—(with whisper)—Satan: "No need for you to become possessed figure until it comes time for you to speak here—why go in for missionary insults and suffering—masochist—well, perhaps just as well, gives you an idea of what men are when they become merely slave citizens of the State, Our Holy Mother of Cannon Fodder and Conquest."

(Satan: "Moment—after this conquest, I'll have to foment rebellion for his soldiers—must be one in human sacrifice.")

In box, he makes Christ start at a sign—announces speech by Christ to convert you—jeering replies—to Christ: "I will give you a tip. Look how familiar their faces are—always rational fools—keep subjects awake"—Christ remains silent—so does the crowd staring at him—Savior uneasy, makes him say his foolish prattle—all eyes are turned on him—there is a growing respect in this silence—Christ remains silent—then Satan starts to speak for him: "Sermon on Mount" (?)—his tone is declamatory and singsong imitating the boring style of priests and ministers—then Christ takes up, simply and meaningly—the Savior fidgets jealously: "They are really listening of their own free will. They never listen to me unless—"—Satan soothes him. "But we want to put on a good show which interests the audience. Otherwise, they will pay little attention to the ironic joke of it. If he makes them care, they will feel their own degradation and hate him for reminding them of it." Christ finishes—a pause of silence—Leader: "Why don't they laugh? Make them laugh! Make me talk—explain the joke to them." He rises—stammers—points out the joke—organized laughter (incident Whose Weasel sings here?).

<u>The Last Conquest</u>   Nov. '42
Notes—Scenario

?—loaves and fishes—Christ gives each nothing, merely makes the motions—Savior's wonder: "Gives nothing and yet each departs as with a gift"—to Satan: "Can you see what he is giving them?" Satan: "Nothing tangible." Savior: "Oh, all right." Satan: "Just a tiny piece of faith, a bit of realization that they are not inwardly born to be monkeys. That will make them better subjects. We need a slightly higher breed of subjects so they live in your manifest Divinity and appreciate it at its true worth."

At last, as Satan directs Christ back to the ass and helps him mount—whispers in his ear: "You are a fool to take my taunt seriously and come back—to hope they will remember your words and see any meaning in them—you are a crazy freak to them—listen to their cruel and jeering laughter as you go out."

Tears amid spontaneous resentful laughter—tears not of pity—Satan: "I will meet you in the Temple. It was corrupt enough when you saw it last but you will be amazed at the modern realistic impressionist we have made in its symbolism and corruption"—Tank leads Christ out—Satan chidingly to Savior: "You had laughter—hope you are satisfied—etc."—Savior grumbles: "Maybe they hate him for leaving them"—Satan regards him queerly: "You have been too long under my spell. You have intuitions which pick my brain. (He makes a face) Go now and play a while, and forget him." The Savior romps like an adolescent—broad jump—Savior: "That is the farthest any man ever jumped. Only a god could do it"—cheer leaders lead crowd: "Hail, Divine Jumper!"—etc.

Curtain

Scene Three—Interior of the Temple—Goddess of State as Our Mother of Bureaucracy and Procreation—Satan enters holding Christ by the elbow—Savior with them—Satan's manner is that of a Minister who acts as guide to show an honored visitor the sights of the city—Savior restless, bored, suspicious that Christ is clever because he walks—wants him killed at once—Satan soothes him—all magician's trick, old stuff, like mechanized chess player, etc.—Satan carries ringmaster's whip.

He explains like a guide the changes since Christ last saw—Master's attributes in this aspect—mother of bureaucrats—her priesthood—fertility—she bears them by the dozen—temple prostitutes—Satan: "I confess I have fetched from former religions of the East—Fantastic cult—a touch of Moloch—Cybele—all priests castrated as befits bureaucrats who must be distinguished from men—prostitutes [are] symbols of the Mother in the aspect of Babylon, the Great Whore, etc.—so many changes in the Temple now—only the Elite are allowed to marry—slave traders instead—aspect of Our Mother as Goddess of Slavery."

Hymn—choir of pimps—the Whore's Weasel sung—Satan: "Dates back to one of the first dictators—not a God—like a Titan—a pimp and murderer who was murdered—on his birthday every year procession of Madams and whores[15] comes to lay flowers at his shrine and weep—an ennobling spectacle, which I suggested as a reminder of the innate practicality of human nature—that any profitable end justifies any means.

"Service to Our Mother of the Holy Face of Insatiable Famine—slaves thrust in a furnace in the belly of the Goddess—the old and useless to the State—would be killed anyway—so sold to priesthood as sacrifices—ceremonies of the State—Our Mother

The Last Conquest · 109

Who Drowns Her Own Children—a truth of Satan in that, but why shouldn't I steal from [my] own ideas."

Savior becomes wildly excited at sacrifice—snatches whip—runs amuck lashing everyone—denounces his Mother—Savior: "It is I. I created Her. Bow down to me!" etc.—finally he starts to beat Christ but Satan takes the whip away—Savior in fury: "Throw them both in flames"—but Satan chides him: "Look at me—you are behaving senselessly—you might damage my handiwork—wreck my plan—if you want to be autocratic"—etc.

Savior subsides sullenly: "Never mind. You are a good minister but not indispensable. You take too much upon yourself. I made you what you are and I can unmake you. I have already dreamed of a pretty revenge." (He laughs and Satan smiles) Satan: "I know. I put it in your head. It would indeed tickle your famous sense of humor—and mine." Savior (nervously): "You mean you would consent—" Satan (ironically): "I consent? You forget you are omnipotent and your will is the law. But do not interfere yet, or you will have to manage the conquest alone." Savior: "No, I am afraid of him."

Satan regards Christ tauntingly: "You must not fear him—if he comes alive. He was too meek and mild and forgiving." He puts whip in Christ's hand. "Here. Repeat your old legendary whipping act—if this time, you can grow angry. But I think you will understand that these poor vermin would not understand why you whipped them, since no knowledge of good and evil remains in them. (He smiles) No, you will not whip these slave changers who are themselves slaves. They have nothing but bodies to punish. They are poor dumb beasts, whom you will pity. Knowing you, I think you might repeat what you once cried." He starts jeeringly: "Father, forgive—" Christ speaks: "Father, forgive them for they know not what they do." (A pause) Satan: "Do you mean me, too, Brother?"—to Savior who is hiding behind him—Satan: "You see. No need to fear him. He would only forgive you."

Then Savior notices no move—again threats—slaves, bureaucrats—jealous of mother—Savior: "She is I—adore me—statue of me on altar"—etc. Satan calls him down—cautions him: "Do not get them too mixed up about the nature of your divinity or there will be domination—men will begin murdering each other in the streets over agruments whether you were first or she was first—whether you created her in order that she might begat you—Our friend here could tell you a lot about that," etc.—Savior again sullen: "You started it. You suggested I create her. You are her real Father. I will repay you for that, sometime—sometime soon."—Satan: "I merely followed precedent. A Mother Goddess is always necessary to stabilize a father. Even in democracies. What was Liberty but a female—a singular superstition, that. And now we will visit the concentration camp where disobedience and disbelief were segregated and discoverers eliminated." Savior: "Will not go. No use for them now—no fun—and I have my duties as host to prepare a last supper for you both." (He rushes away, laughing.) Satan smiles: "He is going to poison us both, the little fool. Come. Let us go. When you have seen the maps and imagined what took place, you will not be able to say 'Forgive them.'" He helps Christ walk. (Irritably) "I wish you would not pretend you are not present in this figure. I know better—you know it. It is not seeming for Evil to support a living Good. It makes me look weak. It makes me seem without pride," etc.

Curtain

Scene Four—Hall of the Last Supper—faces of dead—glasses slipping from hands—Statue of State in aspect of Our Mother of Passion (Thirst), like a frightful Goddess of Liberty, maddened by thirst, holding a poisoned chalice in her hand, toasting herself as Goddess of Death—gallows—galleries around hall filled with invited guests to witness spectacle—Apostles seated around the table, arms handcuffed behind backs—two, Judas and Peter, are played by dwarfs.

Satan comes in leading Christ, supporting him—(Christ appears progressively more like a living man but his movements are still like a mechanical figure)—Satan explains the room: [I] "let the Savior's imagination run riot—his view of this Feast of Life—improved upon his inheritance—the room redecorated—I suggested a few touches—old favorites of mine from the past—He lives history—parts of it which he interprets according to his own desire—this room inspired by many banquet halls in which people were poisoned—Caesars and the Borgias, etc.—Liberty to die."

Satan explains why the Apostles do not rise: "Legs [are] manacled to the chair legs—wrists [are] handcuffed behind them—cautionary with guests—Savior usually waits until the prospective guests are dying of hunger and thirst—feats—finally lets victims drink poisoned wine which he warns them is poisoned—[they] cannot resist." Satan washes his hands of blame: "Allowed free will in such tricks—why should I interfere when man is so base he is without help lower than I could have imagined— the victim, too—not even brave enough to throw the goblet into the Savior's face—afraid for families, although they know he will have them murdered anyway—I have no sympathy for them—no pride, no indomitable spirit of rebellion—they are your own, the damned cursed meek, who inherit nothing but a broken promise when they forget to hope in the long ago because it has never happened—our modern beatitudes: 'Blessed are the meek for they shall inherit death.' Dull."

He sets Christ down—sinks beside him—overcome with loathing and disgust: "You are alive. Do not pretend. You are doing that to mock me because I boasted I was not all of man. And I am. Surely you have seen enough today to prove it, etc. again pleads—it is over—tell your Father—I have won—but he is avenged because I take no joy in victory—spiritless man, I desired that as little as you did—uneasiness and disgust—wipe them from the face of the earth—let us retire to the Isles of Oblivion for a million years—(angry at Christ) You won't answer. I'll make you speak." Again starts a quote which Christ finishes—Satan: "Ah. But that wasn't what I meant"—then incident he saw that day—"Women lying on railroad tracks"—Christ looks now—"It is ordered to run over them or over self—but exceptions prove the rule—men that selfish—love possessions"—returns to his lament: "All base—wipe them out—set free."

"For example, your own Apostles here—they are loyal, of course—You Peter, you have not forgotten your instructions." Peter: "No, your Excellency, I shall deny him three times before cockcrow." Satan: "And your reward?" Peter: "I shall be allowed to live." Satan: "You are old—not serious of a reward, etc." Peter: "Oh, even a moment more at any cost. I am afraid to die."[16] Satan (to Christ): "You see? No, I shall get him a job in the Diplomatic service."—to Judas: "And you?" Judas: "Yes, Excellency, I know my orders—30 pieces of silver—I can buy my way into the Elite—30 pieces of silver justify any means. I shall have no guilty memories this time. I shall not be a damned fool and hang myself." Satan: "I had considered that the only decent thing you ever did. But no matter." Judas: "It was you who made me do that." Satan (confused): "I? Yes, now I remember. But, you see, as He will tell you, I have had to believe in the punishment of the damned. (To Christ with disgust) Tell your Father, as evidence you have seen, these experiments have failed—the earth which is the reason, leaving a smell of rotten souls—let him rush a new, quick Black Death—or a flood with no Noahs—let the earth be clear again with the innocent savagery of beasts—it is a beautiful planet where as a poet said: 'Only man is vile.' "

"Well, must dress for supper—I think you may expect the Savior—in hiding waiting for me to go—remember I have given him back free will for a while—his free will is an adolescent love of murderous intrigue—he may stab you in the back, or propose an alliance with you against me—or both." (He laughs and goes.)

Immediately the Savior appears—sneaks up behind Christ—conspiratorial whisper, bold and fearful of Satan's return: "You are alive. I am not drunk. His magician's trick has turned out a trick on the Magician. I think you are aliver than he, or as alive—rid me of him—I hate him—sometimes I believe he is my father—I suspect his bringing you back is to play a trick on me—I hate his smile—You never know why he smiles but you always know it is at you—Listen—I like you—you are meek—I can use you and some of your ancient sayings—'Blessed are the meek for they shall inherit the earth—tomorrow'—my subjects are meek under penalty of death—what a joke to convince them they are blessed now by God—that is, by me—for being meek, a reward which is never paid—I will appoint you High Priest of the State—in full charge of her worship—invent a new series of divine slogans for you if you like—an illegitimate son of the State Goddess—offer power over religious doctrine—within limits—a king, as [such] keep yourself out of worldly affairs—he always admires me and I always take his advice—get best of him for once, etc."—the figure of Christ remains silent and motionless. He flies into hysterical rage: "You defy me. We will soon see if you are alive, etc." (He stabs [Christ] in back—blood but no change in figure—he runs to Goddess, flings arms around her in turn.)

Savior: "Mommy. There is something—I am afraid." (Then immediate reaction) Savior: "As if you could help me, when I created you." (The arms begin to close on him with mechanical jabs. He cries out in turn.) Savior: "Help! Magician!"—the Magician, in full dress with ribbons, medals appears—presses button—Magician: "Just in time—that button you have is often pressed to crush opposition—you forgot it—by accident—that is the trouble with machinery—it has a life of its own, a lust to vengeance still upon the Tyrant inventor."—Savior pretends: "How much she hurt me. I alone am Health and the kiss of Death!"—then to figure—Savior: "I was afraid—blood but own contamination—I do not understand"—Magician says: "A very old theatrical trick—a bladder of blood—I knew you would stab—I wished you to get pleasure out of gesture of stabbing a wooden figure"—then in whisper to Christ: "Now I know you are alive."

(Statue sits at head of table, goblet in hand—instead of shrine.)

Spectators crowd in galleries (done by reversing motions)—every seat full.

Then the Last Supper begins—speech to crowd by Satan who acts as toastmaster—Magician: "A banquet in honor of our distinguished guest—probably his last on this earth." (Laughter)—he goes on in a diabolically facetious vein: "You will witness a contest between magicians—Our Master has taken lessons from me—as in everything he learns. Our Lord now surpasses his instructor (Applause)—so you will see the fake Savior repeat his ancient trick of turning water into wine and then wine into his own sacrificial blood—an easy matter of suggestion to those with the credulity they called faith—and then Our Master will cap him by really in fact turning wine into—But you will see what by the results." (Laughter)—he turns to Savior—would he proceed—silence—Magician: "A shy, quiet meek man." Satan explains to gallery, but I was never backward"—he demonstrates to galleries and the stage musicians—"Water. You see it is water because it looks like it and to us modern men realistic appearance is truth—it is water—Now first (He acts for Christ)—always water to wine—then wine to blood"—asks Judas and Peter to taste—"Blood all right"—then Savior takes up—"Miracle of the State—blood to water—but water of miraculous properties—Drink! I command all of you to drink!"—(Peter and Judas have been instructed only to pretend to drink)—Christ and others lift goblets—Satan, too—

A voice from the gallery: "Do not drink Jesus!" Savior orders him strangled, furious—they all drink—10 Apostles killed by poison—Peter and Judas pretend [to be dead]—Christ and Satan remain—Savior bewildered—clings to Satan whom he has just tried to murder—Satan: "Can the Prince of Poison be killed by poison? You are a fool! Or my wooden figure here?"—Savior: "The crowd is disappointed. What shall I say?" Satan: "Tell them you changed to wine for him, because you preserve him for further amusement"—Savior repeats—then Satan speaks ironically to crowd: "Well, it all goes to show, doesn't it? In the midst of life we are in death. The fake Savior here has a little story he used to tell about that, as I remember. Will you relate it again?" (He begins to speak for Christ a parable (?)—Christ takes it up—at end, silence as if audience impressed—no laughter)—Satan: "You must laugh. He meant it sincerely. Can't you see the joke in that, etc."—but still laugh only a little—Savior in fury: "Guards! Lash them until they laugh"—(cries of pain—laughter)—"Now lash them—all the way to their homes."

Savior suspicious of Satan: "You are bungling this Last Conquest spectacle—the audiences do not know their lines—neglect—a poor director—you are old."

Christ rises—walks out—Satan explains to terrified Savior:"[He is under] my control—he goes to meditate in the Garden—at my suggestion—as you do so often."

Scene Five—The Garden of Meditation in the grounds of the Emperor's palace—stage of outdoor Greek theatre—audience cannot be seen—have not arrived yet (as in Scene One)—not time for curtain—moonlight—Goddess of State shrine at left, modern version of Earth Mother, Our Mother of ———.* Christ has trees all turned into crosses.

---

*O'Neill leaves a blank here (written as above), presumably to be filled in later.

Figure of Christ in kneeling supplication—Satan enters with Savior—impatient with him—puts him at once to sleep—Satan: "Enough of your free will for one day"—starts to lay him in his Mother's arms—a touching spectacle when the lights go on—Satan: "But I see she has already someone in her arms—a very unholy Lady—this manifestation—Our Lady of Modern Nature—an insect which disposes of her lover, etc."

He puts Savior with back leaning against another tree—then dialogue with Satan answering for Christ when Christ remains silent—as in Scene One—Satan: "Let us have done with all pretense. You are here, alive as man again—this disguise which I created in your image—alive as man—in war with me, Your opposite—as in the beginning when Your Father, mine Ancient Enemy, My Father, too, created man—you were in Adam, too—in Eve—my first success—for force in man the first taste of knowledge—of the egotistic objective realism—the outward serving which has after conditioned his inward serving—until at last he said to himself in the pride of his ignorance: 'What my ears hear, etc. in their drunkenness, that is truth and the only truth—now I know everything. Even looking through a mechanical contrivance which brings the billion stars nearer to the human eyes, I say, in effect, these are man's. By seeing them, I possess them. By attempting to explain them, I explain them. The cosmos is only a projection of man's senses. All wisdom about the earth which I possess. There is no God. Therefore I am God. I was never created, therefore I created myself. So therefore I begin to feel sick unto death of myself, for all is explained without explaining anything. The surface is me. I cannot see to the bottom of death. Therefore I assume death is an old superstition, and I destroy the mystery of life which is of the soul, because there is no soul. And I am very sick, etc.'— (Satan laughs) The fools! It was I in them who brought them to their wisdom of knowledge. Am I not Lucifer, the bringer of light unto men."

(He laughs) "I saw what your Father had made more clearly than he did. He was too hopeful about his new creature. But You and I who were condemned to live in spirit in this creature, we know better. We knew He had created a thing which possessed a shallow spirit, a mind full of sinister ideas, an immense vanity—the clever greedy animal easily trained to perform tricks for food, but too stupid even to see a meaning in his life except the greed of his belly. I saw that. I knew I could always depict you. As I have. And now he is sick unto death—really this time—and You have come again for the final defeat, at my will!" (Proud Satan here)—exultant.

Then as in Scene One, depression—skip here—Satan: "You have seen—why go on—I am afraid You will feel it Your duty to become entirely flesh—suffer the old agony of sacrifice—this time entirely in vain—to the tune of realistic laughter—as if, in old days, You had been crucified in the arena at Rome, instead of a far-off unimportant province—no, go back—tell your Father to wipe them out—be a good loser, etc.—and give me my parole of a million years in the Isles of Oblivion, watching the warm crests, etc.—Or let me go through with the rest—easy to fool them with magician's art." Then pleads—Satan: "Let me take your place—I can stand crucifixion—easy—fake nails—red paint—anyway, what is pain to me an obvious affliction—or I'll agree to feel it as a man would."

<blockquote>
Notes made after writing 2nd draft
of Prologue
The Last Conquest   Dec. '42
Notes
(with new character)
</blockquote>

Introduce new character—Man, the Perfect Subject-Citizen of the State, The Tribune of the People. Hulking, low-browed, submissive, cowed, shoulders bound, eyes on ground—of huge gorilla-like strength but so completely enslaved [he] doesn't need manacles any more—cannot read, cannot write, corrupt and slavish obedience, dignity—etc.

Satan has chosen him as the perfect specimen of The People—a joke to be their representative, to give them sense they have a voice in the government but his is only a clinging silence, uninterested, his eyes vacant—without a hope or dream or thought—his great strength always exhausted—all he seems to desire is sleep which he does at every possible moment.

He, on order, is cheer leader of the people—he starts their cheers or laughter.

In prologue he sits on floor in corner—Court Fool?—and tests around to try all propaganda on, etc.

Satan asks: "Do you remember Christ?" Perfect Citizen: "No, what is Christ? Never heard of it." Satan: "He was, so He said, a Son of God, who became a Son of Man." Perfect Citizen: "Never heard about it, or I've forgotten maybe—like to forget. (Then cringingly afraid he has made a mistake) Oh, you mean our Savior of the World"—then abject terrified apologies to Satan and Leader—"Of course, I know—worked so hard today—so tired—but I know—you are the Divine Son of our Holy Mother, the Blessed Whore, You are her Father, too, etc. Listen, I pray every morning and night, as ordered"—He starts to recite prayer.

After Satan sets up figure: "Come take a look at his face. Do you remember?" Perfect Citizen: "No." Satan: "Shut your eyes and try to think." Perfect Citizen: "Yes, believe I did once see a picture of him—a book—old book my grandfather had hidden under mattress—I knew all books were forbidden—got afraid police would find—so went and told—they let me off with 50 lashes, me and my mother—hung grandfather—made me watch—funny to see him laughing—I laughed—the police patted me on back—gave me a glass of beer—cold beer—never forgot that—so kind, the police—(Suddenly) In picture in book this guy was nailed on a cross—or someone who looked like him. Are you going to crucify this fellow?" Satan: "Not at the moment but eventually we may have to." Perfect Citizen: "Hope so. I'd like to see that. I don't see many shows any more—remember saw a picture of you in book, too—or someone like you."

Satan: "You see, Divine One. There is a memory even in our Perfect Loyal One. That is dangerous. He might remember sometime something his grandfather said." Savior: "No, no. He was disobedient subject—about keeping that book. Desired death."

(Changes—The Perfect Citizen has a dim sure instinct that Satan is his real God and Slave-Master—in his moments when he forgets Savior, he turns to him, begs his forgiveness, etc.— Satan has to remind him of Savior and the State—there is the underlying jealousy of the Savior for Satan—which Satan turns off by saying: "You see, Master. That is the result of my duties as Minister of Spiritual Affairs—my mingling among men. They see the Symbol and mistake it for the real Power and Glory and Divinity, Yourself.")

"Love one another"—Perfect Subject laughs: "Excuse, thought Satan gave signal to laugh."

At end—Subject kneels and prays to Satan—Satan has to tell him to face Goddess.

Prologue—Scene One—Satan tells Savior: "To enjoy this spectacle the more, you may have free will—that is, of course, within certain limits—you must not quarrel with your mother and daughter in public—bad for morale—nor give way to bored sadism—but you can act freely otherwise—I know how you love to act—in the night scene I will arrange for a thousand spotlights, now there is much—."

Scene One—Satan explains to figure of Christ: "I wanted age of Savior stopped at seven—age of playing slaves and soldiers—aiming to try to guess at everything—boring and fantasizing pet—cruelty."

Scene Two—[Perfect Citizen] is put to sleep with Savior until drama begins—Later, he leads the laughter, when proposition is explained to him—(Mouthpiece for Propaganda or any other Ministry).

Scene Three—He is director of tasks—(as he passes he gives signal for laughter)—laughter at Christ after he gets cut—he keeps talking as if Christ were alive—obstinate about it until threatened—laughs at Son of God, pretenses: "Where's his army, police force."

Scene Four—He appears with Christ and Satan—cringing terror of slave declined—sold as sacrifice—put in fiery belly—Satan: "Not you, but you may be allowed to throw survivors in"—Perfect Citizen: (eager) "Yes, that'd be fun"—Savior bullies and torments him: "We might just stick his feet in. He might be more respectful." [Perfect Citizen] turns—grovels—Savior: "Kiss my shoes and I might not"—etc.

Scene Five—He doubles as Peter and Judas—impressed by Christ's miracles—water into wine—Savior: "Put him to work—wine for all"—Perfect Citizen starts to drink—remembers warning—whispers warning to Christ: "Frame-up—water poisoned."

Scene Six—In Garden—Perfect Citizen: "I'd offer to take your place, used to pain, but too scared of death—long for it but scared—scared of pain, too—I know what pain is—you don't."

Scene Seven—Christ [is] judged by the Perfect Citizen, Representative of the People—Pontius Pilate—when he asks: "What is truth?" Perfect Citizen: "I don't know (He is genuinely confused—then quickly) Yes, I know. Truth is what I hear on the radio—like every man in the world is constipated except [when] he takes (this or that cure) and each cure is only cure—so, I take 'em all." Then official announcement over radio—it has been discovered [that] Christ is a dangerous conspirator against the Savior and the State—Crowd: "Let him be crucified"—The Perfect Citizen: "Yes, let him be crucified—people's voice—I mean your voice (Savior) and your voice (Satan) and the Minister of Propaganda—but I want to wash my hands—I ain't responsible."

Scene Eight—Calvary—mount—dying groans of Christ—the people groan in sympathy—orders to lash—make laugh—the move [ordered] to leave—but insist on staying—Satan speaks for Christ: "I am dead but I am alive. Look in your hearts and you will find me alive. I die a million deaths then but still I live, etc."

Scene Nine—(toward end) Satan: "They are burning the palace—afraid he [Savior] is in it—one of best puppets I ever lived in—too bad—fate of perfection in this world."

At beginning, worn out, "Talking all night—every word he ever said—had to—couldn't stop—that was his joke on me—he used me—I said: 'Give unto Caesar,' etc.—and they began to give them to him—palace burning—utter defeat for me. Temporary—they are mad with goodness—giving to each other all each possesses—even I gave my pride to God—along with my resignation—but He would accept neither."

Final scene of Scene Nine—Satan alone—remarking sardonically on the failure of his Last Conquest—wonder at himself—what made him—disgust for men and himself as man—pity for men, etc.

Couple, ordinary simple men and women come to visit the spot. Satan says: "I will make myself invisible—listen—edifying to hear what these crucifiers think"—Couple:"It is good to be free—to have a soul again—to know there is good and evil in our hearts and we can choose." Satan: "But it was Satan who tempted you. He is strong and you are weak. So why blame yourselves when you have such a good excuse."—Couple: "No, the God in us is stronger if we choose. Christ is our refuge and our strength and evil cannot prevail." Satan:"Perhaps, but you will forget. The spirit is intangible, unseen while greed and power are realistic facts to anchor dreams upon." Couple: "We will not forget this time." Satan: "I seem to have heard that before."—Couple: "At least, we will try. We have destroyed the World State and its hideous religion and its evil fake Son of God who was the Antichrist, the partner of Satan."

Satan: "Devotionalism is easy. You were always apt at that." Couple: "We will build new temples of the real where we will worship the spirit of God in man." Satan: "You had better erect temples to Satan, too—just so you won't forget and be caught, as always, unprepared, by the evil in you—so you may come to know yourselves at last." Couple: "Oh, we do now. We have learned our demons. We will never forget God again." Satan: "Why, God bless you. I hope you do not believe; then my occupation is so easy it is boring. I just walk in and take possession." Couple: "No more pagan Gods of Death." Satan: "God, I am sick of making mechanical toys to frighten fools." Couple: "You, Sir?" (terrified) Satan: "Come, come, do not fear me. I am merely a poor human who is still a bit bewildered by the sudden change. I am a stranger from the moon just arrived by the latest plane—to know yourselves at last."

(Note) In Temple scene, there is smoldering resentment of bureaucratic priesthood against Savior of the World as origin of State's Daughter—she is Goddess Mother to them, who gave birth to Divine Son—that is, he comes second to her—no rift between Church and State—Satan warns Savior against doing anything (lashing Mother statue) to widen breech with historical commentaries—Savior [is] defiant—will have all the bureaucratic priesthood executed—Satan: "A good idea. I would like that myself. But you will find even in the Army and Police, there are fanatical worshippers of your mother, etc."

· 3 ·

BLIND ALLEY GUY

Introduction

Eugene O'Neill seems to have come full circle in his final creative years, using in one of his last unfinished plays, *Blind Alley Guy,* characters and ideas similar to those in his first "Play in One Act," *The Web,* written in the fall of 1913. When the author completed the second draft of *A Moon for the Misbegotten* in May 1943, he began a final set of notes for *Blind Alley Guy* in late May, concluding them with a short section, dated "June 1st '43," that is perhaps the last passage O'Neill ever wrote as playwright. His Work Diary entries had ceased a month before on May 4, 1943.

The central male figure in both the early and late plays is a gangster: the crudely drawn Steve, O'Neill's first criminal and pimp, in *The Web,* and the complex dualistic Walter White/Black, the name used in the final version, known to his underworld friends and foes as "Blackie," in *Blind Alley Guy.* Their two so-called molls are also similar: in the former play the twenty-two-year-old prostitute, Rose Thomas, who is sickly and destitute and looks thirty; in the latter drama, the twenty-four-year-old Dora Bond, a "Peroxide blonde," who is ill, haggard, and abandoned. She, like Rose, has lived in mortal fear of the brutal man with whom she has cast her lot. The two men beat these women at the slightest provocation; neither man wants to be tied down with the burdens of a child.

These are but the first and last of O'Neill's large gallery of outcasts. Criminal types and references abound in other works: *The Dreamy Kid, The Iceman Cometh, Hughie.* In his 1918–1920 notebook O'Neill includes an idea for a "Gunman Series." Twenty years later, in 1940, he conceives a series of monologue plays, "By

Way of Orbit," which, like *Hughie*, the only one completed, contain underworld figures. Narrator Erie Smith, in *Hughie*, which O'Neill outlines on November 20, 1940, just two weeks before making the first notes for *Blind Alley Guy*, is described as a Broadway "Wise Guy," a "small fry gambler," who lives "on the fringe of the rackets." The word "Guy" has for O'Neill connotations of underworld life as he uses it in the title of his gangster play. One interpretation of the words "Blind Alley" is given in *The Last Conquest* when Satan says: "The blind alley into which materialism [leads] (put into their nature by Lucifer)—naught is there but what you see." The words can also symbolize, as does the early play title, *The Web*, man's hopelessly trapped condition.

A question obviously arises: what prompted the author to focus consistently on characters and situations from the underside of life? Incidents in his own life may have contributed to his choice. Shortly before writing *The Web*, O'Neill had lived for almost a year (1911–1912) at Jimmy the Priest's, which housed an assortment of low-life figures. Later in another stay of approximately a year (1915–1916) in New York, he was befriended at a dive called the Hell Hole by a group of small-time gangsters, the Hudson Dusters. He had also heard stories about colorful New York characters from his brother Jamie, a Broadway dandy. O'Neill's own nature and inclinations contributed to his interest; like the criminal, he was always a rebel against society, trying often to defy its code of proper behavior and placing himself on the side of the poor and rejected. He would also, doubtless, agree with Bertolt Brecht, who equates the bank owner and the bank robber, holding that each is, in his own way of conducting business, a thief.

By a strange coincidence, Brecht is working in 1941 on *The Resistible Rise of Arthuro Ui*, which shows the similarities in the rise to power between a Chicago gangster and Hitler.[1] In July 1941, when O'Neill changes the concept of *Blind Alley Guy* and its characters, his central figure becomes a Hitler-like gangster. In his original plan and first notes, however, the drama is but another in the long line of autobiographical vehicles.

In the autobiographical *Long Day's Journey into Night*, O'Neill concentrates primarily on his parents: his mother's growing alienation and revenge through her return to drug dependency, his father's remorse for lost artistic, rather than commercial, theatrical success, and their highly charged quarrels with each other and with their two sons, Jamie and the author's self-portrait, Edmund. In *A Moon for the Misbegotten*, O'Neill's last completed full-length play, the focus is on his brother's "revelation of self." As a kind of cathartic purging of his own deep-seated problems, O'Neill apparently planned, initially, to use *Blind Alley Guy* as his own "revelation of self" and his complex relationship with his parents.

When O'Neill begins *Blind Alley Guy*, he labels this work the "Ricky H. Play Idea" and uses this heading for it until the very last set of notes dated "late May '43," although he injects possible titles throughout the manuscript. "Ricky" is a nickname for Richard, the name the author gives the seventeen-year-old self-portrait in *Ah, Wilderness!* who goes off to Yale in 1905, the same year O'Neill enrolled at Princeton.

Blind Alley Guy was started in December 1940,[2] exactly two months after the dramatist had completed *Long Day's Journey into Night*, which depicts incidents that occurred in the dramatist's life in 1912. The setting in the early outline for *Blind Alley Guy*, 1918, suggests the author wanted to take his own story beyond 1912 into 1918. The emphasis is on a family much like the O'Neills. The play's hero, who was born in a small town in upper New York, breaks away to go to New York City, "where he embarks on a life of crime." The author, after his recuperation period in 1913 following a bout, supposedly, with tuberculosis,[3] seemed to make a psychological break with his parents as he sets out on a new career and lifestyle and spends a lot of time away from them, writing plays in Provincetown and assisting in staging them in New York.

Tess and Ed White, the parents in *Blind Alley Guy*, resemble Mary and James Tyrone, the parents in *Long Day's Journey into Night*, whose prototypes are Ella and James O'Neill, the author's mother and father. Tess, like Mary, has big eyes, full, sensitive lips, a youthful figure and is "still an unusually good-looking woman for her age." Also, like Mary, she has a "strange, withdrawn, ingrowing quality—dreamy and detached." She has Mary's peculiar dual personality: Tess is "a contrast—by turns complete relaxation into a vague, day-dreaming quietude [resembling Mary's condition when on drugs] or alert and aggressive." In the play's early draft Ed is similar to James Tyrone in nature (he resembles him in physical appearance in later versions); he is a good, simple, uncomplicated man, has a "sense of what is right and wrong, religious in a mild way," but is "bewildered by any display of passion."

After a passionate romance with a roving ranchhand, Tess had married Ed, whom she views as a father figure (Mary Tyrone thinks of her husband this way) or "friend, never thought of him as lover." Tess has a childbearing history like Mary's: her first child is a disappointment (the author's older brother Jamie could be similarly described), the second child died, "then at last a son—and she stops having children." She "has never been able to mend her way of unequal love" and has "come to love her son more than her husband." Both James and Jamie Tyrone are convinced Mary loves her younger son more than them, another case of art imitating life.

O'Neill neglects to describe physically his self-portrait in *Blind Alley Guy*. His name is quickly changed from Ricky H.[4] in the first notes to Harvey White, whose alias is Howard Black or "Blackie" in the notes of January 20, 1941. As a child, he is given some of O'Neill's youthful characteristics: he is "quiet, reserved, solitary, obedient, and compliant on the surface. He hates the small town where he knows everyone." There is another side of his nature, which may or may not resemble O'Neill's: he has a "callous ruthlessness" that regards human life, even his own, as valueless; he is "devoid of any feeling" for his family and resents family love and ties.

The first set of 1940 notes is devoted entirely to the "character, upbringing, etc. of Ricky." In the January 20, 1941, notes, O'Neill lists the dramatis personae and then writes three different outlines for Act One. In the first Harvey and Dora return to his parents' home after a "gambling house stick-up." It is said to be the one place the "police will never look for him." The emphasis here is "the gradual effect on them and the family of their being there." The author then describes "another angle for play" in which Blackie does not appear; yet the play remains the story of his life and a revelation of his character as brought out "in their memories, jealousies, frustrations, conflicts, guilt, all due to their relationship with him." Actually, this statement sums up the basic premise of even the final draft of the play before the Hitler-like connection is made. In this early version "the play takes place in twelve hours before [Harvey's] execution." The second version of Act One tells the "story of play (with Blackie in it)," although he never appears. This is followed by a vague synopsis of the first three acts.

O'Neill changes the setting to July 1924 and moves one step nearer to his final concept of the play when in the July 1941 notes he states: "Tie-up all through interpretation of his character with that of Hitler—aversion and fascination at freedom of the utterly immoral . . . insights by women into emptiness, non-belonging, emotional sterility."[5] The parents are paragons of virtue, religious and morally upright. Their daughter, Cassie, can't marry the man she supposedly loves because of her abnormal fascination for her brother who "had got her to state where she consented to give herself" when he slapped her face, calling her a "dirty bitch." Her hatred for Dora is tinged with jealousy. In the Act Two that begins this draft, Dora tells Ed and Tess that their son is dead. Act Three contains a flashback, depicting, supposedly onstage, a scene between Dora and Blackie, with the latter describing a recent "gambling house stick-up," during which he neglected to wear a protective handkerchief and gloves. It is just a matter of time before he is captured. He wants to wait alone for the police and forces Dora to seek safety with his parents. For some reason O'Neill then changes the setting of the play from a farm outside Albany to a "home in California." Blackie is to be electrocuted now on the east coast in Sing Sing, rather than on the west coast in San Quentin.

The dramatist spent twelve days in July, between the 15th and 30th, on the "R. H. Play." He then set it aside in early August to work on "Time Grandfather Was Dead" but returned to it on August 21 and worked on the preliminary notes until August 30. After a few cursory notes, as he takes up the work in August, he devises a more elaborate dramatis personae, which includes Cassie's fiancé, Jack Tabor, who actually never appears in the play, and changes the setting to 1941 and the central character's name to Walter White, alias Harvey Black or "Blackie." O'Neill's play now is to "tie up with world situation." Walter believes "that he alone understands Hitler," and he tells Dora: "that guy and I could be pals." He hates Christ and Jews. Ed White, an ardent

Methodist and violent antiunionist, "thinks Hitler has some good ideas." While his wife, Tess, now the owner of a ranch having grazing land and orchards, thinks Hitler "ought to be hanged," she is extremely prejudiced, hating "Papists and kikes."

Walter leaves town and goes back years later, just after Dora returns from her honeymoon with an older man, whom she does not love. Walter reawakens her earlier attraction to him and persuades her to run away with him. Walter inspires a "strange conflict of emotions" in all three women in the play: his mother, sister, and Dora. Throughout the play O'Neill stresses one characteristic about the central figure: his "lack of feeling," his "emotional sterility." This emotional flaw can also be detected in the four Tyrones in *Long Day's Journey into Night* and seems, most certainly, a characteristic of the four O'Neills. If theirs is a love-hate relationship with each other, where are the words, the actions to indicate deep love? There are numerous examples bearing testimony to their acrimony and deep-seated hatred. Their tragedy was caused not merely by a failure of love but an inability to articulate whatever emotions they did experience. In spite of their reputation, as Irishmen, of being gregarious, they conducted their relationships as one would play a game of poker, displaying little or no emotions. The majority of O'Neill's characters in other plays react to each other in a similar manner, particularly those in *Blind Alley Guy*.

In late August 1941 O'Neill expresses for the first time some enthusiasm for the drama he is working on and states in the Work Diary on the 25th: "this can be unusual, thrilling play." In the heading above the latest version of Act One are the words: "Outline—New conception." There is little to distinguish this three-act draft, which occupied O'Neill from August 30 to September 19, from earlier ones, the exceptions being Dora's intense desire to read the day's newspaper in the White home, to conceal one section from the family (about Blackie's execution), and to hide her anxiety about the time, especially the time difference between California and New York.

In the final version of Act One, which the Work Diary establishes O'Neill started on September 22, 1941, the author writes what is to be the last dramatis personae, which includes only four names: Ed, Tess, Cassie, and Dora. He then establishes the specific time of the first, second, and fourth acts, indicating he will borrow a device he used successfully in *Long Day's Journey into Night:* to have these three acts begin just after the family had eaten a meal and was dispersing. The setting does differ, however, for only the exterior of the house is shown in these three acts rather than the interior. (The remaining act, the third, apparently is set in Cassie's bedroom.) The dining room is located at the right of the front door, and the voices of Ed and Tess are raised in an argument. Few clues are given about the cause of the argument until a section on a page near the conclusion of the notes for the play is read: "Recurrence of argument between Ed and Tess about Hitler—opening Acts I, II, & IV—follow same pattern. Each ends on a note of affinity to Walt."

The time of the play's action is also crucial to understanding the vague references. O'Neill has moved the time of the setting back to July 1934. The cause of the parents' running argument is not known until the very end of the 1941 notes when O'Neill states: "News in day's paper adds fuel to argument—best friend, Röhm, murder—new revelations, his refusal to commit suicide, etc." The exact date in O'Neill's July setting can easily be established: Röhm was shot at 6:00 p.m. on July 1, 1934; the specific "day" of the action of the play is either July 2 or 3.[6]

The play remains without a central focus until the Hitler connection is made and the specific reason for the tension between the parents revealed. They argue because they have different opinions about Hitler's role in Röhm's execution. Ed White calls Hitler a "lousy gangster murderer." His wife claims Hitler acted in self defense, that Röhm and his closest followers were planning to double-cross the Nazi leader.[7] The quarrel is rekindled again later in Act One when Tess reminds Ed he used to admire Hitler, that he "wished we had someone with his guts at the head of our government to smash the Communists like he smashed them." The fact that the men killed were not Communists but people who had started with Hitler irritates Ed. It had been a betrayal of loyalty and trust.

Rarely before in any play had O'Neill expressed political views of such importance and with such vehemence as in this unfinished play. His deep concern for the then current world conflict may provide a reason for his slow progress with this play. He states in a September 29 Work Diary entry: "I can't move it—same old stuff again—too many ideas in head—lose interest not in idea of play but in writing it—a why bother in this world feeling—too much war preoccupation." Even though he dates the very long new version of Act One "Sept. '41," the Work Diary reveals that he worked on this from September 22 to October 27. The several remaining pages of notes, apparently the last ones he wrote for 1941, are exceedingly fragmented.

O'Neill accurately predicts at the end of these 1941 notes how Hitler would die three and a half years later on April 30, 1945. The characters are discussing how the Allies will "get Hitler." Dora, believing that Walter is being electrocuted for murder because he was deliberately careless and wanted to get caught, makes the last remark of the play that links him with Hitler: "in the end he'll get sick of himself and commit suicide. They'll think they killed him but it'll only be because he killed himself."

Three new tentative titles head this set of notes: "Gag's End," "Rocket's End," and "Exit An Enemy Alien," each displaying a total lack of imagination. O'Neill jots down a few notes for the third and fourth acts and then returns to the first act again. In the very last paragraph of the 1941 notes, he makes startling and cynical changes in the White family, stating: "loss of all ethical and moral values by Ed, Tess, and Cassie—complete scepticism in which they take pride," "no faith in old religion," and "sex morality of no meaning, ancient bigotry." The reader is left to ask, after the autobiographical similarities of physical characteristics are recalled, if this, or any part of it, is an actual description of the inner natures of the O'Neill family. Despite their supposedly deep-rooted Irish Catholicism, none of them, except at times the father, went to church in their New London years. The father and his two sons were dedicated alcoholics. The sons were also frequent clients of New London and New York bordellos. The mother was so weak in character that she could not break a twenty-five-year morphine addiction.

On October 27, 1941, the author decides to put *Blind Alley Guy* "aside till its time comes," and records his first notation the next day for *A Moon for the Misbegotten*. He continues to work on this drama, written lovingly for his brother, for the next year and a half and completes the second draft of it on May 3, 1943. In "late May '43," the author makes what he calls a "3rd set notes" for his unfinished third play. For the first time in the notes he adds after the heading "R. H. play," the title "Blind Alley Guy." Strangely, he disregards this title totally throughout the manuscript. On January 21, 1941, in the Work Diary, he states: "some notes—tentative titles "Gag's End"—or "Blind Alley Guy." From that point on, in every entry made in the Work Diary when he refers to this play, the author calls it "Blind Alley Guy."

In the May notes O'Neill works out a plan for his most dramatic use of sound since *The Emperor Jones*. A cuckoo clock now serves, as the tom-tom did in the earlier 1920 drama, as a reminder, a device marking time until the offstage death of the play's central character. "Its silly sound punctuates the growing tension, becoming the voice of death." The notes are again fragmented with an assortment of ideas intended to be incorporated in the first and fourth acts. The notes here on Act Four provide about the only indication in this entire manuscript that the work could be, as O'Neill had stated in the Work Diary, an "unusual, thrilling play." As the clock strikes seven, the moment of Walter's death in the electric chair, the tension mounts within Dora and contrasts ironically and tragically with the calm of Tess and Ed White, who are totally unaware that their son is about to die.

The short paragraph the dramatist wrote on "June 1st '43" is apparently the last one that O'Neill ever wrote as playwright. The notes were designed, seemingly, for Act Two and contain a short exchange between Tess and Dora. The subject, like that of his first very short sketch, *A Wife for a Life*, is concerned with the man-woman relationship. It is not one of O'Neill's great philosophical moments, for it merely points out how foolish women can be "when love gets 'em." And so, to borrow from T. S. Eliot, the O'Neillian dramatic world does not end with a bang but with the slightest of whimpers.

It is impossible to assess the merits of a play merely on the basis of an author's early fragmentary notes, outlines, and partial scenario. Going over the same kind and amount of materials for *Long Day's Journey into Night* or *The Iceman Cometh* would elicit about the same tentative reaction from a reader as a perusal of these notes for *Blind Alley Guy*. O'Neill usually took a play through many more creative stages and drafts before pronouncing it "finished."

Blind Alley Guy has in its central focus perhaps the weakest developmental process of the three last unfinished plays. It cannot be said that O'Neill had played out his autobiographical hand with *Long Day's Journey into Night* and *The Iceman Cometh* and had found it impossible to continue in this vein in *Blind Alley Guy*. The dramatist interrupted work on the play to complete the highly autobiographical *A Moon for the Misbegotten*, laboring in a period of great illness and being able, at times, to produce only a page a day. O'Neill had to examine his priorities in his last creative years and to make a choice of what was most meaningful to him. He bypassed the three more complex political dramas, two with large casts of characters, and concentrated on a simple primarily two-character play that was a loving, poetic, and highly humorous eulogy for his brother Jamie.

Perhaps *Blind Alley Guy* could have been a successful play had O'Neill continued with it after he changed the autobiographical emphasis to make it a satirical political propaganda play. It is particularly significant that O'Neill here smashes the mother mystique, the play's early sentimentalized view of Tess White. In the last notes for the play she is totally amoral, selfish, aggressive—a snobbish bigot and supporter of Hitler and his Nazi regime. She is in this propaganda play the precursor of the "Divine Mother" of the World Savior in *The Last Conquest:* the "Mother Goddess of Destruction and Death." Her husband Ed would like to see Hitler's thugs in this country breaking up the unions. At the end of Act Two as the note of Hitler's affinity to Walt is made, the father brings in the gangster-mob similarity: "Ed's old admiration for Capone (and Walt's)—(and anyone's)—justification of his killings—kill or be killed."

By changing the autobiographical characterizations of the Whites and portraying them as godless materialists and racists who support the ruthless German dictator and mob violence for specific purposes, O'Neill delineates the prototypes of apathetic Americans who later make possible the totalitarian World State of *The Last Conquest*.

The Whites have, in Walter, spawned a monster, an insensitive brute who hates society and religion, scorns the concept of justice, and is so indifferent to human life that he kills an innocent drunk in a gambling house robbery for no reason. His great heroes, in addition to gangsters, are Lenin, Stalin, and Hitler. "His longing for death is sublimated into a desire for destruction." It is fairly obvious that O'Neill would have had little difficulty identifying Walter with Hitler in subsequent drafts. There is one point that O'Neill fails to clarify in his notes. He gives this character two names, Walter White, alias Harvey Black, "Blackie," to signify, it may be assumed, as he had done with the split John/Loving in *Days Without End*, that this central figure would be involved in an internal Good-Evil conflict. No such dichotomy emerges; Evil reigns supreme here.

On October 27, 1941, after a three-month intensive working period, O'Neill laments in a Work Diary entry: "it still won't come right." Perhaps the fact that his gangster hero was an offstage character, who could not be said to be truly dualistic in nature, limited O'Neill in his creative imagination. Perhaps the author was simply too ill and weary to make the effort needed to continue with this work. However, the theatre was the major beneficiary when O'Neill put aside *Blind Alley Guy* to write *A Moon for the Misbegotten* before it eluded his capacity forever.

Gag's End
R. H. Play Idea
(Notes and Outline)

(original conception)	Ricky H. Play Idea	Dec. 16th '40
Character, upbringing, etc. of Ricky	[Born, brought up in small town upper New York—education high school until middle of senior year—then breaks away to go to New York City—after involvement in scrape. His parents keep a small candy store—hard-working, decent, honest, ordinary people who just manage to	

make ends meet. He is an only child—(or one sister?)]*

Even as a small boy, he is [quiet, reserved, solitary, obedient and compliant on the surface because he is indifferent, but]* subject at times to fits of a strange, cold formidable fury which frightens everyone—contrasted with a total lack of emotional reaction to people, he has an extraordinary sympathetic, sentimental sensitiveness where animals and plants are concerned—a vague, dreamy awareness of nature—a thwarted yearning toward kinship with nature.

As a boy his periodical running away from home to ramble along through neighboring countryside—which cannot [be stopped] because no complaint against parents or him—impulsion he cannot control.

Later, as he gets older, he goes off for weeks—hops freights—gets to know hoboes—feeling of kinship with them as outcasts who can't belong to social structure—through them contact with non-moral attitude about property—theft, etc. but always solitary inside him—contempt behind his outward amiability—for their dirt and slovenliness of mind and body, for their fear of law.

From a small boy, he possesses the utter fearlessness and later on the callous ruthlessness of one to whom human life, particularly his own life, has no value—murder becomes meaningless because it seems to him to be of no importance whether he or anyone else dies.

He achieves a reputation in school because he deliberately seeks danger—as if he hoped it had something to give him—he even becomes hero in high school fire—one of those he rescues is girl, Dora, who falls in love with him, whom he seduces later on—although he gets terribly burned in legs and body, he bears the pain with a strange

---

*O'Neill crosses out with curved lines the entire first paragraph in brackets and the material in the second paragraph in brackets.

stoicism, as though he relished it as a chance of proving not so much his superiority as his differentness from others—at the same time a queer regret—wishes he could cry, scream, give way, express pain.

He becomes an enemy of society not from any sociological motive—he has the same scorn for radicals he feels for all politics or parties—he is entirely devoid of any feeling of ties to any sort of social organization, even his family—he feels himself an alien who cannot share feelings—he appreciates his father's, mother's, sister's love in a detached, impersonal way, but resents it, too, as a tie which seeks to keep him bound—he hates the small town where everyone knows everyone—he hates his father's store, the small sufficient lower middle class sufficiency which is neither poverty nor wealth.

The small yard of the house becomes a symbol—small, bad soil, hard to raise anything, fenced in—on wash days he detests it—once in a cold fury he had torn down all the wash and stamped on it—after his fit he had helped his mother rewash, hang out—refused to explain.

His father had given him woodshed lickings but finally gave up in defeat—because Ricky always accepted them without resentments or crying—as something fathers do to sons—but finally one day he coldly states, no more—too big—I can lick you now, if I want—and if I get started I might lose temper and kill you—I wouldn't want to kill you—got nothing against you—you're all right—so it comes to this, either you give up licking stuff or I'll pack up and leave home so I won't run the risk of killing you.[1]

Jan. 20 '41

Characters

Edgar White
Tess, his wife

Cassie, their daughter
Harvey White (alias Howard Black, "Blackie"), their son
Dora

Act One
(1918)

Home, small town-type lower middle class sitting-room—White, his wife and daughter—around ten at night—start to go to bed—sound of car—hunch it is Dora.

(Talk before this about son—never has written—but Dora has—regularly four times a year—it is now five years since he left home—letters from all over United States—the story she tells them is that Harvey's job is with a big construction company which builds the bridges all over the country—she makes it plausible (he was always fascinated by machinery) and they accept it with outward relief and satisfaction that he has settled down and is doing well—but inwardly they are afraid—she always promises they will come for visit next summer—but [it] never happens—outwardly they regret but inwardly they dread visit and are relieved—she never gives any address but General Delivery and has good pretexts for this.)

(White has, a year or two before, sold their home in town and bought a small farm a couple of miles outside—his hardware store has grown quite prosperous in a small way and [he] is semi-retired, going to the store a couple of days a week, leaving the business to be run mostly by Cassie and assistant who has been with him since a boy and whom he has taken into partnership since [he is] engaged to Cassie.)

(Cassie keeps putting off a definite date for marriage on various excuses—she didn't know why herself—it is really because she still feels tied to brother, whom [she] has loved and still loves and later because he stands between her and love for parents; she feels she could feel—in her character is a strong streak of Harvey's strange lack of feeling which she took over from him in order to defend herself against his indifference.)

White is a good, simple, hard-working man, uncomplicated, sense of what is right and wrong, religious in a taken-for-granted mild way, an affectionate family man—a typical good bourgeois in every way a moderate, kindly good citizen, doing his duty with satisfaction in a good world, bewildered by any display of passion.

Tess, his wife, is his perfect, congenial mate on the surface—loves him—but deep underneath this is a disappointment in him—she had dreamed of him as romantic, passionate lover—the reality had been too mild, too much—she had come to love her son more than her husband—her daughter, too.

He and Dora beat it [home] after gambling house stick-up—the one place police will never look for him—he is convinced about this—so is she until she gets there. The gradual effect on them and on the family of their being there—the family soon sees something [is] wrong with the marriage—they begin to take sides.

He [Blackie] is lame from jump from window through skylight—family told it is rheumatism.

It is Dora who tells all the lies—all he does is acquiesce indifferently when she asks him to collaborate.

All the past begins to him again—his strange callous lack of feeling from a boy—his complete immorality.

Mother and sister taunt and sympathize with Dora—she couldn't make him feel either, even though she could possess him physically—they resent and hate with her his rejection.

He mourns over the memory of a cat he had which has died—he becomes absorbed in affectionate care of pigeons, descendants of ones he owned—so proud of his ability to tame them quickly—no fear of him.

Their hatred of him for this—derisive laughter—until it brings on one of his quiet murderous rages—then abject turn of him.

Mother and daughter tell Dora they guess now all about his job, etc.—might as well tell the truth—Dora (vindictively): "I'd like to. Shall I tell them, Blackie?" Blackie: "Sure. Go ahead. Why not?" Dora: "He says that but he'd kill me if I did—like he'd squash a fly"—but he says sincerely: "No, tell them—I've never been afraid of the truth—always admitted it, about myself and everyone else—about life—I'm the only one I ever knew who had the guts—so go ahead—you tell your side, I'll explain my end of it—maybe that'll get us somewhere, although I don't believe it can."

She tells the story of their life together.

Another angle for the play—Blackie never appears although he is chief character—only his father, mother, sister, and Dora—yet play is the story of his life, revelation of his character, as brought out in their memories, jealousies, resentment, frustrations, conflicts, guilt, all due to their relationship with him.

Play takes place in twelve hours before execution—begins at nightfall—blinds down—groups of the morbid curious outside on the street—cop—newspaper reporters, etc.

Furniture all piled up, ready to move to storage—home sold, business sold—ashamed to stay in the town—going West somewhere—vague—the trains, buses, here and there until [they are] no longer news—in spite of grief and despair, there is a gleam of compensation in this for mother and daughter—mother from farming people—wants a garden, vegetables and flowers—at last a drying yard!—her hatred for yard on Monday, no room for anything but clothes—subsistence farm not for profit—she remembers slaving and insecurity of farm as business—daughter glad of excuse to get away from fiancé—she has broken engagement for his sake, but he refuses—she dreads marriage—her ideal [is] a filling station at the crossroad—father sad about his store, his dutiful, respectable, God-fearing good citizen stability and routine—saying in town you could set clock by him—but underneath, to his own fascinated horror, is a relief and an irresponsible resolve never to work hard again—let women work.

As the action progresses it is Blackie's attitude of ruthless lawless realism that takes possession of them[2]—his lack of feeling, too, for other lives or his own.

Father at one point: "Do you want to take my God from me?" when they sneer bitterly at prayer.

The deep affection, sympathy, understanding, compassion between them at the start—the closeness of the family.

Their horror (and bitter resentment) at interview with Blackie after the condemnation—resisting, pleasant—no feeling or fear about anything—indifference about [his] death in the [electric] chair—his terrible attempt to console them, point out the silliness of their grieving or remembering—his only interest [is] in plans for moving to the country—their reaction, would have been better if he'd blame them—even cursed them.

Their antagonism toward Dora and at the same time sympathy—justice—she's not to blame—it is he who is to blame for what she is (only one thing they'd hate her for—if she was the one who turned him in).

She returns after Governor has refused a reprieve—after seeing Blackie for the last time—he has told her he knows who made the mysterious phone call to the cops revealing his hiding place with her—of course, she has known all along he knew—she has claimed some stool or some tart must have tailed him.

Bitter antagonism against Blackie's lack of feeling extends even to his lack of fear of death—to a hope he will be terrified at the last moment—they know he won't—will remain indifferent—so they hope there is a hell.

Warden's talk with Dora—never encountered anyone as fearless as Blackie—their pride—and their hatred and scorn—not afraid because he can't feel—isn't courage—no credit—as if he'd been born without a heart—or castrated.

R. H. Play   Jan. '41
Story of play [with Blackie in it]*
Act One

Family at the farm—memories of son and Dora—interrelations brought out by attitudes toward him, her—secret resentments, etc. Cassie's fear of marriage, longing to get away from town, etc. Father about business—etc.

Arrival of Dora in car—her pretended surprise at not being expected, lie about letter with postscript written by Harvey—will he come? She says if he can get away.

She [Dora] is glib but very tense and nervous—only Cassie is suspicious. Cassie's attitude toward her, sympathetically drawn to her because of antagonism for brother, but at the same time, jealous, hostile because of love for brother—glad she's lost her looks—and Cassie guesses the truth of the seduction before marriage for which she blames her (scheme to get him)—

---

*O'Neill crosses out these four words in brackets.

blames him because she knows from experience his unscrupulousness (has felt he would have seduced her—sister-brother taboo meant nothing to him).

Dora [is] glib about the story of the marriage, trial [is] so exciting at first—but when the novelty wears off, no home, she unconsciously emphasizes the strain of the uncertainty, never knowing from week to week what's to happen to you—she tries to keep a secret—slips into argot in talking—laughs nervously about it—learns from Harvey—construction gang talk—tough men.

Dora asks with too casual casualness about the morning paper—delivered?—when?—explains Harvey bought a couple of shares of stock.

Finally, she pleads [being] tired—bed—they are sympathetic—father says [it is] late, time they all went—women go up—he goes around locking up—Cassie reappears. Father's unsuspicious but worried wonderings—Cassie starts to sneer but stops at once and reassures him—he's worried about Dora's eagerness about the morning paper—stock gambling—he starts for bed.

Mother comes down—Dora seemed so anxious to get her out of the room—and yet kissed her, hugged her, is affectionate—so tired and sick, poor girl—then she shows suspicion—but she fears the marriage [is] in trouble—Cassie again repeats reaction of Father—sneer—starts but then reassures.

Act Two   Jan. '41

The following morning—breakfast—Dora can't eat—Mother comments on hearing her restless all night—smoking—guilty rebuke—Dora apologizes—first night in country—not used to quiet—Dora (strangely): "But I'll sleep sound tomorrow night, I hope"—Mother: "Why not tonight?"—Dora: "Takes two nights to get used to."

Paper arrives—Dora knows: "I'll get it"—insistent—they notice—Father remarks about the gambling, the wait: "What's keeping her?"—Dora comes in—all start, expression on [her] face—she tries to laugh off—stock gone down two points—never intended for gambling—not like Blackie—slip of tongue which she hastily covers up—Dora: "Forgot you don't know him—friend of Harvey's, a gambler—never shows feelings—[I] don't believe he ever had any."

Cassie notices—and Dora sees she does.

White remarks: "Well, Harvey always was a great one for hiding his feelings, too"—he soon goes out—to see [if] pigeons' place is clean, etc.—descendants of Harvey's pets—Mother: "[They] multiplied—ate a bit—but don't tell Harvey that—does he still have those quiet fits of rage?"—Dora: "I don't know—I mean I haven't noticed lately"—Mother: "Bad. I was always afraid he'd do something he'd be sorry for"—Dora: "Oh, I don't think he could ever do that"—Cassie says: "She means he's sorry for anything he ever did"—unconsciously they agree with secret resentment—then quickly pass off and deny.

Father goes—mother gives paper to Dora—says she's only interested in local gossip and she can read that anytime—she goes to wash the dishes.

Scene between Dora and Cassie—Cassie's cross examination—Dora frightened and resentful—lets [her] hardness and slang come out—Cassie [is] more and more suspicious—Dora appeals to sympathy—Dora: "I'm sick Cassie, etc.—why [are you] so hostile—we used to be good friends"—Cassie sympathetic: "Yes, we were. If you still feel that way, why can't you tell me the truth—[I] know you haven't—if you've had trouble with Harvey, we'd understand it wasn't your fault—we know he's not easy to live with—not like anyone else—something inhuman"—Dora jumps at this: "Yes, it's true we did have a quarrel—he flew into one of his rages over nothing. You remember."

Mother comes in—scene her and Dora with Cassie mostly a listener—memories—starting as fond and then betraying bitterness and lack of love.

Father comes in—ditto with him.*

Cassie reads the paper—comes on a notice of refusal to reprieve for a murderer "Blackie"—to go to the chair the following morning—[reads] when she is alone.

Synopsis: Play begins the morning before the morning of Blackie's execution—on a small farm outside a village of 3000 or so inhabitants.

---

*Beside this passage in the margin, O'Neill writes the following notation: General notes—Dora has dyed [her hair] blond as disguise—never did before—because that was like a moll.

Act One

Family scene before going to the store—get mail on the way—hope for a letter from Harvey—wish he'd write instead of Dora—resentment against her—thus far—[he] never has except through her—Cassie envious of the traveling life—Father's only moves [are] two miles—[you would] think he'd been going to the North Pole—resentment—dreams—maybe something [will] come up—Mother says: "After you marry Albert"—Cassie contemptuous—"[he is] like Father—[that is] why he likes him—then [tries to be] fair—Albert [is] all right"—Mother: "Then why keep postponing the marriage?"—Cassie wavers—Mother makes a remark: "Something of Harvey in you"—Cassie: "No, I feel, he never felt anything—he'd wander off as if [he] couldn't help it, like a tomcat"—both women show resentment of Father's sentimentality, no real feeling—preoccupation with store, duty, church (they wonder if he really knows what he believes)—being a good man, etc.—but at once contrite and affectionately humorous about Father—case Harvey's game chickens, etc.—scene with White in—reveals his character—good, kindly, sentimental and yet hard as iron about what he regards as the right way of Christian living.

As [they are] getting ready to leave for the store, Dora arrives, having driven all night.

Scene with all—then White and Cassie leave—Dora and Mother—Dora to take a nap—her talk of the paper plants curiosity—Dora: "[Do you] still take any village paper?"

Act Two

After dinner (middle of day)—Cassie finds the Albany paper in Dora's car—Mother's fear, marriage on the rocks—her hope Harvey will come after Dora—Cassie objects: "This marriage [is] not important enough to be in the newspapers."

Act Three

Supper—discussion to sell the place—move west—plans, dreams—Father: "You better come with us, Dora—one of the family"—until she confesses she was the girl who turned in Blackie—Father—this sadly: "Not that we don't understand—but I guess maybe you'd better not come."

At the last—Dora: "I—I—I'll bet the poor sap loved him right to the end"—Mother says: "His mother and father, too"—Cassie: "And his sister—if he had one."

<u>R. H. Play</u> July '41
Notes—(new conception without Blackie)

He [Blackie] does not appear in play—but he is dominant character in it as his whole life is recorded through his effect on each of the four members of his family, his father, mother, sister and wife.

The end is the moment of his execution in San Quentin (difference in time, 4 hours (and daylight saving)—(business of cracking waves—check on the exact time to the moment via radio, etc.).

Tie-up all through the interpretation of his character with that of Hitler—aversion and fascination at freedom of the utterly immoral (and assertive and prudish), the unscrupulous and ruthless who dominate at any cost—at the same time, insights by women into the emptiness, non-belonging, emotional sterility behind this—resentment, bitterness, contempt and pity—recognition he makes a weapon of the inability to feel while at the same time his greatest secret longing is to feel—boring, sad appreciation of his loneliness and isolation from his kind—revenge on them as if they had rejected him—etc.

He is the reason for the move to the farm (through mother, principally)—reason why she keeps pigeons, pets of all kinds—her memory of his reaction as a baby and in town.

[He is the] reason his sister can't marry the man she loves—can't trust or believe—Ricky had got her to a state where [she] consented to give herself—then he had slapped her face—Ricky: "Dirty bitch!"—then [he] apologized—but not really sorry, simply puzzled, wondering why he did it—doesn't want her—who would want his sister?—Cassie: "Guess he thought it would give him a kick because forbidden, awful sin—but it doesn't—seems silly, meaningless"—sister confesses this to Dora—whom she hates and yet feels a deep identity and understanding with.[3]

Before Dora appears—discussion about Ricky and Dora—yesterday Ricky's birthday—always hard day for them—hope for surprise—his return but dread, too—afterward relief and disappointment—Dora's letters over the years—Father and Mother make themselves believe but have secret doubts—sister doubts but pretends to believe for their sakes—but this time she comes out with scepticism—her tension, keeps putting off the date for wedding, at the end of excuses, and then fiancé is growing tired of waiting, etc.

Father—bitter resentment against Ricky because no one to help or succeed him running store—in family in the same town four generations—he is obsessed with family pride, tradition, continuance—his respect for this, duty to society, to God, humble acceptance—but behind this he envies son his unscrupulous denial and self-assertions—as a youth, he had wanted to break away—Spanish War(?)—father had to approve patriotism—only 16.

Father and sister's secret resentment against mother because of her greater love for Ricky.

Mother [is a] fine simple honest character—religious—but her honesty a defect—insists always on openly facing secret facts—none of us perfect, all weak and sinful—confess openly so no misunderstanding—try to mend one's ways—face the truth about self—ask forgiveness—trouble is she never [has] been able to mend her way of unequal love for Ricky—and her honesty had been carried to extreme by Ricky—face what you are and be it regardless—no sin, what is, is right, because it's truth, etc.

[Father's business—dry goods store (?)—cord and lumber (?)]*

R. H. Play   July '41
Notes

Act One—Sitting room, the White house (or porch)—moonlight—around 10 P.M. (bedtime)—July 1924

Act Two—Later that night (around 1 A.M.)—the same

Act Three—The same (around 6 A.M.)

Act Four—The same

---

*O'Neill crosses out this line in brackets.

Execution time at San Quentin (?)—ll P.M.?—if 11 then 3 A.M. Eastern time (and daylight saving)*

Act Two

Mother and Dora (and Cassie?)—Mother always getting psychic hunches—usually wrong—but proud of her quality—Mother: "Harvey† is dead, isn't he?"—Dora: "Yes"—Mother: "What did he die of?" Dora: "Pneumonia—construction jobs"—Mother then excuses [her] lack of feeling, after trying to cry dutifully—after a while—Mother: "Have to buy mourning"—reproves Dora for no mourning—younger generation—Dora says: "Didn't want you to know." Cassie: "Why?" Dora: "[It would be a] shock if I came in all in black—besides Blackie wouldn't want me to—cared nothing about death—I mean, he didn't care"—Cassie who was convinced for a moment—penitent and sympathetic—becomes suspicious again—Cassie: "Blackie?"—Dora: "His nickname in the construction racket."

End of act Dora and Cassie—Cassie: "[I] don't believe he's dead. What are you waiting for?"—Dora [is] hard—Cassie: "Like a crook's moll in movies."

Act Three

Mother breaks the news to the Father—rebukes him for lack of feeling—this leads back to old quarrel as to who is to blame for Harvey's character—"You never should have married me when you still loved another man"—(or woman), whichever—talk as if Harvey were still alive—then realization deep sadness—Mother really breaks down, sobs: "My baby"—he consoles—suddenly she stops and bursts out: "He'd think I was a fool. He'd say: 'For God's sake, Ma cut out the sob act. What's there to cry about?' And he'd mean it. He just wouldn't understand"—Father agrees.

"Always wanted to be dead" (Father says?—or Mother—or Cassie?—or Dora?—all have gotten this from Harvey?).

Then scene Father, Mother, and Dora (Cassie's room [is]

---

*Below this passage O'Neill drew a rough draft of the setting, the White home.

†For some reason O'Neill cannot decide on a definite name for this character.

lighted—Mother tells Dora—found her in kitchen looking for the paper—can't sleep—most of the paper used but she took what was left).

Scene Father and Dora.

Last scene Dora and Cassie—the truth comes out.

Dora (at one point—with deep pity): "Poor Harvey. He never could belong to anything—or anyone—not even himself. He never had a chance."

Dora—her story (at last)—he made her be unfaithful: "Maybe he thought that might make him love—maybe I thought so, too—always between us a sort of secret understanding, a conspiracy—and I hoped it would free me from him, too—perhaps he hoped so, too—he was fond of me—but nothing came of it—I remember us both sitting in a room—nothing to say—finally I screamed: 'Why don't you beat me up? Why don't you kill me?' He said: 'What for?'"

Cassie: "Yes, that's what he'd always say about everything: 'What for?'"—Dora: "I said: 'I left you flat and ran off with Red, didn't I?' He smiled that crooked bitter grin of his: 'I don't blame you. I've always wanted to run away from myself.' I said: 'I slept with him, didn't I?' He said: 'Well, why not? What of it?' I said: 'You dirty son of a bitch.' He said: 'Don't put on an act. What's the use of talking when nothing happened.' 'Nothing happened? I've just told you—' He got sore: 'Don't stall. You know what I mean. Here we are the same as ever. Nothing has changed, has it? It didn't work.'"

Very last—Mother: "I'm psychic—I know he's in heaven—I know he can feel now." Cassie: "Yes, that would be heaven for him"—Mother and Father go in—Cassie and Dora left—Dora's last outburst: "I loved the son of a bitch. I still love him."

Dora's story of the final days: "He was sick of the game. No kick in danger anymore. He'd pulled every stunt there was to pull. He'd taken every chance and gotten away with it. Sometimes I used to feel that he hoped on the next job he wouldn't get away with it. He got this hunch about a small place, raising fancy pigeons—retire from the business—he'd never been picked up, never been mugged or printed—but no money—always threw money away—gambling, horses—so a few more jobs.

"Feverish activity—you know how he was when he wanted something"—Cassie: "You mean when he wanted to want something"—"Yes, that was it. At first, he had me kidded because I wanted—said I could have a kid—but I soon saw something desperate—trying a last bit—we went looking—He said he had exact picture in mind"—Dora describes—Cassie: "But that's this place." Yes, I got that right away. He wanted home. Or he thought that was the last chance—to try to go back."

"Finally in Vermont (or Berkshires)[4]—Blackie: 'This isn't it but maybe it'll do. Careful buildup of a new life—say [it's] a summer place at first—then decide to stay all year because [we] like so much—tell the truth, [we're] from California—[I'm a] mechanic—left money by uncle who'd gone to Mexico—the trip to celebrate—put up a barn as a mechanics shop—try to invent something.' First it [went] across big—[he] got a friendly garage man—helped fix cars for nothing—you know what a shark Harvey was—and made everyone like him—you know how he could do that when he tried."

Cassie: "Yes."

Dora: "But underneath desperate—saw he'd failed before he started—didn't mean anything—except the pigeons—but I kept hoping—[I] got pregnant—told him—he was glad for me—but didn't touch him—I hoped after it was born—

"Then gambling house stick-up—forgot a handkerchief—forgot gloves—pulled a fool trick—killed a drunk—but [he] got clean away—but now he was on a spot—a crowd of witnesses.

"His conscience [bothered him] about killing the drunk—but only for a couple of days.

"[I] got rid of the kid—[I] told him—he was fooling with the pigeons—all he said was: 'Yes, I knew that was what you went for—a wise stunt.' " Cassie: "A wonder he didn't say: 'What of it.' Dora: "That's what he thought—I went crazy—killed a pigeon—for a second he was going to kill me—then we just stood looking at each other—then I said: 'God, you were only faking about that, too. You don't even give a damn about the pigeons any more.' I thought he was going to cry—mouth drew down—like a kid—God, it broke my heart—I put my arms around him—I kissed him—I said: 'God, I'm sorry. Forgive me, Blackie.' He said: 'Forgive what? You're right. Hell. It's only a god damned kid. What of it? I used to like them once, but I guess that was dumb of me.'"

She gets brooding over this—can't forgive—last straw—she'd been fond of the pigeon, too—guilt—connects with killing the child—revenge—feels she will some day murder Blackie—finally goes out and phones the New York police—afterwards remorse—tells Blackie—escape—but he understands. Blackie: "Thought maybe you'd do that—don't blame—no bargain for you, married to me"—but he shows no feeling—justice—refuses escape—lethargy—too tired—Blackie: "[I'll] shoot it out." (Dora offers to stay with him—die together)—Blackie [is] irritated at her: "Don't be dumb—where's the percentage in that for you? Hell, you like life. Don't put on an act. That's what I've done but I had to—because nothing else—all a gag to me—and I'm not going to shoot it out—what's the use?—too tired—(with return of old defiance)—[I'll] go to the Chair—show them they can't faze me with that little act—make me care a damn about life—or fear death (then ugly)—the papers will say I kept an iron nerve to the end. Iron nerve, nuts! The saps! There's no nerve to it when you don't give a damn."

Dora: "So you won't even let me die with you?"—Blackie: "No, beat it—license plates—go home—forget it—and don't try to see me in jail—won't see you—this is the end—goodbye now"—furious, she tries to goad him: "I won't! I'll forget—marry—have kids—everything I never got from you."

Blackie: "Now you're talking sense. That's the dope. Easy for you. You're still a good-looking doll. You've got 'it' "—suddenly he wants her—on floor—she fights—he says: "Don't put on an act. You like it. Come on. Last time. I won't be getting any of this again, you know"—Dora: "So I gave up. I let him. I even liked it. Then afterwards he said: 'Thanks now beat it quickly. Goodbye'—I was crying so I couldn't hardly see—I said: 'You son of a bitch! I still love you!' He said: 'It's no time to start gabbing about love. Get the hell out of here, Baby. Keep moving around. Keep changing plates—cars—don't go home right away.' [He] grabbed my arm—hustled me to the garage—started the car—pushed me behind the wheel—kissed me—like you'd kiss the statue of Washington in the square—said: 'Good luck, Baby. Play your cards right and you'll be set for life. And for Christ sake, don't waste time thinking of me. I'll soon be dead and glad of it. Stop crying. What's there to cry about? etc.'—I drove and drove—headed south—crying so hard I couldn't see."

At the end—for a moment she and Cassie [are] proudly defiant—best hope for fear—Dora: "They can't make him afraid—he'll show 'em! etc."—they both grip chairs as the clock strikes—(similarity to an electric chair position)—the believer's baptismal—no nerves—just doesn't care—joke on them—but he wanted them to explain how it works—interested in electrical gadgets—Dora pictures the scene—knows because [she was] always afraid he'd come to it—as clock strikes, pack of hysterical derisions—then stiffen and slump.

Mother comes out—(Father later)—Mother: "What is it?"—Cassie: "We're hot—terrible heat"—Mother says: "Just had the strangest feeling on brother—Harvey there—almost see him—changed—kissed me—really kissed." Cassie: "Guess you are really psychic, Ma"—Dora: "I wish I could believe that. I still love him, you know. The poor kid. The poor lonely lost kid."

R. H. Play   July '41
(notes)
(reverse home to California)

Time—He is electrocuted at Sing Sing at 11 P.M.—7P.M. California time—

Dora arrives after breakfast—around 7:30 A.M. after driving all night—eager to get home, she says—lovely moonlight night—etc.

Scene—Valley in Northern California—blazing hot day in late August—*

R. H. Play   July '41
Notes

Suggestions for title: "Put On An Act"—"No Sentimental Sob Stuff"—"What Of It?"—"A Realistic Attitude"

---

*At this point in the notes O'Neill drew a detailed sketch of the White home in the California setting.

Dora: "He liked music—only blues—makes orchestra play—[he] listened and looked sad—but puzzled—as if he couldn't make out what he was sad about—as if that was what made him sad."

Mother [possesses] strange, withdrawn, ingrowing quality—dreamy and detached—sentimental about Nature appreciation—lover of sunsets, etc.—sense of superiority in this over husband and daughter—insists on pointing out—"You don't see"—abrupt transition from this side of her nature to other practical side—fine housekeeper and proud of it—husband always follows advice on business matters—fine cook, obsessed with food—but eats little herself—slender, has kept figure—fine rider—jealous sense of own property, won't have servant except to help her, because can't endure their imperfections—hard to get servant because she expects so much—religious by nature but has gotten away from narrow Methodist creed in which she was brought up into a vague God-Is-The-Spirit-Behind-Everything—believes she is psychic—and she is in a certain way of sensing happenings—but always wrong on nature of happenings—usually opposite to her guess—if she feels there is to be abrupt change in weather to cold, there *is* abrupt change, but to a heat wave.

The ranch [is] near a village (small, about 100 acres of orchards and fields on hills) is her property—remnant of big ranch her father inherited—he was a failure at ranching, careless, had to sell lot of land.

But she and her husband are descendants of gold rush pioneers—her ancestors from South, Georgia, his from Ohio—husband is ten years older than she is—his family and hers were intimate—she married him after her great romance—she had fallen passionately in love with roving ranch hand—no good, drinker, no ambition except to wander and live, etc.—full of charm, singer, writer of verses, etc.—her practical side told her no future in it, couldn't change or hold him, impossible as a husband—and wouldn't let him seduce because of her Methodist attitude—now regrets—justifies—surprised when husband proposes—friend, never thought of him as lover—accepts on rebound after lover left—imagines it's no good in bed with her—only way to permit, react—not unfair because he never knew and good for his happiness—but all love turns to child—

first is daughter, a disappointment—next child dies—then at last, a son—and she stops having children, her purpose accomplished.

Husband—big, ruddy muscular man—proud of butcher shop, of doing own slaughtering, of quality of meat—folks even come from city to buy it for special dinners—tradition of business—butchers in Ohio.

<u>R. H. Play</u>   Aug. '41
<u>Notes</u>

Tie-up with world situation, this year or last—in strange way—character of Walter, the son—resemblance in frustration (unconscious), inability to feel, which is the driving motive behind criminal, anti-social career—hatred for society in which he feels alien, longing for death sublimated into desire for destruction—no real belief in social program—owe it to own mob, etc., etc.—hatred for Christ, unconscious ambition to supplant, become victor Anti Christ—reason he hates Jews—liberty means his liberty alone as supreme master.

(Walter an anti-Semite—became [Socialist, then]* Communist, then Fascist—admiration not for social theory but for leaders, Lenin, Stalin, Hitler—none for Mussolini—"Wop loudmouth ham"—first attracted to Communism as an agent to destruction of United States as is—but always a lone wolf[5]—never wants to belong—won't be used by party line—use.)

In Dora's story about Walter, she quotes what he used to say about Hitler, Stalin—his strange confidence that he alone understands Hitler—Walter: "That guy and I could be pals. I know what makes him tick. Only I guess he'd never stand that from anyone. He wouldn't admit, scared to face himself. That's where I've got it over him. I've got more guts. I'm not even scared of myself." Dora says: "Can you believe it, honestly thought he was greater than Hitler."

[Walter said:] "Dames—he's scared of them, too—he'll fix 'em—keep 'em locked up in the house—do it only to bind soldiers—for me to use—slaughter 'em—he's scared of dames because he knows if he loved one, he'd find it didn't mean

---

*O'Neill crosses out these two words in brackets.

anything to her—nor what'd be more, to him—but I'm not scared—and it does mean something to you, don't it, Baby?—and to me, too—for what it really is—just lust—what's the matter with lust?—we gave it a bad name, that's all—priests and ministers—old men and women did."

The Father—omnivorous reader of magazines and newspapers—now mostly radio—no books—favorite expression: "I got a theory"—his wife always amused: "Oh, you and your theories!"—He is in many ways the typical American—complacently superior as to Europe: "Tell 'em what to do—but no involvement."

A great lodge member.

Good-natured tolerance—about Hitler—Father: "Crazy, ought to be put in an asylum"—Wife: "Ought to be hanged"—but he demurs: "Not responsible"—Hitler has some good ideas, he thinks—regarding Unions—and suppression of religion—he says this to tease wife who is ardent Methodist—when she protests: "That's the trouble with the world. Lost God"—he replies provocatively: "Portugese—they haven't. Nor the Wops." Wife: "Oh, them streamlined niggers. Better have religion suppressed than Catholics"—Father: "The Jews—orthodox, I mean, they're still mighty religious." Wife: "You can say that to me—them Christ-killers. I'm ashamed of you. You're a no-good American. Papists and kikes ruined the country."—Father: "It's not American to feel like that, Mother—and you know you like most of the ones you know"—(mentions the help she gave them in town)—Wife: "I don't say there aren't good ones—but all the same, never should have let them in here—bad for the country. Look at gangsters—all Wops, Jews and Irish and Pollacks." Father: "I'm part Irish." Wife: "Well, I meant shanty Irish. You're not shanty descended. Your grandfather had 100 pounds when he landed—if you weren't lying when you told me"—Father: "No, that's true. He owned his own land—and shanty—sold out.: Wife: "Well, then he wasn't shanty, the way Americans mean it."

This [is] all in opening after-breakfast scene.

Strange blight on walnuts—

Father volunteers in 1st War—disillusion—but also pleasant sly memories of Paris—and in quartermaster corps—became butcher.

He says: "If we want war, let's fight right here at home—smash unions—revive vigilantes—I'll volunteer first of all—I hate them bastards worse than I hate any Germans—let's make the United States safe for democracy at home."

	R. H. Play	Aug. '41
Setting 1941	Characters	

Ed (Edgar) White (49), semi-retired proprietor butcher shop (big, husky but bad heart)
Tess Ingels, his wife (50), owner of ranch, grazing land and orchards (100 acres)
Cassie, their daughter (24)
Dora (Bond), their daughter-in-law (24)
Walter White (26) Dora's husband (alias Harvey Black, "Blackie") ⎫ do not
Jack Tabor (27) Cassie's fiancé for 3 years, runs butcher shop ⎬ appear in play

---

Ed and Tess married in 1914 (Ed 22, Tess 23)
Walter [was] born in early 1915 (26)
Cassie [was] born in late 1916 (24)

Ed volunteers in the army in early 1917—gassed and wounded at Argonne—returns in 1919—inherits butcher shop, 1925.

Tess inherits ranch in 1928 and they move there from town.

Walter [is] a senior in high school in 1932 (17)—disappears in spring a few weeks before graduation—previous secret association with bootlegging gang—drove truck and guard.

[Walter was] an athletic hero in high school—football quarterback, basketball, baseball s. s. and captain in senior year—small but dynamic and fast and field general—his characteristics, noiseless, quiet-like, indifferent lethargy which suddenly explodes into action—given to fooling in games—wins no matter what—any means justified—rules for saps.

High school fire in which he is a hero, saves Dora, in early winter of 1932, senior year.

As a student [Walter is] lazy, uninterested—falls behind, then makes up in a burst of intensive study—always passes final exams—but no meaning to him except as [a way to] prove to display superiority in beating the game—a cinch.

He turns up home again after several months' absence (Fall 1932)—hoboing—he had been drawn to Dora's love for him—loves her for that—but uneasy at any tie—really leaves to get rid of it—works at butcher shop—drawn back to Dora—vague, baffled, reaching out for sentiment, he feels [he] ought to feel—imitation of others courting—inarticulate, silent—finally explodes in action—seduces her—(In describing this, she says: "As if he wanted to finish with her—convince himself that's all it is. What of it?")—demonstrates the power to conquer—to possess and thus show disdain for possession by throwing away—this happens in spring of 1933 when he is 18 and Dora 16—(Episode with Cassie at this time, too—plays on jealousy of Dora—gets her to the point where she knows and he knows he can—then drops it—[Walter] can't understand why [it] means so much to Dora—resents her clinging—no further intercourse with her—practical about this—she might get caught—Walter: "I wouldn't marry you—I'd beat it—going to anyway—you get more—count me out—grab some guy that belongs where you belong and forget me, because I'll forget you.)"

He disappears again in fall of 1933—leaves goodbye letters for family and Dora—indifferently, objectively sorry.

For a while Dora goes to pieces—gets a reputation as a wild girl, parties, scrapes, booze, affairs which mean nothing—fired from high school—Dora: "I guess I became just a dirty little tramp"—Cassie: "Yes, and I was glad and ran you down but I knew why and didn't blame you. I'd have liked to do the same, etc."

Then abruptly Dora gets sick of herself—the memory of Walter fades—she meets a man ten years older—Dora: "Stupid, I guess, no class, just dull and hard-working and good—he falls in love. I guess like Walter with me, I fell in love with his love because it gave me back my self-respect"—[Dora is] engaged in fall 1935—her family scornful of his unimportance, but resigned to anything that keeps her settled down—but insist on long engagement—he wants, too—expects a raise—Dora wants marriage right away.

They are married in early spring 1936—return after a month's honeymoon to find Walter back. (He has turned up suddenly—has money—story of working for construction firm—truth is he comes there as a hideout after a bank robbery in which he shot a cop—has kept his real identity a secret in underworld—plausible fake life story—home in Ohio town—etc.—and born a wolf anyway)—he is fed up, too—sated with lawless thrills—again reaching out to belong—lethargy—talks of buying a garage.

He and Dora avoid each other—but she feels a prisoner—reaction, she avoids pregnancy.

At last, a meeting—and then, now—intercourse—his admission—Walter: "I never forgot you—don't know why—guess I need you, Baby"—[they] arrange to elope—finally he tells her—warns her, [she had] better not"—Walter: "I'm what they call a crook."

But she goes—fall 1936—Walter 21, Dora 19—her husband waits, then moves away—divorces her two years later—she waits for Walter to suggest marriage—he never does until the attempt to settle down.

Her family disowns her.

The strange conflict of emotions Walter has inspired in the three women, his mother, sister, and Dora, who loved him in a deep maternal protective tenderness toward the boy who can't mature, who was born crippled in his inability to feel[6]—as if he [had] been born blind and deaf and dumb—the feeling of his lonely isolation—the intuition that he tries to overcome his infirmity—that he isn't to blame—can't help it—something in them always understands and excuses him.

Coupled with this an aversion for a born monster, an ugly and maimed man—"Like a beggar without a face you avoid looking at while you drop two bits in his tin cup—to keep him from following you, crying silently for your flesh to save him from starvation"—a scornful antagonism of mystified passionate worm toward an impotent lover—superiority, a desire for revengeful taunt.

But this is made incongruous by the fact that Walt is anything but impotent—physically handsome, has power of attracting all females—enormous nervous vitality in sex, as in other things, when he explodes in action—but it is the lust of an animal, divorced from love, for any desire to breed, divorced even from pleasure—has no meaning—leaves him apathetic, forgetful—each act [is] isolated as if it never happened before, never would again—a woman as temporary means for a physical function.

And yet Dora knows he tries to establish a relationship through sex—desperate attempt to break through to love—savage.

This resentment—and horror—and hatred for his realistic attitude which dooms them—dooms love—defeats them—leaves them meaningless—their attempt to believe this is only a defensive pose—but know better.

And yet, it inspires them also with desire to be as *free* as he is—to be ruthless—to use any means to get what they want.

R. H. Play
Notes—description of characters

Ed White is 49—about 5 feet 7 but looks shorter because [he is] so broad—fat, big stomach, beefy arms but still immensely strong—round head, thinning blond hair, bald spot, fat face, double chin, fair skin baked red, sunburn dotted with freckles, bleached brows, lashes, hardly noticeable—light blue eyes, round—small, full-lipped mouth, good teeth—attractive grin—general boyish expression of face—likable energetic personality.

Heart trouble—should take care [of himself] but doesn't—pronounced limp, left leg [is] stiff from kneecap shattered by shell fragment—went in 1918 (Argonne).

Education, high school and 2 years State agricultural school.

Tess—fifty, thick gray hair almost white, inch taller than husband, thin but not scrawny, has kept figure pretty well—dark complexion, high cheekbones, hollow cheeks, big dark eyes, long lashes, heavy brows, trace of a mustache, wide full-lipped mouth, angular jaw—still an unusually good-looking woman for her age.

Personality a contrast—by turns, complete relaxation into a vague, day-dreaming quietude—where anything outside the limits of her ranch-housewife activities are concerned, she is insensitive, detached, wondering, full of contemplative comments, usually pointless and banal, but with flashes of intuition.

A relentlessly efficient housekeeper—obsession with order,

neatness, cleanliness, exact routine—can't keep servants long because they can't or won't live up to her demands—really doesn't want a servant, stranger in the house, handling her things—but, on the other hand, work [is] too much for her alone (the way she works)—so this is a perpetual source of conflict in the house—she would have liked (that is, the housekeeper part of her) to train and keep Cassie as an assistant—but Cassie rebelled, made herself independent—arguments but no hard feelings in this, because Tess recognizes her obsession, wishes she could be free of it—rebels herself, fits of deliberate self-defiant slovenliness, laziness (enforced).

Education—high school and 2 years at California [college].

Great reader of newspapers, magazines—articles, not fiction—interested in all popular science, invention of articles, psychology, etc.—firm believer in vague theory of electric waves (proof, radio)—brain electric—power of telepathy, etc.—Walter [is] alive—etc.—convinced she is psychic.

Superior distinctive pose about townswomen—does not go to the movies—reads.

Cassie—resembles both parents—strong, ruggedly built, 5 feet 5—good figure, thin type—chestnut hair—hazel eyes—quiet, thoughtful, intelligent, dreaming—affectionate sense of humor regarding parents—but inwardly there is conflict—a confusion of not knowing what she is or wants to become—school teaching is only a saving activity—source of the conflict goes back to her brother—secret hostility to Mother because Walter [is] her pet—extremely prudish attitude about Walter and Dora—ultra conventional reaction—social disgrace, immoral conduct, etc.—and condemns in every other way—sceptical of Dora's letters, how well [they are] getting along—no intuition about this, simply doesn't want to believe—all this conceals real reason, which she won't admit to herself—Mother guesses—very touchy on the subject of why she has kept postponing marriage—big conflict here—loves him but feels barrier—feels unfair to him, ought to release, but can't bear to let him go—vague hope something will happen so one day it will be all right—problem will suddenly be resolved.

Dora is about 5 feet 6. She must have once been exceptionally pretty but now she looks sickly, her body thin and wasted, her face so haggard, drawn and deeply-lined that she looks at least ten years older than she is—dry, sallow skin stretched tightly over her jaw and cheekbones—a straight thin nose, a sensitive mouth with full lips, big gray eyes. Her hair is obviously peroxided. Hollows in her long slender neck. Her expensive clothes on the extreme of the latest style fit her badly as if she has lost ten pounds since they were fitted. Her hat, also in extreme style, or too youthful and gay, rakishly masks her ravaged face.

She tries to assume and maintain a natural, simple, familiar manner of a wife paying a long-postponed visit to her husband's family, confident of her welcome, except with Cassie. But a terrible strain she is under cannot be concealed. She is conscious of this and constantly tries to explain it away with various glib excuses.

Her face is too old not only in appearance but in the quality of its expression. There is the hardness and sorrow and pain and defiance of years of bitter experience in it, and, at the moment, a tough defensive cynicism that gives her the look of a prostitute.[7] Her eyes, which should be beautiful, have a flat, depthless look as if they were merely organs of sight cut off from registering thought or feeling, and this makes them appear repellent and cruel.

At first extremely ingratiating—no make-up except on lips—remembers Tess didn't approve. Tess: "Oh, I got over that—years before you left."

Jumps at sickness—didn't like letters—pneumonia—one reason Walt thought [she] better come—rest.

Cassie and Dora at one time close friends.

<u>Outline—New conception</u>[8]   Aug. '41
Act One

For a few moments after curtain, argument on Hitler, unions, etc. clearly heard through open windows of dining room (right of door)—it continues as the three come out on the porch—Cassie goes to the gate for newspaper—talk between Tess and Ed—snatches—hope [there's a] letter from Dora—her postcard—funny only postcard—usually long letters—postcard said she and Walt might come soon—hope so—their attitude toward Dora—always liked—not to blame for her actions in the past—Walt's fault—in love with him—love [is the] reason pro-Dora—actions of her family—as if a disgrace to marry Walt.

Tess: "Who are they? We're from pioneers. They're just interlopers from the Middle West—etc.—Dora had been so good for Walt—settled down, if you can call his wandering that—but doing so well, from her letters"—resentment against him for never coming—then excuse—Cassie comes back reading the paper—joins in—antagonism toward Dora and Walt—accepted Dora's letters—hopes she won't come—Tess and Ed rebuke—she is ashamed—justifies antagonism against Dora—way she acted after Walt left the first time—after he came back and she eloped with him. Tess: "All of us make mistakes—you're always telling me don't be proud, don't judge, etc." Cassie says: "Not moral grounds—she was so weak—ought not to have shown she was hurt—pride—and when he came back, should have ignored—instead all he did was wave [his] little finger and she was his slave." Tess: "I can't remember when you—Walt had a way with him." Cassie: "I got bravely over it"—then says: "Oh, don't be afraid I won't be nice if she turns up—really pity her, married to Walt—I'll bet he's made her pay, no matter how happy [her] letters sounded—too happy to be true, if you ask me—hope she won't come—I think best for all of us no connection."

She goes in the house—Tess and Ed lower voices—worry about her—more and more nervous and dissatisfied—can't imagine why [she] doesn't marry—engaged so long it's a joke—Ed: "Why don't you talk to [her]—get him to make her"—Tess: "No use. He's tried"—then talks about Walt—memories, etc.—resentments—Ed: "Maybe it is better [he] never comes home—he wouldn't stay—now we're forgotten, etc."—then ashamed—"But why?—if Walt were here, he'd act surprised—say 'What if you have forgotten? Only natural. You ought to. Don't be sentimental. What of it'" etc.—they become sad and bitter—then ashamed, hopeful—Tess: "He must be changed—young, then—must love Dora"—etc.—they drop subject—he looks at paper—again talk about Hitler—Ed: "Walt [is] like Hitler—no feeling for others' feelings."

Then noise—car to the barn—someone who knows the place—Cassie [comes] out—they wonder who—woman gets out—Tess: "[She] sees us. She's waving. You go and see what she wants, Ed"—he goes—Cassie: "I guess it must be Dora"—Tess: "If it is, she's alone"—Cassie (strangely): "You sound relieved, Ma."—Tess indignant: "No such thing. Oh, I hope it is Dora. Must be. Ed's kissing her. Oh, I'm so glad. Now we'll hear all about Walt." Cassie: "The truth? I wouldn't be so sure, Ma"—Tess rebukes [her]: "Come along. Let's go and meet [her]"—she starts—Cassie doesn't follow—Tess: "Don't be that way. Come on"—Cassie: "Don't worry. I'll be nice to her—as nice as I can be"—Tess goes—Cassie waits—bitter, apprehensive.

They enter with Dora—Dora [is] talking nervously with forced gaiety: "I must look like nothing on earth—no sleep—drove all night"—greets Cassie, kisses, effusive warmth—Cassie responds stiltedly—shocked at Dora's appearance: "You drove all night? Why?"—Dora: "Nearer I came, more eager to get home—kept saying [I'll] go to next town—beautiful moonlight—knew [I] couldn't sleep, anyway—too excited"—Tess and Ed fussily solicitous—Cassie watchful—Dora goes on: "I was telling Ed—Walt was so disappointed—looked forward—last moment—told me to come alone—do me good—[I've] been sick—didn't tell you—had pneumonia—down to skin and bones—can't seem to recover strength—etc."—Ed and Tess tell her: "You will here—just rest, etc."—Cassie: "How is Walt?"—Dora: "Oh, fine—never better—working head off—but it agrees with him—doing so well—can't get along without him—etc."

Ed: "Had breakfast—we'll have coffee"—Tess says: "Lie down, take a nap after"—She and Ed go in.

Scene Dora and Cassie—Dora feels antagonism—appeals for old friendship—Cassie moved in spite of herself: "What is the truth about Walt, Dora?"—Dora stiffens: "What do you mean? What I've written, told you. I've been sick—still am." Cassie: "I wasn't doubting you're sick"—Dora repeats story mechanically—then suddenly exhausted: "I'm sick."—sees newspapers—Dora: "What's the news? Anything exciting?"—Cassie: "It's all the war"—Dora: "You know, Walt has the craziest hunches. He isn't pro-Nazi, he isn't pro anything, but he really admires Hitler. He thinks he has the right idea about people"—Cassie: "Yes, Walt would"—Dora: "Yes, he would, wouldn't he?" Cassie: "He hasn't changed then?"—Dora: "Yes, he's changed a bit in one way. Or he's tried to. But not in his opinion about people and life. He believes you've got to be realistic and not sentimental and face the truth and not feel anything one way or the other." Cassie: "Not feel anything. That sounds unchanged."

Dora breaks: "Don't ask me any more questions now. I'm too all in."—etc. (After a pause) Dora: "Any other news?"—Cassie: "I didn't notice"—Dora: "Can I take a look?"—explains stocks—glances through [paper]—awareness Cassie is watching, poker face, but does hesitate on one headline on inside page—covers up by reading another about taxes—Dora: "What I'm really looking for—stock market—(she puts paper aside—shudders)—fever—and my stocks went down—no gambler, can't take it." Cassie: "You gambled a lot when you fell in love with Walt." Dora: "Yes, I did, didn't I? But I won that time"—exhausted pause—shudders again—Dora: "What time is it?" Cassie: "Going on to 8"—Dora: "With all the traveling Walt and I have done, never got used to change of time." It's three hours off New York, isn't it?" Cassie: "Four now in daylight saving"—Dora: "It's nearly noon there now" (shudder) "Chill. Have you got aspirin? Never mind. Some in my bag. I'll go in. Better take a nap"—Tess appears: "Coffee ready." Dora: "Good—warm me up—caught a cold, etc.—It's so good to be here. You're all so good"—goes in—Cassie picks up the paper—starts to look through—Ed comes out: "Poor kid, look likes hell. Pneumonia takes it out of you. Same age as you, 24, isn't she? Looks 35—a sick 35." Cassie: "Well, that's what comes of marrying Walt." Ed [is] angry: "Cut out the bum cracks, Cassie, etc."—goes to feed the pigeons—Ed: "Too bad Walt didn't come see what a flock from his pets—etc."—he goes—Cassie searches the paper—Tess comes out: "Tucked her in—cold, day like this—fever—etc. What you looking for in paper?"—Cassie: "I don't know. That's the truth. I mean, just glancing over the headlines—nothing in particular"—Tess grows ruminative: "You know how psychic I am." Cassie: "Oh, Ma!" Tess: "You always laugh, but I am. I've got a feeling it isn't only she's sick. I'm afraid something happened between her and Walt."

End, Dora comes out on porch above—looks down at Cassie searching the newspaper—Cassie senses—looks up—Dora asks for the paper—excuse, always reads self to sleep—nothing to read—Cassie hands paper up to her—Dora goes back—Cassie [is] more suspicious, afraid.

Outline
Act Two

Opening same as Act One—they are heard from dining room, arguing—three come out—thermometer—heat—Dora hasn't been able to eat anything—excuse, nervous, indigestion—Dora: "Better not to—rest and peace [are] what I need—It'll be all over by tonight—I'll sleep well tonight"—Cassie: "What will be all over?"—Dora: "Why, I mean, rested by then"—Ed asks: "Where's the paper?"—Cassie: "I gave it to Dora"—Dora goes upstairs to get—their talk about her—Tess' prophetic hunch: "Trouble with Walt"—Ed matter-of-fact: "Drove all night—let down—nerves—too tired to sleep—natural—why look for other reasons"—they stare at him.

Dora comes back with paper—goes to Ed—he starts looking through—Tess [goes] in to help wash the dishes—comments on her obsessive housekeeping—Ed notices part of the paper [is] missing—Cassie stares at Dora—Dora says: "Yes, I noticed that too. Did you give me all of the paper, Cassie?" Cassie: "Yes, it was all there." Dora: "Couldn't have been. I guess you didn't notice"—Ed dismisses it—doesn't matter—inside pages—he speaks of heat again—only one thing to do on a day like this—take a siesta—Ed: "You, especially, Dora—guess you'd like another nap"—He begins questioning her about Walt—Cassie notices how guarded and forced her answers are—he doesn't—he is relieved and pleased by information—confesses he had fears for Walt—way he used to be—Ed: "I thought he'd never get really interested in anything (memories)—my son but never knew him—didn't want me to—father didn't mean anything—wouldn't have been surprised to hear he'd become a stunt flier, or daredevil with a circus, etc.—or maybe worse—when he got to driving rum trucks for bootleggers, I was afraid he'd wind up a gangster—loving you is what saved him, Dora." Dora: "Don't. (Then as he is surprised) I mean, I don't deserve any credit. (Asks what time. He looks at watch, tells her) That makes it 5 in New York." Ed goes in—like to work but doctor's orders.

Dora and Cassie—Dora asks: "What's the matter with Ed?" Cassie: "High blood pressure—has had a heart attack." Then scene between Dora and Cassie beginning with Cassie asking why Dora [is] so concerned about Eastern Time—Dora glibly explains away—then about the paper—etc.—until Dora [is] frightened and angry—and revengeful—turns on her—under Cassie's questioning—Dora: "Look out, Cassie. I don't like you—because I know you hate me. So cut out the old 3rd degree stuff. If you keep on, I might get sore and let you have it—then you'll wish you'd minded [your] own business." Cassie: "Let me have what, Dora?" Dora: "Well, you seem to think I'm lying—so maybe I'd let you have the truth. You know what Walt always says: 'We're all too yellow to face it'—except him, he meant, of course." Cassie: "Yes, of course"—Dora: "You couldn't take it, Cassie. You're soft and sentimental—just a small town schoolteacher who's never been around, etc." (This with a strange superior hardness)—Cassie: "You don't seem able to take whatever it is yourself, Dora. (defiantly) Have you and Walt broke up?" Dora (grasps at this): "Yes, if you want to know."

Tess comes out, embraces [Dora]—her psychic hunch—sympathetic: "Tell us about it, Dora. Cassie and I know what Walt's like, etc."—Dora (tries to discuss with generalities): "Same old story—both to blame I guess—tried to make it work—but finally decided no go—no hard feelings. You know Walt. He doesn't bear hard feelings anymore than soft feelings." Cassie: "No, I don't think he's ever felt anything at all." Tess (rebukes, then agrees): "Yes, but he always wanted to—he'd have given anything—done anything." Dora (bitterly): "Do anything is right." (finally she breaks) "Can't talk now—I'll tell you all about it later. Tomorrow I'll be all right—or even tonight—any time after seven." (She stops appalled—catches)—Cassie (stares): "Why after seven?" Dora tries to explain away—Tess suggests a siesta—Dora grabs at this—goes in with Tess—Cassie alone—Ed comes out—can't settle down on his siesta—mind keeps milling around—smoke a pipe—worried about Dora—changed so—Cassie tries to reassure—Tess calls Ed from indoors: "Doctor's order he rest after lunch"—he goes in.

Dora (comes out on balcony—leans over—hostility): "I'm sick

of your questions. I'll shut you up so you won't ask more—reason I left him—I found out he's a crook—you're not surprised, are you?—I guess you knew he'd wind up a crook—and now he's in jail[9]—that's the truth and I guess it'll hold you for a while."

Act Three*   Sept. '41

Dora's room (and upstairs porch?)—shutters closed to keep out the sun and heat—dim light with glaring heat outside—Dora on bed, nothing on but a bra and slip ins—suitcase half unpacked—clock—Dora's desperate fright and horror—finally decides to run away—gets up, starts repacking suitcase.

Cassie (enters, catches her at this—has newspaper—is terribly shaken—but forgets for a moment): "Why [are you] going?" Dora says: "Realize never should have come—not when you're here—but let's not get sore at each other again—shouldn't have come anyway—take advantage of Tess and Ed's kindness—ought to have guts to face this alone—did for a while—but suddenly had to go home—can't go to own home and this used to be like a second home—his—don't mind what I said about Walt being a crook—you know how I meant it—crook with me—unfaithful—always knew but finally he got too rough." Cassie says: "Don't lie, Dora. You were telling the truth." Dora (defiant and angry again—tries to go—Cassie stops): "[It's] best for all [if] I go—you'll be sorry if—and I'm not lying—he's been unfaithful all along—shouldn't think you'd be surprised—you know Walt—he had a way—we all fell—and he'd make a pass at any skirt around, even his own sister."

Cassie: "Why d'you say that?" Dora: "Because he did, didn't he—just to show he was realistic—beyond any laws—and to prove he could—prove his power—oh, I don't say anything happened—he wouldn't need that—only to prove he could, if he wanted—to himself—then he wouldn't be interested much any more—it would be finished—he didn't want you—I'm the only woman he ever really wanted—I know that—and only

---

*O'Neill has drawn a small one-inch-by-half-inch rectangle in the left margin opposite the first paragraph to represent Dora's bedroom. In it are small lines to suggest a bed, doors, and windows.

because he thought I was the only one who might make him feel—well, he failed there, too—never got beyond lust—he couldn't love even me—and I failed."

Cassie breaks down—denies—Dora: "Nuts! I know better. That's the reason you can't marry—you hate me—hanging on to Walt—can't free yourself—well, you'll be free soon."—etc.—Dora again sorry, tries to go—Cassie says: "Yes—to—your duty, etc."—Dora taunts than apologizes—starts to go—Cassie stops: "Got to know the truth"—shows the paper—Dora alarmed but pretends scorn—Dora: "So that's what you drove to town for! I saw you. You always were a little sneak, spying on Walt and me, hiding in the bushes—you're a fool—nothing in the paper—I'm right, aren't I? You didn't find anything." Cassie: "No—nothing I could imagine—" Dora: "I told you! You're crazy"—Cassie: "Nothing but one item"—Then scene in which Dora becomes more and more distracted. Cassie more and more suspicious and frightened, gets Dora to contradict self in story—Cassie: "You're lying, Dora, you said he was a crook"—Dora: "Yes, that's true but not—" Cassie: "Not what? You mean not a murderer"—Dora alternates between extreme defiant lying and pleading: "Stop it—for your own sake, you damned fool!"

Cassie asks again why Dora [was] so insistent on Eastern and coast time—finally, in fascinated terror, she comes to an item in the paper—that a criminal named Walter Black, "Blackie"—opposite to White—sounds like Walt—he always chose the opposite—he'd like to be Black[10]—he'd feel that was having guts to face the truth"—Dora distractedly proclaims ignorance—Cassie: "It says he committed many killings—a hired killer—says [he] never would have been caught if it hadn't been his wife informed the cops—it says Gangster has refused his lawyer's plea"—Dora: "All right. You're asking for it! That is Walt. That's me. Now how do you like it?" Cassie, hoping against hope, so crushed and broken—first thought father and mother must never know—Dora: "Never know through me. You'd never have known either except for damned prying"—Cassie says brokenly: "Says caught through wife's information. How could you—I know you loved Walt"—Dora: "Because of a lot of things. Because he made me. He wanted it. You'd have done the same." Later. "I've got to tell you the whole story—got to tell someone—and you're the only one who'd understand."

Knock—Tess—both put up great pretense—Dora: "Cassie's been telling me about engagement"—etc.

Curtain

Act Four

Same as I and II—Exterior—and opening is the same—voices from dining room—Tess and Ed arguing about world crisis—then Ed and Dora come out.

Ed and Dora scene—his urging her gently to forgive Walt and go back to him—Ed: "I know you must be in the right—I know Walt—we'd always be on your side, same as we always were—but you [have] got to forgive a lot in marriage, got to make allowances for Walt"—memories of what Walt did to him and Tess—Ed: "We forgive him—or at least we try to—because [he was] born that way"—(Then his uneasiness)—Ed: "He might go all to pot without you—or make it an excuse—lord knows what he mightn't do—you're the only person he ever loved, I think—etc."—she finally can't stand it—asks him to stop—he is contrite—sad—sorry.

Tess and Cassie come out—finished cleaning up—Tess asks: "What you been saying to Dora?"—Ed (sheepish): "Only saying I hope she'd make it up with Walt"—Tess says: "No time to bring that up—no tact—you go attend to those famous chickens of yours (and cows and pigeons)"—Ed says: "You mean Walt's"—he goes.

Tess takes up where he left off—Walt's livestock leads to Walt—apologizes for Ed's tactlessness, then goes on herself—memories of Walt—livestock—incident of his killing animals he seemingly loved ruthlessly to free himself from the tie—but at the same time crying bewilderedly as if he didn't know why and couldn't believe own explanation—Dora again starts to break—Cassie interrupts: "Leave her alone, Ma," etc. Tess goes in to do dishes.

Then Dora-Cassie scene—and Dora's story (strange suppressed intensity in this scene—necessity to speak low—and several interruptions—Tess and Ed—their contrasting small talk—no chance for Dora to tell story before—always Tess or Ed around).

Recurrent waves of hatred, jealousy, sympathy, identity between two as story progresses—at end, when she tells about turning Walt in—Dora: "Don't look at me as if I were a murderer. What would you have done in my shoes? You'd have done the same. You know damned well you would—only thing to do—what he wanted—in love with death now—all he ever loved anyway[11]—you couldn't help yourself"—Cassie agrees, first in identical spirit of revenge, then in a spirit of pity—Cassie tells Dora what she must do: "I'll send an air mail letter to a friend to send me a wire from Walt asking me to beg you to forgive [him] and come back—and you'll go—keep writing once in a while—finally write Walt [was] killed instantly in an accident—all this for parents' sake—they won't ask questions—too relieved—sad, but they'll be relieved, too"—they suddenly remember the time (motive all through the play of Dora's smashed wrist watch)—nearing seven—Cassie: "If they hope Walt will show fear [they'll] be mistaken—pride"—Dora: "Nothing can faze him—he'll be hoping that the chair may make him feel something—but it won't—his last failure—the poor bastard!"—they cling together, terrified—stare at Cassie's wrist watch.

Tess comes out—glad Cassie and Dora [have] made up—placid—her prophetic hunch that all will turn out for the best—she sits in an old-fashioned rocker—Ed turns up—does the same—Dora and Cassie in straight-back armchairs—rigid clutching the arms—Tess remarks: "Why don't you relax?"—Ed: "Yes, this time of evening—long shadows—beautiful—life is beautiful, if we only had the sense to see it, we'd only hold it close, etc."—then cuckoo clock from the hall—Dora [is] pitiful and nervous—alarm—she says pain like an electric shock, like rheumatism—[they] solicitous—nerves—silence—Ed's philosophic soothing—Dora begins sobbing: "I loved him, I tell you, Cassie, I loved him no matter what he did. I couldn't help it. I still love him." Cassie: "I know, Dora." Tess: "We all love him—even if he never wanted it." Ed: "I'm sure he knows how much you love him, Dora—and appreciates it." Dora: "Yes, maybe he does—now!"

The White residence in Northern California; lighting directions are provided at the bottom to indicate the time of day for the acts. (Courtesy Yale Collection of American Literature, Beinecke Rare Book and Manuscript Library)

<u>Gag's End</u>   (?)
<u>Blind Alley Guy</u>   (?)

Characters

Edgar White
Tess, his wife
Cassie, their daughter
Dora (Mrs. Walter White), their daughter-in-law

Place: A small ranch of about 100 acres of pear and walnut orchards and pasture land located in a valley in the southern part of northern California about five miles from the nearest town.
Time: 1934—a hot day in July
Act One   Exterior of the house—around 7:30 A.M.
Act Two   The same—around 12:30 P.M
Act Three
Act Four   The same—around 7 P.M.

Act One

Scene: Exterior of the house. It is an old white two-story frame building, with a porch on the ground floor and a railed balcony above extending along its entire front. It is situated on top of a hill, and faces in a westerly direction (front) with a view overlooking the valley, which runs north and south.

At extreme left-front, a big densely-foliaged black-walnut tree, half off left is a frame for the house on this side. A gravel path from the garage and barn, off left, skirts its trunk at the rear. Three steps lead from the path to the porch round the screen front door. A similar door directly above opens on the balcony. There are two screened windows on each side of these doors. At right of the porch a large oleander, heavy with white blossoms. Wisteria vines at the other end of the porch climb up the supports of the balcony and stream to the roof and are twined along the edge of the roof and the balcony. On the porch are three chairs, an old-fashioned rocker before the window at the left, two wicker armchairs before the windows flanking the doorway.

At the rear of the house the hill slopes sharply to a cañon where in the rainy season there is a brook. At right rear, beyond the oleanders, there is a vista of rolling foothills rising to a range of low mountains. The hills are turned a light brown or faded corduroy color by the sun of the dry season studded with deep green hemlocks solitary or grouped in small grove. The mountains beyond the hills are dark with chaparal.

The window trim and solid shutters and doors of the house are a bleached green. The white walls will soon need a fresh coat of paint. But there is nothing rundown about the place. Everything has a well-kept look. [The atmosphere is one of sufficient prosperity.]*

It is around seven-thirty in the morning of a day in July, 1934. The sun has risen above the mountains at right-rear. The sky is a cloudless pale blue. There is no breeze and it is already extremely hot but still comparatively cool in the shade of the front of the house.

From the dining room, at right of door on the ground floor where the family has just finished breakfast, the voices of Ed White and his wife, Tess, can be heard, raised in an argument which, though emphatic enough, holds no trace of acrimony. Evidently this couple still like each other, and do not pick arguments for arguments sake, just to give vent to a concealed boredom and antagonism. Every once in a while, their daughter, Cassie's voice, is heard bored by the subject but affectionately amused by her parents. As all doors and windows are open behind the screens, what is said is as clearly audible as if they were outside on the porch.

Ed: Well, I say he's no better than a lousy gangster murderer!

Tess: And I say you can't blame him. He had to. It was self-defense.

Ed: Self-defense, my neck. You know that's damned nonsense, Tess.

Tess: It's the plain truth, from what I've read. They were planning to double cross him weren't they? And he found out about it. Well, what would you want him to do? Wait and do

---

*This sentence in brackets was crossed out by the author.

nothing? He knew if they got hold of him, they'd kill him in the end to get rid of him. The only way out was for him to kill them first. Just try putting yourself in his place, and be fair. I'd do exactly what he did.

[Ed: That was years ago. (Resentfully) What you want to rake that up for, Tess?]*

Cassie: (amusedly) Yes, you would! You can't bear the thought of killing one of the chickens, even. (She laughs) Goodness, Ma, you're hard-boiled this morning. (This breaks up the argument for the moment.)

Ed: (Kidding affectionately) Yes, she's plumb ferocious, Cassie. I don't know if it's safe for us to be around her.

Tess: (Laughingly) Oh, all right. Get out of here, then, and give me a chance to clear the table. (There is a scraping of chairs pushed back and a moment later Ed and Cassie appear in the hall behind the screen door and come out on the porch. Tess follows them but remains for a while just inside the screen door.)

Edgar White is forty-seven, six feet two, weighing around 250, an old Aggie varsity tackle run to fat, and also a veteran of the first World War. He walks with a decided limp, his right leg stiff as a result of a kneecap shattered by a shell fragment in the Argonne. He has a round, freckled face, thinning sandy hair, grey-blue eyes and a stub nose—a homely, commonplace face. He is easy-going, generous, a good neighbor, a hard worker before high blood pressure put a curb on his activities, and is liked by nearly everyone in the community. He wears baggy old khaki pants and a short-sleeved blue mesh cotton shirt, unbuttoned, showing his hairy, freckled chest.

Cassie is twenty-four, tall and slender, with large brown eyes, dark brown wavy hair, a short straight nose and small firm mouth. She is near-sighted and wears bifocal spectacles. In appearance and personality both she is attractive. She is simple and direct, warm and affectionate, has a sense of humor, and her smile is charming. She has not been a school teacher long enough for it to put its stamp upon her. She is dressed in colorful cotton print and wears an engagement ring.

---

*O'Neill crossed out this line of dialogue in brackets.

Cassie: (As they come out) I know it's no use offering to help you with the dishes, Ma, but I wish you'd let me. You make me feel so lazy and guilty.

Tess: (From behind the screen door) Well, I won't let you. You're on vacation, and heaven knows you've earned it teaching a lot of lazy brats that don't want to learn anyway. I'll have them done in no time. (She comes out on the porch—smiling) Guess I'll loaf with you a second before I start.

Tess is three years older than her husband, tall, thin, with a wiry body that is still strong and active. She is very dark, her skin dry and swarthy, her hair straight and jet black but streaked with white. She has a long thin nose, finely modeled, deep-set black eyes, high prominent cheekbones, a wide, thin-lipped mouth. One would suspect she had Indian or Spanish blood somewhere in her ancestry but, like her husband, she comes from a choice strain of American pioneer stock, her remote forebears being Scotch-Irish. In manner and personality, she is like her daughter, naturally warm, simple, direct and affectionate, with the same charming smile and sense of humor, and like her she wears a colorful cotton print dress but has an apron over it.

Ed: (Approving affectionately) That's the stuff, Tess. Come on and loaf. Sit down and relax. (He pushes her with smiling bullying into the rocking chair at left of door) Now stay put a while.

Tess: (Immediately begins to rock) Only for a minute. (She draws a deep breath.) My, the air's nice and cool here now. (Ed sits down on top of the steps where Cassie is already sitting.)

Cassie: It won't be cool later. We're in for a good blazing heatwave, I think.

Ed: (Lighting a cigarette, with a glance at the sky) Yep. Time we had one, and by all the signs this is it. You watch yourself, Tess, and keep out of that damned oven of a kitchen all you can. (A bit irritably) I wish to God you'd listen to reason and get another cook and save yourself.

Tess: Now don't start on that, Ed. The last five we had were all lazy, dirty and couldn't cook, either. I'm much more content doing the work myself than worrying about some shiftless woman who breaks my dishes and ruins my good stove and gives us all indigestion. No more servants for me. I've told you that a hundred times and I mean it.

[Ed: Hell, Tess, they weren't as bad as all that. You expect them to be as good as you are, or be thought no good.]*

Cassie: (With amusement) Yes, it seems to me I've heard this argument before. It's no use, Pa. You're right but you can't convince her. I've given up trying.

Tess: (To Ed) And don't worry about the heat bothering me. You're the only one who has to be careful, and not go running out in the broiling sun because you suddenly get a notion something's not being done exactly the way you'd do it. There's no excuse. You know very well Tom Avery[12] [is] looking after everything as well as you could. Your business right now is to take it easy and get your blood pressure down where it belongs. You know what the doctor warned you.

Ed: Oh, damn the doctor.

Cassie: (Smiling) Seems to me I've heard this argument before, too. Never mind, Ma. I'll keep an eye on him when you're not around and see that he doesn't do anything foolish.

Ed: Two bosses. Swell chance I've got in this house.

Tess: (Smiles teasingly) Yes, isn't it dreadful. I don't know how you stand us, Ed.

Cassie: (Puts her arm around his shoulder and gives him a playful hug) Poor Pa! Can't seem to call your soul your own, can you? (They laugh and he grins contentedly. There is a pause.)

Tess: (Slowly—in a tone she tries to make casual but which sounds a bit strained) Cassie, your Pa thinks Walt and Dora might arrive this morning.

Cassie: (Her tone the same quality as her mother's) You're just guessing, ain't you, Pa? Dora's letter said sometime this week, and it's only Tuesday.

Ed: (His tone is also too casual) I figured out on a map the distance from Galveston, Texas, where the letter was postmarked. If they took the most direct route and didn't stop any place more than overnight and made early starts, and if Walt still drives as a hell-for-leather heathen as he used to, they could get here by tonight.

---

*This line of dialogue was deleted by the author.

Cassie: Too many "ifs," Pa, and you've left out the biggest one—if they're really coming. Dora had us expecting them last year, remember, and the year before, and they never arrived.

Tess: She never said definitely. All she wrote was we could expect them if Walt could get a vacation. This time she says they surely will come.

Cassie: Well, I hope they can. I'd love to see Dora again. (She adds quickly) And Walt, too, of course. But I won't believe it until I see them. The same thing may happen again.

Ed: I don't think so, Cassie. If I know Walt, he's had enough of being promised a vacation and then having it called off at the last moment. I'll bet this time he's told his bosses he's taking one no matter what, and if they don't like it—Well, you know Walt. He'd mean it. He wouldn't give a damn what.

Cassie: No, he never did. I don't think he'd even bother to warn them. He'd just go. They'd wake up one morning and find he'd disappeared—the same as he used to.

Tess: (Slowly) Yes, Walt never cared—he couldn't understand—(She catches herself guiltily.) But let's not rake up the past. It isn't fair when we all know from Dora's letters how completely he's changed in the past three years.

Cassie: Yes, imagine Walt becoming a model husband. He's made Dora happy, that's sure. For me, that's the best thing he's done. He certainly owed it to her after all that suffering—(She stops abruptly).

Ed: (Hasn't been listening—defensively) Hell, I don't mean to rake up the past, Tess, I was only saying how free and independent Walt's always been from the time he was a kid. I'm sure he hasn't changed in that because it was born in him. (This with a wink at Cassie—teasingly) Got it from you, Tess—stubborn as hell and bound to have his own way or die trying. Me, I've always been a weak, submissive guy—but I don't have to tell you that. (Tess smiles.)

Cassie: (Takes up his teasing tone eagerly) Yes, you have. That's why you volunteered in the World War, isn't it—because you were so weak?

Ed: (Frowns) No, I did that because I was a sucker for a lot of lying slogans, like a lot of other damned fools. (He indicates his stiff leg—bitterly) And look what it got me—a bum stiff leg for the rest of my life. (Then he grins good-naturedly.) Taught me a lesson, though. Never have looked for an argument since then.

Cassie: (Teasingly) That's funny. I thought I heard you in one not long ago.

Ed: Oh, that. Forced into it, Cassie. (With a teasing glance at his wife) You wouldn't have me stand by and listen to your mother admiring that rat without a word of protest, would you?

Tess: (Roused) It's no question of admiring him. I was just claiming that if you face the facts of the position he was forced into, you have to admit in his boots, you'd do just what he did.

Cassie: (With comical protest) Oh, gosh, have I started you off again?

Tess: (Ignoring this) It's you who used to admire him. I've heard you say time and again you took your hat off to him, and you wished we had someone with his guts at the head of our government to smash the Communists like he's smashed them.

Ed: All right. Sure, I said that. I still say it. But these men he's just had killed in that purge weren't Communists. They were nearly all people who'd started with him and helped him get to the top. One of them was his best friend. (Indignantly) That's what finished him for me. It shows him up for what he is—a yellow, double-crossing, murdering rat! By God, I hope one of them he didn't get gets him! Someone will, too, wait and see.

Tess: I'll bet they don't. He's got too much brains, and they're too scared of him.

Ed: (Angrily) If I was one of them, by God, I'd find some way to take a shot at him!

Cassie: (Amused) I thought you'd become meek, Pa. Who's being "plumb ferocious" now?

Tess: (Laughs) Yes, isn't he a tough guy. (She ruffles his hair affectionately) You're a nut, Ed. Don't get so excited about nothing. It's bad for your blood pressure.

Cassie: Then why do you argue with him, Ma? (With a tone of irritation) It's too silly. What do either of you care what happens in Germany?

Tess: I don't. (Smiling) I was only looking for an excuse to put off washing the dishes.

Ed: (Grinning good-naturedly now) Hell, I don't give a damn, either, Tess. Let 'em all kill each other off, and the more the merrier. It's their business. They're not killing us. There's only one guy over there I'd really love to hear had got his and that's Stalin.

Tess: (Decidedly) Me, too! He *is* a rat. (Then she laughs.) Well, now we've agreed on something. I'll go back to work. (She gets up and yawns.) Excuse me, I can't help it. I didn't get much sleep. (She goes to the door—irritably.) Oh, I do wish Walt and Dora could tell us exactly when to expect them. It gets on my nerves, waiting and not knowing—(Quickly) But it's not their fault, of course. (She opens the door.) See you later. You make your father stay out of the sun and behave, Cassie. (She disappears inside.)

Cassie: All right, Ma. (She puts her arm through her father's.) You heard my orders. I hope you'll be meek.

Ed: (Grinning) I sure will. As it happens, all I want to do is loaf. No pep whatever. (He stifles a yawn.) She's started me doing it. I didn't sleep so well, either. Your mother is right. It gets on my nerves, too, waiting and wondering—

Cassie: Well, it was always like that with Walt. You never could tell—(A pause) You mean, wondering what he'll be like now?

Ed: (Too decidedly) No, I didn't. I meant wondering when they'd turn up here. (A pause. He speaks argumentatively as if he were convincing himself as well as Cassie.) We know pretty well from Dora's letter what he's like now, don't we?

Cassie: Yes, but—he's never written once himself.

Ed: Well, he wouldn't. He always thought letters were foolish. He couldn't see any need for them. But he has written postscripts to some of Dora's.

Cassie: A few lines. [Telling us nothing.]*

Ed: That's a lot for him—to take the trouble. [It's a sign he's changed.]*

Cassie: I'm sure Dora got him to do it.

Ed: Well, that's more proof he's changed—to let anyone persuade him to do anything he doesn't believe in. [It shows what you've said, that she succeeded to turn him into a good husband, must have changed.]*

Cassie: (Slowly) Yes, that's true. (She gives a short bitter

---

*These three passages in brackets were crossed out by the author.

laugh.) The trouble with Walt was, he never believed in anything, as far as I could see.

Ed: (Slowly) Couldn't, I'd say—would if he could, but couldn't. There was something born in him—

Cassie: I know—hard and cold, not able to feel what anyone else would feel.

Ed: He tried to, Cassie, remember that.

Cassie: Maybe, at times.

Ed: He wanted to feel it.

Cassie: But most of the time he was proud he didn't. It made him feel strong and superior and scornful.

Ed: (Bitterly) Don't I know! (Then relentingly) But still—well, it's a funny thing to say about your own son, but I never could get to know Walt—I mean, the real Walt.

Cassie: Neither could anyone else. I don't think he could himself.

Ed: But I did realize you couldn't hold him responsible—the way you would any other boy—for all the crazy things he did and said to hurt people. He never deliberately tried to hurt anyone. The way he looked at things—we're stupid to feel hurt or angry.

Cassie: Oh, I know that, all right. And he didn't care, either.

Ed: (Suddenly contrite) Hell, Cassie, here we are digging up the past again. Let's cut it out. We'll be in a swell mood to welcome him home, if we keep holding old grudges against him.

Cassie: (Sharply defensive) [Who said]* I have no grudge against Walt, Pa. Why should I? He never hurt me. All I ever held against him was the cruel way he treated Dora for a while after he— (She stops—then blurts out) What's the use of beating about the bush. You know. I mean after he'd made her love him and seduced her and—

Ed: That's all past, Cassie. You've said yourself he's made up for all that. He's been a good husband. She's happy. It all ended for the best. Forget it. (A pause) The greatest miracle to me is the way he's buckled down to work at this job he got with the construction company, and the success he's made of it right

---

*O'Neill deleted these two words in brackets.

from the start. Four promotions in three years. That's going some.

Cassie: Yes, he's certainly made good. He must be getting a fine salary now, judging from the expensive Christmas and birthday presents he's sent us. Of course, it was Dora who did that. I'm not criticizing Walt, Pa, but you know he'd be the last one to remember, if she didn't remind him.

Ed: Yes, but remember he wouldn't pay any attention to reminders unless he wanted to.

Cassie: Yes, I admit that.

Ed: Come to think of it, his success with the company isn't such a miracle at that. He always had brains—when he wanted to use them right—and he was never afraid of hard work—whenever the job interested him. He was just restless—got bored—couldn't stay put long. The job he has now fits his nature—keeps him moving all over the country—new places all the time—new problems to work out. No home, no settling down—that would just suit Walt.

Cassie: I shouldn't think it would suit Dora, never having a home, but she evidently loves it. She must have changed a bit, too.

Ed: Of course she has. She's a woman now, not a girl. And Walt has become a man, shouldering a man's responsibilities and doing it damned well. I'm damned proud of him, Cassie.

Cassie: Well, Ma is, too, and so am I. He's made Dora happy, and even if he hadn't done anything else, I'd love him for that. (She looks off left front.) There's the postman. (She gets up.) I'll go down to the box. You stay here, Pa—and stay put. I'll be watching you, remember.

Ed: You couldn't get me to move on a bet. More likely, I'll fall asleep. (He stifles a yawn.)

Cassie: Probably there's nothing except the paper, but there might be another letter from Dora. (She starts walking briskly and disappears off left behind the walnut trees. Ed gets up lazily from the steps and yawning openly now sits in the chair on the porch at right of door in a sprawling, relaxed position. Tess appears behind the screen door.)

Tess: (With satisfaction) Well, the dishes are all washed and dried. It's no job at all when you keep your mind on what you're doing. The cooks we've had would have dawdled an hour over it and acted like over-worked martyrs. (She comes out on the porch and goes to her husband.) I'm glad to see you're showing more sense for a change and resting.

Ed: (Lazily taking her hand—with an affectionate grin) Always obey your order, don't I? It must be love. (He kisses her hand.)

Tess: (Pleased) My, but you're mushy today. (She pats his cheek.) Where's Cassie?

Ed: Gone for the mail. She thought there might be another letter from Dora.

Tess: I hope so. (She moves away to sit in the rocking chair.) What have you two been talking about?

Ed: Oh, Walt and Dora, of course. I hope they'll show up soon and end the suspense.

Tess: So do I.

Ed: You know, Tess, it's funny the way Cassie keeps harping on Dora's being happy and giving her all the credit for what Walt's done. Not that Dora doesn't deserve a lot of credit but Cassie talks as if that was all she was interested in.

Tess: (With an indulgent smile) You mean to tell me you don't see through that?

Ed: Oh, I know Dora was her best friend ever since they were kids together, but still—

Tess: There's more to it than that. The important thing is, she was very fond of Walt, too, and when she discovered he was gone on Dora, she was darned jealous. But you know Cassie, how decent and fair and honorable she is, from that moment, she started leaning backwards to show she wasn't jealous—became friendlier than ever with Dora and when the scandal about them came out, she took Dora's side and was bitter against Walt. Of course, she was right about that after the way Walt acted, suddenly disappearing and leaving Dora here to face the music. No one could excuse him for that. No wonder Dora went to pieces and made a fool of herself and got herself disowned by her stupid, stuck-up family, and lost all her friends except us.

Ed: Well, Walt found he really loved her and he came back and married her, didn't he?

Tess: (Slowly) Yes. I've often wondered why. It wasn't like Walt to care—He couldn't see—(Quickly) But we're talking about Cassie, and I'm saying she was leaning backwards defending Dora and down on Walt before he disappeared—when I couldn't see so much to be excited about. After all, it takes two. Dora never claimed he raped her.

Ed: No, and people don't look at such things the way they used to before the World War. But I think Cassie does. There's a straight-laced streak in her, no matter how tolerant she talks.

Tess: Yes, but the point I'm making is she got used to leaning over backwards to take Dora's side—and she's still doing it. She's still ashamed because she once felt jealous.

Ed: Yes, now I come to think of it, she was always close to Walt until he got mixed up with Dora—used to take his part and excuse him even to us, although she'd scrap with him and argue against his crazy ideas.

Tess: And cry when you gave him a licking, remember.

Ed: A lot of good lickings. He'd never cry or admit he was sorry. Didn't hold hard feelings either. Just seemed to regard it as something we both had to go through until he got big enough—(He shakes his head.) He was a strange boy all right.

Tess: (Slowly) Yes, he was. There were times when you couldn't believe he was human.

Ed: Oh, I wouldn't go that far, Tess. He was plenty human when he wanted to be. Don't forget he was a big hero around here once, after the high school fire when he risked his life and saved so many kids, including Dora. That's what started his falling in love, don't you think?

Tess: No. That finished it. She had a case on him before—like all the girls at school. He was a football hero, too.

Ed: (With sudden enthusiasm) He sure was! Small and only weighed 140 but he was the finest halfback I've ever seen, and I'm including all the university teams I ever played against. Wiry and tough, strong as a bull and quick as lightning—a fine driver, a grand power, a wonderful open field runner. He had everything. If he'd gone to Cal, as I wanted him to, he'd have made the varsity easy—and All-American before he was through. (Bitterly) But, of course, he wouldn't.

Tess: (Amusedly) That's still your greatest disappointment isn't it? (She laughs) You and your football! You'll never grow up.

Ed: (As if he hadn't heard) He wanted to show he was

different so he did what no other boy on earth would do. Resigned without warning as captain of the high school team. Wouldn't listen to persuasions, or give any reason except he'd had all the football he wanted. That stopped his being a hero around here until the fire made him one again, and he soon squelched that, too.

Tess: Yes, being a hero bored Walt after a few days. Not because he was modest. He wasn't. But he wasn't vain, either. He just couldn't feel anything. He had to go his own way, alone. (This almost desperately) Oh, Ed, can't we keep off the subject of what Walt used to be? It isn't fair to him. (A pause) Speaking of Cassie, Ed, I'm beginning to be really worried about her and Tom Avery. If she doesn't soon agree to set a definite wedding date, she's liable to lose him. He tries to hide it but he's getting tired of being put off, and I don't blame him. Engaged for two years now. That belongs in the old days, not today.

Ed: (Frowning) I'm worried, too, Tess. You ought to speak to her again.

Tess: I have. And she promised she'd set a day soon, but she's promised that before. You know Cassie. She always says yes to avoid arguments, but underneath she's as stubborn as Walt to do as she pleases. I told her I'd been watching Tom and I could see how sore and hurt he's getting. He's beginning to suspect she doesn't love him. But she does. I know that. And she's scared to death she'll lose him.

Ed: She better be. Plenty of girls around here would like to get Tom.

Tess: Yes, he's damned good looking.

Ed: Better than that, he's steady and a hard worker—knows his job and is reliable. You don't find many like him these days, not on fruit and walnut ranches, that is. Apart from the fact I like him personally, and know he'd make Cassie a fine husband, I have selfish reasons, too. If he and Cassie split up, he'd feel bound to leave here and I'd never find another foreman half as good. That wouldn't have mattered so much a while back before my heart started to act up. I could attend to everything myself in a pinch. But now I'm a good-for-nothing.

Tess: (Leans over to pat his hand tenderly) Shut up. You're no such thing.

Ed: And there's another thing. You know my feeling about

this place. It's home—the house of my family since the early fifties—not just a ranch.[13] Tom likes it, too. He wants to stay here and, married to Cassie, it would still be in the family after we're gone. It may be foolish and sentimental to have such ideas, nowadays. (Bitterly) I'd hoped that Walt—But he was never interested except in running the tractor—anything to do with machines. The land might belong to anyone, as far as he cared. I tried again and again to explain my feeling to him. He'd just look bored and puzzled. He couldn't get it. When the boom was on, he asked me why I didn't sell out at the top. He thought I was a damned fool. (With an abrupt change) Oh, to hell with it.

Tess: (Slowly) We can't help always coming back to Walt, can we? (A pause) Here comes Cassie. I hope there will be a letter. (Cassie enters left front along the path, folding the newspaper she has been glancing through)

Cassie: Nothing from Dora, darn it. No word at all. Just the paper. And no news in it worth reading, as far as I can see in glancing at headlines. (Teasingly) A lot about your old pal in Germany, though. I'm going to keep the paper away from you two if I have to sit on it—that is, until it's cool tonight. It's going to be no day for heated arguments. (She sits on the steps) Gosh, but it's hot in the rooms. And no breeze. By this afternoon, we'll think we're in a furnace.

Tess: We better close all the blinds and take siestas after lunch.

Ed: (A bit defensively) Well, it will be a dry heat. We won't be knocked out by the humidity like the people in the East are.

Cassie: (Laughs) Do I have a good Native Son boasting, or don't I? Isn't he the limit, Ma? (Tess laughs)

Ed: (Grins sheepishly) It's true, all the same. (A telephone rings inside the house. Cassie jumps up) You sit where you are. I'll answer it. (She hurries in. Her voice can be heard clearly) Hello. Who? Oh, all right, read it. No this is her daughter but I'll take it for her.

Tess: A telegram, Ed. Must be from Dora. (They listen. Cassie's voice is heard as she listens to the reading of the wire) Cassie: Yes—Yes—Yes—Yes—All right. Thank you. (A moment later she comes out on the porch. Tess asks anxiously): It's from Dora, isn't it? Oh, I do hope it's not the same old story—

Cassie: No, Dora says she'll arrive this evening sometime. It was a night letter from Los Angeles.

Tess: Why, then they're almost home.

Cassie: I said Dora said *she'd* arrive. It's the same old story about Walt. He can't come.

Tess: Oh! (There is vexed disappointment in her exclamation, but at the same time she seems relieved).

Ed: (Disgustedly) Hell! (But underneath, he seems relieved, too).

Cassie: Dora says a wire from the head office has just reached them. There's some trouble on a job in Oklahoma. They asked him to go there at once, and offered him a bonus if he does. He feels he's got to but he insists on Dora coming so we won't be too disappointed. He hopes he'll get his work done in time to join her here for a few days anyway.

Ed: Well, that's something. Let's hope he can make it. We mustn't feel too bad about this, Tess. It's a tough break but Walt's not to blame. These big corporations ask you if you can oblige them, but they really mean you do it or else. Walt knows that and he likes his job and wants to keep it.

Tess: (Dejectedly) Oh, I know that. I'm not blaming Walt. But it does seem—

Ed: Proves how valuable he's become to the Company. We've got to look at it from that angle and feel proud.

Tess: Oh, I do. And Dora's surely coming, that's a blessing. She'll tell us all about him. It will be just as if he were here, almost.

Cassie: Yes, it will be wonderful to have her around again. I hope she can stay a long time.

Ed: Yes, I always had a soft spot for Dora, ever since she was in pigtails, playing around with you.

Tess: Yes, I always felt she was like a member of the family—especially after the scandal—

Cassie: She always was to me—like a sister. Well, we proved how much we thought of her. We defended her when everyone was telling the vilest lies about her. We gave her a home when her family wouldn't have any more to do with her. We took her side and blamed Walt—as we had to do in justice, knowing him.

Tess: And one thing you have to say about her, there's no streak of ingratitude in her. She's never forgotten. I know she likes us better than she ever did her own folks, and she regards this as her real home.

Cassie: Of course, she does and she ought to. You're forgetting, Ma, that she is a member of the family now—as Walt's wife.

Ed: And sure damned proud to have her, them's my sentiments. (A pause. Somehow they all seem relaxed as if a worrying strain had been removed. Suddenly Cassie laughs.)

Cassie: How relieved we are, all of a sudden! Why haven't we the honesty to admit that we simply can't picture Walt as he's changed and we'd still be afraid to have the old Walt around again. (Tess and Ed look shocked and rebuking.)

Tess: Afraid? That's a strange thing to say, Cassie. It isn't true—

Cassie: Oh, yes, it is, and you know it, Ma. I mean, afraid he really didn't want to come, afraid he'd get bored after a day or two and yet couldn't conceal it or wouldn't bother to. But afraid most of never knowing what he might suddenly say or do to hurt you—accuse you of horrible things so matter of factly, and you could see he wasn't deliberately trying to hurt. He was surprised and a bit contemptuous when you got shocked and angry. He couldn't see why. (She gives a bitter little laugh) Remember how he'd say: "What are you making such a fuss about? It's a fact, isn't it? Why do you have to pretend and put on an act." Or: "I was only asking you a straight question. Why can't you answer it straight? I know the answer anyway. So what of it?"

Tess: (Slowly) Yes. The horrible questions he could ask—as if he was just curious to know.*

Ed: (Notes bitterly) So what of it. I remember him saying that all right. It was his favorite pet slogan. He ought to put it in his will to have that engraved on his tombs—(He checks himself and curses angrily) God damn it, can't we quit harping on what Walt used to be like? We've admitted it's rotten and unfair. (A pause. He speaks with forced casualness) Speaking of Dora, I wonder if *she's* changed. I hope not.

Tess: Not in how much she thinks of us. You can tell from her letters she looks on this as her real home and us as her real family.

---

*O'Neill erased the next two lines, but the final words can be deciphered: "off and lonely at times."

Ed: Well, that goes for us, too, don't it? (He pauses) I hope she hasn't changed in looks. She sure was pretty. (He grins) All curves and every curve in the right place, that was Dora.

Tess: Yes, she had a fine figure. And with her big blue eyes and her curly chestnut hair she was certainly attractive. Her hair was her best point, I always thought—such a lovely shade of brown.

Cassie: (Assertively) She was more than just pretty or attractive. She was really beautiful. (A pause).

Ed: Her wire said she'd arrive this evening, Cassie?

Cassie: Yes, Pa. In time for supper.

Tess: Then she'll be here for supper with us. We can hold it if she's a little late. [Do you remember anything she especially liked, Cassie?]

[Cassie: Why no—except chocolate cake. She liked everything, Ma. Dora was healthy.]*

Ed: She'll have to keep rolling to make it. That's a long hard drive for a girl alone. (He shakes his head) It's dangerous. She ought to take it easy and get here any time tonight. No sense in risking her life to save a couple of hours. [Look at that speed lunatic tearing down the highway. (They all look. He exclaims excitedly) Wow! Did you ever see—Cut into our road—on two wheels—just made it without running over—it's a miracle he didn't—]†

Tess: Can you think of anything she particularly liked to eat, Cassie. As I remember, she had such a hearty appetite she liked everything.

Cassie: Let me see. Well, chocolate cake, for one thing.

Ed: (His eyes on the road in the valley) Speaking of fast driving, look at that lunatic tearing down the highway. (Angrily) By God, I hope he gets pinched. (Suddenly they all gasp. He exclaims) Wow! Look at that! Who the hell—By God, I'll tell him off, whoever he is! Damned maniac!

Tess (Grabs his arm. The car is heard roaring up the twisting road):   You'll do no such thing. You'll sit right down again and stop losing your temper. It's the worst thing for you.

Cassie: Yes, Pa. You cool off. I'll go to the garage and see

---
*O'Neill erased these two lines of dialogue in brackets.
†This speech in brackets was crossed out by the author.

who it is—probably got the wrong road. I don't recognize the car." (She goes quickly off left along the path.)

Tess: (Pulling at her husband's arm) Sit down, Ed. (He does so.)

Ed: (Grumpily) You'd think I was a damned invalid, the way you go on.

Tess: (Humoringly) No, but you got to act as if you were for a while. (They are both looking off left. The noise of the car stops.)

"Gag's End"   "Rocket's End"
"Exit An Enemy Alien"   Sept. '41
R. H. Play
Notes

Act Three   Dora: Something about Walt sets you free—makes you want to dance down Main Street naked and thumb your nose at everybody[14]—that [the] only real thing to do in life was whatever you damned pleased—no rules except what I want—etc.—but when you get to know him you saw he wished there were rules he could believe in—he didn't want to believe everything was nothing—that was only his revenge because he was born so [he] couldn't feel.

Act Four   Dora: Perhaps the reason I came here was [I] wanted revenge—hoped you'd grieve—blamed you for what he was.

Last—Dora: They think they killed him but he really committed suicide.

General—From the first, their uneasiness—still afraid to get news of Walt—overcompensate for this.

General—Change date to year of Hitler's purge, 1934?[15] seizing power—approval—what we need over here.

Act One: In spite of their love for Walt, they also hate, dread him—afraid of letters, afraid he will come home—not only dread what he may do, but effect his character [has] on each of them—his realistic attitudes—as if he were an evil freedom which tempts, fascinates and horrifies—and at the same time a poor cripple who makes them feel ashamed—and a nihilist who makes life meaningless for them, because as it [is] really doesn't matter whether you do or don't do any particular act.

These different attitudes are revealed in scenes between Ed and Dora, Tess and Cassie, Ed and Tess and Dora, Cassie and Dora in their memories of Walt even when he is a child.

For example, when Tess had been tempted to run off with a man—physical infatuation—she knew Walt knew—knew and he watched—curious but detached—seeing her as a woman, not as a mother, no feeling—her resentment at this—after long silence between them, her protesting cry: "I am your mother"— his contrite: "I know." (Hugs, kisses her—tries to be her son— gives up, frustrated—she says pityingly, instinctively): "You poor boy." (Then he hardens defensively): "Why don't you run away with him, Ma. You might get a big kick out of it. When you get sick of him, you could always come back—put on a sob act— Pa's a sentimental slob—he'd forgive and forget—anyway, why shouldn't he? What [is] the difference?"

Similar experience with Cassie and Ed with one particularly striking one, as above, which gnaws at their memory.

Walt's recurrent livid, cold fits of fury—never against anyone but against life—in high school fire he saves Cassie as well as Dora.

His generosity about money or any possessions—but because he didn't care. Walt: "Doesn't mean anything to me." You never felt he gave you anything—and he didn't. He rejected gratitude, it puzzled him and you felt he was right to reject.

Recurrence of argument between Ed and Tess about Hitler— opening Acts I, II, and IV—follow same pattern.

Each ends on note of affinity to Walt.

Second one brings in the gangster-mob leader similarity— Ed's old admiration for Capone (and Walt's—and anyone's)— justification for his killings—kill or be killed.

Last one—will they get Hitler? Ed's affirmation—Tess' negation—ask Dora's opinion—Dora: "In the end he'll get sick of himself and commit suicide. They'll think they killed him but it'll only be because he killed himself."

News in day's paper adds fuel to the argument—best friend, Röhm, murder—new revelations, his refusal to commit suicide—etc.

(Dora had suggested to Walt he kill himself at the end.)

Dora's story to Cassie—physical hold of Walt—so strong might have been able to accept it as love but for knowing he couldn't—and for periods when he wouldn't even want that—then I'd feel I didn't exist at all—no use to him.

The loss of all ethical and moral values by Ed, Tess, and Cassie—complete scepticism in which they take pride—(although in private relations each is honorable)—no faith in old religion—government all grafting politicians—sex morality of no meaning, ancient bigotry—don't vote except on special local issues which affect selfish interests—etc.

Cassie sings in the choir (own church—for money reason only).

R. H. Play—Blind Alley Guy
Notes*   late May—43

Effect—the cuckoo clock which Tess has bought husband for Christmas present—a joke on his escape into memories of old house and family life—keeps striking at intervals throughout the play—its silly sound punctuating the growing tension, becoming a voice of the doom of passing time—and at the end the voice of death.[16]

Dora finds it is two minutes slow—sets it to radio.

Dora cannot help showing inner strain—all three watch this—Edgar and Tessie come to the conclusion [she had a] fight with her husband—she grasps at this—any explanation to hide the truth—they keep after her, console—on her side—know what he's like in his spells—but good boy at heart—she agrees to anything—then they begin to confide in her—their feeling of his inability to feel—his complete unawareness of all moral values—examples.

Cassie remains suspicious of something more.

In Act One, Mother says amusedly: "You still have a grudge against her, haven't you?" Cassie indignantly denies: "Always liked Dora, one of best friends in high school—and when all that trouble came, I stood up for her, etc.—I was on her side against Walt—etc." Tess teases her: "All the same, I always felt you were jealous of her when she and Walt fell in love. You and

---

*O'Neill erases two words here: "before write."

Walt were so close." Cassie: "We were not. I can't imagine anyone feeling close to Walt. He wouldn't let them, even if they accepted—even if he wanted himself." Tess: "That's a funny thing to say." Cassie: "You know what I mean, Mother"—Tess (With a sigh): "Yes, I suppose I do"—Ed: "I do, all right." Cassie: "As for love, he couldn't feel love"—Tess: "No—he couldn't. It just puzzled him, etc."—Ed makes excuses: "Wouldn't say that—certainly loved you and Cassie—me, too, in his way"—Cassie: "He thought love was just—I mean, before he discovered how much Dora meant to him—if he has really discovered it"—they jump on her: "Why say that—three years— her letters"—Cassie: "Yes, *her* letters"—etc.

Cuckoo clock—in Act Four. Dora begs Cassie to stop the striking: "It'd be too horrible to hear that silly sound at seven"— Cassie goes in and disconnects—Dora says with hysterical bitterness when she returns: "Just thinking—maybe [I am] wrong—Walt would have loved that—he'd be amused—give that twisted grin of his—like to hear the cuckoo, cuckoo as they turned on the current—he'd say [that is the] way everybody's life should end—it's all cuckoo."

Dora takes off [her] wrist watch: "[I] don't want to know"— then puts on again—Dora: "[It is] worse not knowing"—it is Ed who turns on the radio—wants to hear 7 o'clock comedian program—cheer Dora up—is at the end of an ad for wine is heard—then: Announcer: "It is now 14 seconds before 7, so-and so-watch time"—Dora breaks: "Turn it off, for God's sake"—he hurries in, bewildered—Dora stares at watch.*

Act One—Dora's note from Texas—surely coming this time unless something happens to stop Walt at the last moment—but she'll come, anyway—then wire last night from Arizona? Los Angeles? saying coming—didn't say if Walt with her—they expect her in the evening.

Ed notices the relief of Tess and Cassie when Walt doesn't arrive—rebukes Cassie (Tess and Dora in the house)—she replies: "You're relieved yourself, Father. Don't pretend"—Ed: "Dora's changed a lot—looks, I mean—and not for the best.

---

*O'Neill draws a wavy line in the left margin to bracket the material from the first word in the May 1943 notes, "Effect" to the word "watch."

R. H. Play					June 1st '43

Scene between Dora and Tess—Dora (about Ed and Tess): "I always felt you had a severe contempt for him because of the World War injury—felt [you were] looking for an excuse to be content with what [you] had—but at the same time [you] loved him more because [he is] more dependent on you—and now his high blood pressure—more contempt and more love"—at the end of the scene, Tess: "Women are all crazy, I guess, when love gets 'em"—

[End of Notes]

NOTES

The Visit of Malatesta

Introduction

1. The letters "W.D." after a passage indicate quotations from Eugene O'Neill's *Work Diary,* in which, from January 1, 1924, to May 4, 1943, the author kept a written record of his daily creative progress working on his plays, of his health, and of personal events in his life. The *Work Diary* was transcribed by Donald Gallup (New Haven: 1981).
2. James Joll, *The Anarchists* (Boston: 1964), p. 226.

The Play

1. The material dated "Jan. '40" is written on one separate page and is not part of the notebook, which contains all the notes written in February 1940 and in February and March 1941.
2. Daniello is included in an early list of potential names for characters in *The Iceman Cometh.* Its use here in the title as a possible alternative to Malatesta is puzzling. One wonders why O'Neill would consider a fictitious name for Malatesta when he knew the name would be known to many who, like the dramatist, were familiar with the life of the legendary anarchist leader. In the first act of *The Iceman Cometh,* Hugo, in his attempt to wheedle a drink from Rocky, says: "The great Malatesta is my good friend."
3. O'Neill uses the fictitious first name he gives Malatesta in an alternative title here; later in a February 12, 1941, Work Diary entry, he changes this title to "Malatesta Seeks Surcease."
4. Tony Daniello's wife is unnamed in the earlier January notes, and neither she nor Malatesta is described, even briefly, there as are the other main characters. Francina replaces Julietta. The two names in brackets have been crossed out: Ralph Lombardo, her husband, and Frankie, the Daniello's younger son, eliminating them from the play. Angelo is, presumably, twenty-five, the age given for the elder son.

5. In my judgment this name, which appears directly under Joe Genaro and is a possible alternative to Gus Bascone, is Dominic.
6. O'Neill's preliminary research to establish Malatesta's age suggests he contemplated setting the play in both 1912 and 1922, as well as 1913 and 1923, the date eventually used. Using *The Dictionary of Dates* by Helen Rex Keller (New York: Macmillan, 1934, Volume 1), the dramatist calculates the following:

$$
\begin{array}{cc}
1912\text{-}54 & 1913 \\
\text{'}22\text{-}64 & \underline{55} \\
& 1858
\end{array}
$$

Even though he concludes his hero would be fifty-five years old in 1913 (a mistaken conclusion as the real-life Malatesta was born in 1853 and not in 1858), the author, after changing the setting to 1923, disregards the actual age of Malatesta, making his fictitious counterpart fifty in order to portray him as a dashing romantic figure, capable of arousing the passions of three women in the play. O'Neill uses the Keller book also to list memorable historical anarchist dates and events beginning in 1872 and concluding with the entry in June 1914: "general strike led by Malatesta and Mussolini."
7. No mention is made in the play of Francina's children, and she is depicted as a grieving widow. Much of this description, however, can be applied to her.
8. O'Neill apparently uses Bascone's trade to evoke the memory of Nicola Sacco, a shoemaker. In July 1921 Sacco and Vanzetti, two Italian immigrant anarchists, were found guilty of killing two guards in a holdup in South Braintree, Massachusetts. Italian immigrants "were to have a cause célèbre with the trial of Sacco and Vanzetti and the six-year legal battle between their condemnation in 1921 and execution in 1927" (Joll, p. 222).
9. The dramatist again seems to have chosen his hometown New London for the setting. The Standard Oil millionaire is probably Edward Harkness, whose Waterford estate was a short distance from O'Neill's family home. The prototype for Gebardi is possibly Charlie Santoro, an Italian-American, who was eighty years old when I met him in 1969 at this estate. Santoro had worked on the estate for fifty-five years. Notes for *A Moon for the Misbegotten* indicate O'Neill often walked over to the Waterford home of John Dolan, a tenant farmer, whose land bordered the Harkness property. In the early notes for this play, Dolan (later Phil Hogan) recruits an Italian friend to serve as a witness in the plot to trap Jim Tyrone in bed with Josie Hogan.

10. In several sections O'Neill mistakenly uses the name Francina when he means Rosa. Before he concludes the 1940 notes, however, Francina's name is correctly used.
11. O'Neill was familiar with the lives and actions of underworld figures. In *Hughie* the two characters discuss the notorious Arnold Rothstein, a bootlegger, gambler, and narcotics dealer. The author's model for the ambitious Angelo was probably the gangster Ciro Terranova, called the Artichoke King because he coerced merchants to sell artichokes only to his produce company. When O'Neill outlines Act One, he describes the speakeasy as being "in back of grocery store." It is, presumably, operated by the Daniello family. There was a definite advantage during Prohibition to being a "grocer." Liquor from several countries, such as Scotland and Canada, was smuggled into southern ports and shipped later, disguised as fruit, in refrigerator cars to northern cities. The liquor was then sold secretly by grocers to buyers who knew the password. A small can of one particular vegetable, such as beans or corn, would signify, correspondingly, a pint of whisky or gin.
12. The real-life Malatesta did indeed acquire a British accent. He left Italy in 1878 and began a life of exile, but he was unwanted in various European countries. "In 1881 he went to London, which became his main base for the next 40 years" (Joll, p. 125). He did not earn his living as a tutor, however, but as a humble mechanic and electrician.
13. These episodes—a return to Italy, imprisonment, and either escape or release from prison—occurred frequently in the life of Malatesta. The particular arrest mentioned here by O'Neill occurred in 1898 when Malatesta and his anarchist friends were imprisoned on the island of Lampedusa. The governor of the island was so impressed by Malatesta's heroic life that he did nothing to prevent the prisoners' escape by boat in May 1899. Aided by friends, Malatesta returned to London, and then made his first, and only, visit to the United States, where he gave lectures to Italian workers in New York, New Jersey, and many Eastern industrial towns.
14. When O'Neill takes up the play again in February 1941 after a lapse of one year, he mistakenly calls the ward heeler "Farrell" in these three paragraphs rather than Connor as he had in the 1940 notes. Because he could deliver the vote, this wily Irishman is an influential ward boss, a leader in the city's political machine that controls policemen and municipal workers in a complex system of graft and corruption.
15. Joll notes that Malatesta was "always 'politically conscious,' without ever becoming, however, a politician" (p. 240).

16. As with the Farrell/Connor discrepancy, O'Neill errs here and in the next paragraph when he again mistakenly identifies Rosa as Francina.
17. Identified earlier as Rosa's cousin, Francina is depicted here as Tony's missionary-minded daughter. This view of her conflicts with other portraits of her as a wife having an intellectual, but normally unemployed husband, who does not have the common sense to perform simple jobs to support his wife.
18. Tony is stating a fact here. Owners of speakeasies had to stand by helplessly while policemen, and sometimes their friends, drank up the profits. The owners also usually had to buy the silence of the policemen on their beats every time a delivery of beer was made.
19. O'Neill errs here on the basic facts of Malatesta's life. Born in the province of Caserta, he was the son of a rich, liberal-minded landowner, who was engaged in commerce. By the time Malatesta made his first contacts with anarchists in Naples in 1871, his parents, brother, and sister had died. The single survivor of the family, by then a medical student, turned over his estate to his father's peasant tenant workers.
20. Various characters in the play suggest more than once that Malatesta masterminded the plot to assassinate King Humbert. The rumor explains why Malatesta is such a charismatic, legendary figure to his former followers. Malatesta's denial in the play that he was involved is probably true. During his visit to the United States in 1899-1900, he did meet King Humbert's assailant, Gaetano Breschi, briefly. While lecturing to a group of anarchists in Paterson, New Jersey, an editor, Ciancabilla, who disagreed with certain remarks Malatesta made, shot him in the foot during a heated argument. "At great risk to his own life Gaetano Bresci sought to shield Malatesta and disarmed the assailant." See Luis Fabbri, *Malatesta* (Buenos Aires, 1945), p. 116.

    Bresci was later selected by the Paterson anarchists to go to Italy to avenge the massacre of a group of innocent beggars mistaken for revolutionists by the police in Milan and killed. Acting on impulse, Bresci assassinated the king on July 27, 1900, at Monza. Malatesta left the United States on March 10, 1900, and arrived in London in April. There is no evidence that Malatesta conspired with Bresci in any way. However, after the assassination Malatesta was placed under close surveillance by the British police but never arrested, either in England or Italy, for the deed.
21. O'Neill gives a negative view of the political situation in Italy where even the old anarchists, once strong believers in freedom at any price, are so demoralized and consumed by greed that they fail to

resist Mussolini's expansionist theories and deeds and his reign of terror.

22. After passage of the Eighteenth Amendment, which prohibited the manufacture, transportation, and sale of alcohol, alky cooking became a cottage industry in the "Little Italy" sections of numerous American cities. Neither the amendment nor the subsequently passed Volstead Act, which covers ways to enforce it, forbade the consumption of alcohol and the manufacture of beer at home. Ten million Americans eagerly began making liquor in the home for their own personal use. At the same time, numerous gangsters and speakeasy owners, like Tony Daniello, installed portable copper stills in thousands of kitchens across the United States. In Chicago, for example, stills were installed in 200,000 Italian kitchens. One-hundred-pound bags of corn sugar, each costing five dollars, were given to the cookers, along with instructions on how to extract the alcohol from them. Collecting fifteen dollars a day (a princely sum in that era), a cooker did little else but keep the fire burning under the still, which yielded 350 gallons a week at a cost of fifty cents per gallon for corn sugar and yeast. The news to the old country of the financial profits to be made from these alky cookers swelled the numbers of Sicilian immigrants.

23. There was in 1923 in O'Neill's hometown, New London, Connecticut, a Front Street located a short distance from the railroad station in the downtown section of the city. To escape detection by law officials, an owner of a speakeasy had a locked entrance with a peephole in it. To gain entrance, a person had to show an admission card or use some kind of password.

24. There is no indication in the play whether Connor refers to Warren Harding, who died while in office in August 1923, or to the silent Calvin Coolidge, the vice president who succeeded him.

25. There are several references in the notes to plans Connor and Tony are making to open a brewery, which during the restrictive years of prohibition would seem to be an illegal venture. O'Neill selected Connecticut for the play's setting, not merely for sentimental, autobiographical reasons, but because it and Rhode Island were the only two states in the union that refused to ratify the Eighteenth Amendment. These and other New England states had an influx of hordes of thirsty Catholic and Jewish immigrants whose scorn for prohibition led to conflicts with their dry Protestant neighbors. Even though saloons flourished in these two states, they could still be padlocked and their owners jailed by federal agents. The proposition Angelo mentions seems

a legal sanction either to convert an already existing brewery to a plant making near beer or to construct a new brewery for that purpose. Brewers could legally manufacture near beer, which contained less than one half of one per cent alcohol. What brewers often did was to send the alcohol that had been removed in the manufacturing process to buyers who, once the liquid was safely delivered, would spike the near beer. Nearly a billion gallons of near beer were made during the first five years of prohibition. Tony speaks several times of cases of Scotch. Either the near beer was used as a front for the illegal manufacture of scotch or the brewery itself would be the front for bootlegging, New London conveniently being a seaport, ideal for smuggling.

26. In earlier passages, Connor's son had been called Michael.
27. O'Neill makes a notation in the margin beside this section: "change about beard." It would have been wrong if he had intended to eliminate this beard as Malatesta is usually shown in pictures, particularly at the age he would be in 1923, as having a beard.
28. The bed trick will apparently be executed successfully in this play whereas it fails utterly in *A Moon for the Misbegotten*, the only full-length drama O'Neill completes during the years he was working on his late unfinished plays. Connor and Delehanty resemble the wily old Irishman, Phil Hogan, in *A Moon for the Misbegotten* in the running quarrel these men have with the English.
29. These few lines on the ending of the play suggest that by the final curtain in either a short second scene for Act Three or, possibly, an added Act Four all the problems of the Daniellos and their friends will be happily resolved. There is some doubt which of the two women O'Neill refers to in this speech when he identifies the woman being interviewed as "Francina." He does confuse the reader in sections following these lines by using the name "Francina" when he means "Rosa." If he does mean Rosa here, the lines do not have much comedic value. What humor the scene would have derives from the ludicrous idea that a woman as fat as Rosa could once have been called the exotic "Passion Rose of the Revolution." If, on the other hand, the author actually means that Rosa's cousin Francina, who now appears to be safely married off to Malatesta, is the one being interviewed by a reporter, there would be ironic humor, in what seems to be the last speech of the play, in having the prim and prudish Francina assume Rosa's colorful role in the old anarchist days and in hearing her boast of being the "Passion Rose of the Revolution."
30. The scattered fragmentary notes that conclude this manuscript

seem to have been written on March 2, 1941, when O'Neill states in his Work Diary that he has "lost grip" on this play. Much of the material here seems most appropriate for Act Two.

31. After he completes the brief attempt to capture the Italian dialect of his characters in this, the last paragraph of the notebook, O'Neill leaves a large space and at the bottom of the page writes his last two mystifying lines of the play.

The Last Conquest

The Play

1. O'Neill actually conceived the first idea for this play two weeks earlier on August 15. He interrupted his work on Act Three of the first draft of *Long Day's Journey into Night* for an idea to develop a drama to "re present world collapse and dictatorships." He was inspired perhaps by a speech given by Hitler, to which he listened a few weeks earlier and which angered him. Years earlier, however, on March 7, 1927, the author had conceived the "Atlantic series" of plays, which was a "history of Christianity beginning with the Crucifixion." The first play was to focus on the life, and particularly the death, of Jesus: "the journey up Calvary"; the thirteenth and last drama was to depict "The Second Coming." Both concepts are incorporated in *The Last Conquest*.
2. The two tentative titles O'Neill assigns this new play, "Straw for the Drowning" on August 30 and "More Than Straw For the Drowning" on August 31, suggest his goal in this new work. In 1919 he completed a play entitled *The Straw,* in which the concept of "the straw" symbolized the last faint "hopeless hope" the hero was given that the woman he loved would not die. The straw imagery here in the 1940 idea indicates O'Neill's desire to offer doomed mankind a "hopeless hope" in an uncertain future.
3. This new title and the later one, "The 13th Apostle," which O'Neill retains throughout the notes until he conceives the final title on June 11, 1942, provide a key to understanding the complex relationship between the two ancient foes. Satan secretly loves Christ intensely; he is sorrowful that he must endure the pain and humiliation of the Crucifixion again. Satan is also, in his own way, a follower or apostle of Christ; his actions in the play, contrary to his expectations, unwittingly seem to advance the cause of Christ.
4. The basic concept here, the Good-Evil struggle played out upon the battlefield of the soul of man in the shadow of the cross of the

crucified Christ, seems to be a continuation of the final scene of O'Neill's 1933 *Days Without End*. In that play the character of John Loving is split: John symbolizes the "good" side; Loving represents the "evil" Mephisthophelian side and is visible only to John, just as Satan in the February 7, 1941, set of notes for *The Last Conquest* is "invisible except by Christ." When John is redeemed in an early version of the final scene, Loving does not "die" bitterly; beneath a large wall crucifix, "he laughs joyfully lying on his back his arms stretched out in the form of a cross." At this point the previous disbeliever John knows Loving is the "Devil he sold his soul to—but if he is the Devil then his opposite, Christ, must be true—he can believe again." (See O'Neill's drawing for this scene in which John stands before the crucifix while his dead self, Loving, lies beneath it, in *Eugene O'Neill at Work*, edited by Virginia Floyd (New York: Frederick Ungar Publishing Co., 1981, p. 164).

5. *A Book of Puppetry*, which Jerome Magon sent to O'Neill in December 1939, may have inspired him to experiment with marionettes. In his letter thanking Magon, the author writes: "The book is [the] most interesting I have ever seen on the subject."

6. The dramatist tries subtly to construct a parallel between the play's anti-Semitic World State and Hitler's Germany. There is the waving of flags with swastikas in the sports arena, "the stadium of the Chosen Superior Race." Several references are made to concentration camps where, Satan assures Christ, if He had "seen the maps and imagined what took place," He would never be able to say "Forgive them" to God. In the last set of notes written in December 1942 after the Perfect Citizen is added to the play, slaves are cast into a "fiery belly" of a furnace.

7. In July 1929, while researching the life of the Chinese emperor Shih Huang Ti for a play, O'Neill found a reference to the "mystic island of P'êng lai" and the "wonder islands." These become in several plays he later wrote the "blessed isles." Caligula speaks of them in *Lazarus Laughed*. All four Mannons in *Mourning Becomes Electra* long to live a carefree life in this warm, exotic refuge and escape their bleak, puritanical New England environment. Again here in *The Last Conquest* Satan exhorts Christ a number of times to be allowed to retire to the blessed isles "for a million years to dream and forget."

8. This reference to cutting the "Pygmalion and Galatea" allusion from the first Prologue supports my belief regarding this missing Prologue: that O'Neill corrected and destroyed the early draft after completing the second draft. Nowhere in the notes is there

any other mention of the "Pygmalion-Galatea" concept. The second polished draft contains some of the finest writing in the play: the material is logically arranged, correct punctuation is used, and the dialogue is well conceived.

9. A number of attributes given this "Savior of the World" appear in Jung's description of Germany's infamous dictator: "Hitler belongs in the category of the truly mystic medicine man. His body does not suggest strength. The outstanding characteristic of his physiognomy is its dreamy look." Quoted in *Adolf Hitler,* John Toland (New York: Doubleday, 1976), p. 525. Note also the similarities between the "Savior" and the malformed Caligula in *Lazarus Laughed,* who has "glazed greenish-blue" eyes; "his mouth also is childish." Its boyish cruelty "has long ago become naively insensitive to any human suffering but its own." Like the World Savior, Caligula tells the people: "I am your God." O'Neill identifies the Savior not only with dreaded despots of the past (Satan describes him as a "manifestation of Caesar") but also with those menacing the world he inhabits: Hitler, Mussolini, and Stalin, portraying the Savior as the "apotheosis and legatee of these modern tyrants."

10. Compare the description of the Magician and that of Tiberius in *Lazarus Laughed,* who is "tall, broad and corpulent but of great muscular strength." He has a "long nose, once finely modeled," and a "forehead lowering and grim." Beneath his half mask, his "lips are thin" and his "chin is forceful and severe." He, too, is bored and weary of battles. His complexion "is that of a healthy old campaigner." In the November 1942 notes O'Neill changes his concept of the Magician, now called Satan, in one detail, making him an "immense corpulent figure" and, therefore, even more similar to Tiberius.

11. O'Neill uses Hitler's military pageantry in this play. Toland states that Hitler borrowed the Roman-style salute "from Caesar by way of Mussolini" but claimed that the stiff-arm salute was German (p. 147).

12. This Nordic Kali, as she is described earlier, seems particularly appropriate in this race-conscious World State. Kali, the "Black One," is an important Hindu goddess associated with disease and devastation and is often depicted bearing a bloody sword.

13. This quotation is, undoubtedly, O'Neill's favorite Biblical passage, used frequently in his work and either quoted in full as here in *The Last Conquest* or woven subtly into plays as a philosophical message, a condemnation of American greed and materialism. In the very last interview he gave just before the première of *The*

Iceman Cometh, O'Neill was asked about his Cycle. *A Tale of Possessors, Self-Dispossessed,* whose title suggests the quotation is its underlying premise. The author criticized the United States for moving too rapidly without acquiring real roots. "Its main idea is that everlasting game of trying to possess your own soul by the possession of something outside of it, too." He adds that the Bible had said it better: "We are the greatest example of 'For what shall it profit a man, if he shall gain the whole world and lose his own soul?'" O'Neill believed that we as a nation have "squandered our soul by trying to possess something outside it, and we'll end as that game usually does, by losing our soul and the thing outside, it, too." Quoted in *Eugene O'Neill,* Croswell Bowen (New York: Ballantine Books, 1959), p. 313.

14. The *Bhagavad Gita,* the "Song of the Lord" or the "path of love," is one of the most important Hindu religious classics. Upanishadic in content, this Sanskrit poem consists essentially of dialogue between Lord Krishna and a prince, Arjuna, on the eve of a decisive battle, actually the battle of life to take place on "the field of Truth," the "Eternal law of the universe." O'Neill cites this poem to parallel his discussion of the eternal Good-Evil opposites and the *Gita*'s central doctrine of the difference between man's lower nature and his soul, between "what is good and beautiful from what is evil and ugly." See *The Dhammapada: the Path of Perfection,* translated from the Pali with an introduction by Juan Mascaró (Middlesex, England: Penguin Classics, 1973), pp. 9–10.

15. O'Neill seems to be recalling a familiar episode that occurred in his hometown, New London, when he and his brother Jamie were frequent clients of Addie Burns' establishment, located just two doors down from the police station on Bradley Street (this famous house is called "Mamie" Burns's place in *Long Day's Journey into Night*). To appease puritanical Yankee New Londoners, twice a year the court held what was called "Ladies Day." All the town's madams, dressed in smart clothes and Lillian Russell hats, paraded down Bradley Street with their "girls" to the courthouse. In an open court, each madam, after pleading guilty to a charge of running a house of ill fame, was fined one hundred dollars. Each girl was fined twenty-five dollars. (Quoted from an interview with Dennis Murphy, a former friend of Jamie O'Neill and a retired police officer who worked in the Bradley Street area in the early twentieth century, July 1969.)

16. Compare Peter's words here and Larry Slade's "let me live" speech in *The Iceman Cometh,* which expressed some of O'Neill's personal ideas. When O'Neill could no longer hold a pencil to write, his

Theatre Guild producer, Lawrence Langner, sent him a Sound Scriber hoping the author would be able to dictate the unfinished plays he wished to complete. In a practice session O'Neill read his "favorite bit," Larry's third-act speech. O'Neill tells Langner: "When I played the record back and listened to the voice that was my voice and yet not my voice saying: 'I'm afraid to live, am I?— and even more afraid to die! . . . O Blessed Christ, let me live a little longer at any price! If it's only for a few days more, or a few hours even, let me still clutch greedily to my yellow heart this sweet treasure, this little life!'—well, it sure did something to me. It wasn't Larry, it was my ghost talking to me, or I to my ghost."

Blind Alley Guy

Introduction

1. O'Neill uses newspaper headlines and articles to parallel historical events and their theatrical counterparts; in contrast, Brecht employs placards primarily.
2. O'Neill dates his first notes for *Blind Alley Guy* December 16, 1940, although he fails to record an explanatory entry in his Work Diary. He had spent part of December 16 "getting out X'mas cards" with his wife Carlotta. His failure to record a reference to the play can perhaps be attributed to the death of his beloved dog Blemie early in the morning of December 17. O'Neill was unusually faithful in keeping up his Work Diary, but the dog may have been ill and needed care on December 16. He does not take the new work up again until January 21, 1941.
3. In a letter to Lee Simonson in early 1938, O'Neill states: "The Docs now tell me that X-rays show no evidence whatever of my ever having T.B.!"
4. O'Neill never completes the word beginning with "H." wherever this initial is used to identify the play or its hero. The "H." could represent "Howard," his evil side, or it could, hypothetically, signify Hitler; however, the early notes contain no political references.
5. Dr. Rudolph Binion maintains that by the time Hitler was nineteen he was "intellectually and emotionally retarded after having lived idly with his widowed mother for some years past at suffocatingly close quarters." Binion notes that the seed of his anti-Semitism was probably planted in 1907 when his mother was undergoing extremely painful iodoform treatments for cancer. Consciously Hitler loved Dr. Block, her Jewish physician, "like a kind father; unconsciously, he blamed Block for his mother's

cancer." Quoted in *Adolf Hitler,* John Toland (New York, 1976), p. 538.
6. The events cited here and elsewhere in the notes indicate O'Neill had researched the rise of Hitler and Nazism. Hitler made his good friend, Ernst Röhm, commander of his paramilitary unit, the *Sturmabteilung* (Storm Detachment), called the SA. Röhm's political rivals in the SS, Himmler, Göring, and Goebbels, convinced Hitler that his friend was plotting to usurp the power of the army. On June 30, 1934, Hitler ordered the SS to shoot SA leaders but omitted imprisoned Röhm's name from the list. Toland states that on July 1 Hitler "was going through one of the most traumatic crises of his turbulent career. It reached a climax that afternoon when he was forced to approve the execution of Röhm. Even Hitler's sentence of death was marked by affection. He instructed Brigadeführer Theodor Eicke to give Röhm the chance to commit suicide" (p. 362). Röhm greeted his SS executioners with the words: "All revolutions devour their own children." He was given a pistol with a single bullet. Eicke and his men waited in a passageway for fifteen minutes and then returned to the cell and shot Röhm, whose dying words were: "My Führer!" (Toland, p. 363).
7. The Röhm affair is used in this version to suggest the similarities between Hitler and Walt. The former destroys his friends; the latter inflicts suffering on his family. "Double-crossing" is again mentioned here and foreshadows Dora's confession of betrayal. Ironically, there were many similarities between Walt and Röhm, who was an extremely cruel, vicious man. As Joachim C. Fest points out, "Röhm had no qualms of conscience; murder did not worry him." Röhm himself stated: "Since I am an immature and wicked man, war and unrest appeal to me more than the good bourgeois order." Quoted in *Portraits of the Nazi Leadership, the Face of the Third Reich*, Joachim C. Fest (New York: Pantheon Books, 1970), pp. 139–140.

The Play

1. The author obviously researched Hitler's childhood, early adult years, and background thoroughly; the parallels between the historical and fictitious figures are too exact to be coincidental. Like Hitler, Blackie excels in sports (he was "an athletic hero in high school") and becomes a "little ringleader"; neither graduates from high school. (Blackie "disappears in spring a few weeks before graduation.") Both fathers of these sons inflict harsh beat-

ings on their sons, who react in a similar manner. Hitler, after reading that silent endurance was a proof of courage, "resolved never again to cry" when whipped. The next time he was punished, he "counted silently the blows of the stick;" from that day on "his father never touched him again" (Toland, p. 12). In *Blind Alley Guy*, the father punishes his son with "woodshed lickings but finally gave up in defeat" when Blackie "accepted them without resentment or crying." He also threatens his Father: "Either you give up licking stuff or I'll pack up and leave home so I won't run the risk of killing you." The sons find a sympathetic ally in their overprotective mothers, who attempt to mitigate the anger of their husbands. Both sons feel a kinship with nature and are reared in a similar environment. Hitler's father moved from the city to a country village, Leonding, having 3,000 inhabitants; Blackie's leaves town for "a small farm outside a village of 3,000 or so inhabitants."

2. Compare Blackie's attitude of ruthless, lawless realism that takes possession of his family and the effect Malatesta, "the outsider," has on the Daniellos in *The Visit of Malatesta:* "the situation in the Daniello family is such that his coming brings out and makes active all the longings for liberty in its members, vague dreams of contented discontent which for his coming would remain that."

3. O'Neill apparently attempts to parallel Blackie's relationships with his sister Cassie and mistress-wife Dora and the women in Hitler's turbulent personal life. Cassie is a combination of Hitler's halfsister, Angela Raubal, and her daughter Geli. Toland observes that Hitler's fondness for Geli "went far beyond that of an uncle. He loved her, but it was a strange affection that did not dare to show itself, for he was too proud to admit to the weaknesses of an infatuation" (Toland, p. 264). Because of her obsessive love for her brother, Cassie is fiercely jealous and antagonistic towards Dora and makes disparaging remarks about her. Hitler's sister Angela disapproved of his liaison with Eva Braun, refused to shake hands with her, and "usually saw to it that there was no room at Haus Wachenfeld" when Eva came to visit (Toland, p. 415). Blackie's wife, Dora Bond, resembles Eva Braun in some respects; both live an underground existence, loving desperately men who are hated and feared by civilized society and are either unwilling or incapable of reciprocating love. The indifference of these men brings the women psychological, as well as physical, pain.

4. Both Vermont and the Berkshires have mountainous areas. Perhaps O'Neill is trying to evoke Hitler's retreat Haus Wachenfeld,

later called the Berghof, on the Ober Salzberg.
5. Before seizing power and acquiring the title "Fuhrer," Hitler was frequently introduced as "Herr Wolf." His first name, Adolf, derives from the Teutonic word meaning "fortunate wolf" (Toland, p. 102).
6. In a Work Diary entry on May 23, 1933, O'Neill writes: "Idea—3 women, 1 man—reverse [*Strange*] *Interlude* theme." He then increases the number to four women, the man's mother, wife, mistress, and daughter, who are symbolically one. Eventually death has suddenly become alive to him, a question mark, and made of his life a question for him. "As the play goes on, the four women gradually approach each other so at end he is with four figures exactly the same—the figure of wife."
7. O'Neill seems to have had a particular woman in mind when he conceived Dora in this play and Cora in *The Iceman Cometh*. Included in the preliminary list of names for the prostitute in the latter is "Cora the Blond." Named simply Cora in the final version, she is, like Dora, a "thin peroxide blonde." Her round face shows "the wear and tear of her trade," but there are still "traces of a doll-like prettiness."
8. The Work Diary entries reveal that O'Neill began this full-scale four-act outline on August 30, 1941 and completed it on September 19, 1941. On September 22 he described in detail the setting, the exterior of the White home. The following day he started the dialogue for Act One and worked on it steadily until October 27, completing a near-final fully developed first act. He put it aside, however, the next day and began work on *A Moon for the Misbegotten*. He ceases writing his Work Diary entries on May 3, 1943, but he resumed work on *Blind Alley Guy* in two later periods: late May 1943 and June 1, 1943.
9. Like Blackie, Hitler had been sent to jail. He spent over a year, feeling he had been betrayed, in Landsberg prison after the failure of the Munich Putsch in 1923.
10. O'Neill strives here in this play to depict the concept of Good-Evil opposites as portrayed in *The Last Conquest* (Christ and Satan). While he obviously succeeds in delineating one half of the dichotomy: the Evil-Blackie side, he fails to suggest any semblance of goodness in the Walter White side. His words and actions in his childhood and young adult years as Walter White were tainted with some kind of malevolence. In the September 1941 outline, Ed White says defensively of his son: "But I did realize you couldn't hold him responsible—the way you would any other boy—for all the crazy things he did and said to hurt people."

11. Compare this statement and that of Edmund Tyrone, a self-portrait, in *Long Day's Journey into Night:* "I will always be a stranger who never feels at home, who does not really want and is not really wanted, who can never belong, who must always be a little in love with death!"
12. O'Neill is not consistent in the name he assigns Cassie's fiancé. He is called Albert in the January 1941 notes, Jack Tabor in the August 1941 *dramatis personae,* and Tom Avery in the September 1941 notes.
13. There is a contradiction about the ownership of the ranch. Here Ed claims it is "the house of my family since the early fifties." In the July 1941 notes Tess is described as having a "jealous sense of own property" and that the 100 acres "is her property."
14. O'Neill once remarked that he would like to shock staid New Londoners, whom he never forgave for rejecting his family, by filling up a car with obvious blond whores and driving down Main Street in New London, encouraging the "ladies" to throw dimes out to the natives.
15. O'Neill seems to have forgotten that in the September 1941 almost fully completed Act One Version he had already changed the date of the setting to 1934.
16. O'Neill begins this last set of notes with a plan for his most dramatic use of sound since *The Emperor Jones.* A cuckoo clock now serves—as the tom-tom did in the earlier drama—as a reminder, a device marking time until the death offstage of the play's central character.

Work Diary Entries

(See p. 205)

1. Excerpts for the three unfinished plays are taken from O'Neill's *Work Diary 1924-1943*, edited by Donald Gallup and published by Yale University Library.

WORK DIARY ENTRIES[1]

The Visit of Malatesta

1940	January
4	Tao House
	Notes on idea for comedy with the tentative title "The Visit of Malatesta"
1940	February
23	The Visit of Malatesta (notes on this idea for comedy)
1940	March
2	Malatesta comedy idea (notes)
1941	February
10	Malatesta Comedy idea (notes)
11	Malatesta comedy idea (notes—like this—never have written about Italian-Americans although in past have known many of them as close friends)
12	Malatesta comedy idea (notes—tentative title Malatesta Seeks Surcease)
13	Malatesta Seeks Surcease (notes)
14	Malatesta Seeks Surcease (notes)
16	Malatesta Seeks Surcease (notes) short shift
17	Malatesta Seeks Surcease (outline I)
18	Malatesta Seeks Surcease (outline I)
23	Malatesta Seeks Surcease (notes—short shift—not up to it)
24	Malatesta Seeks Surcease (notes—but get nowhere, because feel vile, bilious attack)
28	Malatesta Seeks Surcease (a few notes—then p[rostate]. pain lays me away again, a curse!)
1941	March
2	Malatesta Seeks Surcease (outline I—like this idea but have lost grip on it—trouble is too many good ideas—can't settle on one—the war, perhaps)

The Last Conquest

1940	August
30	Work on fascinating new idea I get for duality of Man play—

	Good-Evil, Christ-Devil—begins Temptation on Mount—through to Crucifixion—Devil a modern power realist—symbolical spiritual conflict today & in all times
1941	February
5	Christ-Satan idea (Good-Evil—opposites in Man—Evil conquers the future world (seemingly)—spiritual propaganda play)
7	Christ-Satan idea (notes—tentative title "The Thirteenth Apostle")
1941	March
3	The 13th Apostle (outline)
4	The 13th Apostle (outline)
	[The same entry every day from March 5 to 12 as March 4]
13	The 13th Apostle (finish outline—9 scenes)
14	The 13th Apostle (notes—short shift)
1941	April
2	The 13th Apostle (notes—short shift)
3	The 13th Apostle (notes)
4	The 13th Apostle (notes)
5	The 13th Apostle (notes & start Scene I)
6	The 13th Apostle (Scene I—short shift)
7	The 13th Apostle (Scene I) (not in right mood for this—will put aside for while)
1941	May
27	The 13th Apostle (notes—decide needs Prologue)
28	The 13th Apostle (start writing Prologue)
29	The 13th Apostle (Prologue)
30	The 13th Apostle (Prologue)
31	The 13th Apostle (Prologue) short shift
1941	June
1	The 13th Apostle (Prologue) little done—feel punk bad night p[rostate]. pain
2	try to work but no go—feel too rotten bad night p[rostate]. pain again & develop bad cough
3	in bed all day, coughing head off—if it isn't one damned ailment it's another—should take in stride & work regardless but no can do.
9	The 13th Apostle (Prologue) short am
10–11	The 13th Apostle (Prologue)
12	The 13th Apostle (Prologue) bad night p[rostate]. pain
14	The 13th Apostle (Prologue)
15	The 13th Apostle (finish 1st draft Prologue)

16	The 13th Apostle (Prologue—going over, cuts, etc) short shift to Dr. Meek for tooth
17	The 13th Apostle (Prologue, going over)
18	The 13th Apostle (Prologue, going over)
19	The 13th Apostle (Prologue, going over) short am—feel rotten & dull bad night—pain—chill—little sleep
22	war news—can't work
23	The 13th Apostle (finish going over Prologue—needs still more condensation but that can wait)
25	The 13th Apostle (1st Scene—prelims.)
26	The 13th Apostle (1st S[cene].—start dial[ogue].)
27	The 13th Apostle (S[cene]. I—but bog down—lose interest, not in play, but in working, writing anything—war!)
28	try to work, no go—too much war on mind
29	Lily Gish arrives for visit, accompanied by dog—our cat leaves in disdain, liking dogs as I like Hitler—but dog or not, it is fine to see Lily again.
1941	July
3	The 13th Apostle (a few notes—not up to it)
4	The 13th Apostle (drawing sets for scenes)
5	The 13th Apostle (notes—try to force it but no interest)
6	The 13th Apostle (sets & notes)
7	The 13th Apostle (gone dead on it—a few notes—will put aside, try something else)
1942	April
9	The 13th Apostle (going over what's done—Pro[logue]., notes, outline)
10	The 13th Apostle (going over notes, etc.) Park[inson's]. bad
11	The 13th Apostle (change some conceptions—notes)
12	The 13th Apostle (little done) News comes that Oona has become Stork Club publicity racket Glamour Girl—at this of all times!—I am not amused!
13	Park[inson's]. bad—couldn't control pencil this am.
14	The 13th Apostle (start rewriting Prologue) little done
15	The 13th Apostle (Prologue, rewrit[ing].) little done Parkinson's bad
16	The 13th Apostle (rewrit[ing]. Prologue—little done)
17	The 13th Apostle (some notes)
18	The 13th Apostle (revising P[rologue].—like to do this play—real deep propaganda value, spiritually speaking—but I work so slowly now)

19		The 13th Apostle (rewrit[ing]. Prologue—short shift—fade out)
1942	June	
11		The 13th Apostle (try work but beyond decision to change title to The Last Conquest (more apt) little done)
13		The Last Conquest (Prologue, going over—little done)
14		The Last Conquest (P[rologue]., rewriting) Park[inson's]. very bad
15		The Last Conquest (P[rologue]., rewriting) Park[inson's]. bad
18		The Last Conquest (P[rologue].—rewriting)
19		The Last Conquest (finish 2nd d[raft]. Prologue
1942	August	
20		The Last Conquest (notes) Park[inson's]. bad
30		nerves all gone—bad night
31		Park[inson's]. terrible bad night
1942	November	
19		The Last Conquest (notes—give this a try again—want to do because might do lot of good—real propaganda for the spirit—fine idea, original technique—but develop some inner struggle about it that has held it up)
20		The Last Conquest (notes—I think the inner conflict is because it is at its final curtain a declaration of faith by one who is faithless—like D[ays]. W[ithout]. E[nd].—a hope for faith instead of faith—and also a futile feeling that no one will see the truth, not even the author)
21		The Last Conquest (notes—concentrate on it as play—try to be the objective dramatist—after all, many a thief sincerely admires honesty)
23		The Last Conquest (Scene II—scenario)
24		The Last Conquest (finish scenario, Scene II)
25		The Last Conquest (Scene III—scenario)
26		The Last Conquest (finish scenario, III)
27		The Last Conquest (Scene IV—scenario) short am
28		The Last Conquest (IV, scenario)
29		The Last Conquest (Scene IV—scenario)
30		The Last Conquest (finish scenario, Scene IV) just manage before I fade out)
1942	December	
2		The Last Conquest (some notes—little done)
3		The Last Conquest (Scene V—scenario)
4		The Last Conquest (Scene V—scenario)
5		The Last Conquest (notes—possible added living character—the Perfect Citizen of the World State)

6	The Last Conquest (a few notes—Park[inson's]. bad)
8	The Last Conquest (notes on end of play)
9	The Last Conquest (a few notes—then fade out) Park[inson's]. bad
10	The Last Conquest (a few notes—then fade out)
11	to Meek—he has discovered some pyorrhea, damn him—a bit of scraping—painful business bad n[ight]. little sleep
12	bed till noon—all my ills stirred up
13	The Last Conquest (no go—decide will have to quit on this again—or on anything else—one of my old sinking spells is on me—lower than low—mind dead)

Blind Alley Guy

1941	January
21	R[icky]. H. play idea (some notes—tentative titles "Gag's End"—or "Blind Alley Guy")
22	R[icky]. H. idea (a few notes) bad night p[rostate]. pain
23	in bed till t[ea]. sinking spell again—damn 'em—all in—never get reconciled to these attacks—but ought to because no cure yet
26	Blind Alley Guy (notes—will use this title for R[icky]. H. idea until get better one)
28	Blind Alley Guy (notes)
29	Blind Alley Guy (outline)
30	Blind Alley Guy (outline)
1941	February
9	Blind Alley Guy (notes)
1941	July
15	Blind Alley Guy (notes)
16	Blind Alley Guy (notes—would be good title for autobiography, way I feel now!)
17	Blind Alley Guy (notes)
18	Blind Alley Guy (notes) Oona leaves in eve—has not changed for better
19	Blind Alley Guy (notes—but few—too tired)
23	Blind Alley Guy (notes)
24	Blind Alley Guy (notes)
26	Blind Alley Guy (notes)
27	Blind Alley Guy (a few notes—short shift)
28	Blind Alley Guy (notes)
30	Blind Alley Guy desc[ription]. characters)
1941	August

21	Blind Alley Guy (now this idea is tops again—notes) short am
22	Blind Alley Guy (notes—short shift)
23	Blind Alley Guy (notes—short Sunday shift)
25	Blind Alley Guy (final notes before starting outline—this can be unusual, thrilling play)
27	Blind Alley Guy (desc[ription]. characters)
28	Blind Alley Guy (character desc[ription].—sets)
29	Blind Alley Guy (finish prelim. to outline)
30	Blind Alley Guy (start outline I)
31	Blind Alley Guy (finish outline I)
1941	September
3	Blind Alley Guy (start outline II)
4	Blind Alley Guy (finish outline II)
8	Blind Alley Guy (outline III, start)
13	Blind Alley Guy (III—outline)
14	Blind Alley Guy (outline III)
15	Blind Alley Guy (outline III)
17	Blind Alley Guy (finish outline III)
18	Blind Alley Guy (start outline IV)
19	Blind Alley Guy (finish outline IV)
20	Blind Alley Guy (some gen. notes—short shift)
22	Blind Alley Guy (start on I—scene desc[ription].) short shift
23	Blind Alley Guy (I, start dial[ogue].—but have to quit)
24	Blind Alley Guy (new start on I)
25	Blind Alley Guy bad night p[rostate]. pain again
26	Blind Alley Guy (I—little done—too all in)
27	Blind Alley Guy (I)
28	Blind Alley Guy (I—little done)
29	Blind Alley Guy (I—can't move it—same old stuff again—too many ideas in head—lose interest not in idea of play but in writing it—a why bother in this world feeling—too much war preoccupation (which doesn't help anything)
30	decide put Blind Alley Guy aside for a while
1941	October
9	Blind Alley Guy (go on with I again)
10	Blind Alley Guy (I)
11	Blind Alley Guy (I)
12	Blind Alley Guy (I—little done)
13	Blind Alley Guy (I)
16	Blind Alley Guy (I)
20	Blind Alley Guy (I)
22	Blind Alley Guy (I—rewriting what's done so far)

23 Blind Alley Guy (I—ditto)
25 Blind Alley Guy (I)
26 Blind Alley Guy (I) short shift
27 Blind Alley Guy (I—but it still won't come right—decide put aside till its time comes)
28 (S[haughnessy]. play idea, based on story told by E[dmund]. in 1st Act of "L[ong]. D[ay's]. J[ourney]. I[nto]. N[ight]."—except here Jamie principal character & story of play otherwise entirely imaginary, except for J[amie].'s revelation of self) [This play will become *Moon for the Misbegotten* and O'Neill puts all other work aside to develop this idea.]

O'Neill's last Work Diary entry is dated May 4, 1943, but he dates the notes he made after May 4 in the manuscript itself. He wrote notes for *Blind Alley Guy* in "late May '43" and "June 1st '43."

BIBLIOGRAPHY

Bowen, Croswell. *Curse of the Misbegotten.* New York: McGraw-Hill Book Company, Inc., 1959.
Boylan, James. *The World and the Twenties.* New York: The Dial Press, 1973.
Coffey, Thomas M. *The Long Thirst: Prohibition in America: 1920–1933.* New York: W. W. Norton Company, 1975.
Fabbri, Luis. *Malatesta.* Buenos Aires: Editorial Americalee, 1945.
Floyd, Virginia. *Eugene O'Neill at Work: Newly Released Ideas for Plays.* New York: Frederick Ungar Publishing Co., 1981.
———. *The Plays of Eugene O'Neill: A New Assessment.* New York: Frederick Ungar Publishing Co., 1985.
Fest, Joachim C. *Portraits of the Nazi Leadership, The Face of the Third Reich.* New York: Pantheon Books, 1970.
Goldman, Emma. *Living My Life.* New York: Alfred A. Knopf, 1931.
Joll, James. *The Anarchists.* Boston: Little, Brown & Company, 1964.
Keller, Helen Rex. *The Dictionary of Dates.* New York: Macmillan, 1934.
Mascaró, Juan. *The Dhammapada: the Path of Perfection.* Middlesex, England: Penguin Classics, 1973.
Nettlau, Max. *Enrico Malatesta: Vita E. Pensieri.* New York: Casa Editrice "Il Martello," no date.
O'Neill, Eugene. *Work Diary 1924–1943*, Donald Gallup, ed. New Haven: Yale University Library, 1981.
Perrett, Geoffrey. *America in the Twenties.* New York: Simon & Schuster, 1982.
Sinclair, Andrew. *Prohibition: The Era of Excess.* Boston: Little, Brown & Company, 1962.
Spengler, Oswald. *The Decline of the West,* Volume I. New York: Alfred A. Knopf, 1926; Volume II, 1928.
Toland, John. *Adolf Hitler.* New York: Doubleday & Company, 1976.